SIR HENRY ROYCE

The thirteenth Silver Ghost in a lovely English setting near its birthplace. (Rolls-Royce)

SIR HENRY ROYCE

ESTABLISHING ROLLS-ROYCE, FROM MOTOR CARS TO AERO ENGINES

PETER REESE

To Dr Joanne Shannon,
with thanks

Cover illustrations all courtesy of the Rolls-Royce Heritage Trust
Front: (from top) The first Royce car on the road; Henry Royce in 1907; 1931 Supermarine S6B, outright winner of the Schneider Trophy.
Back: A connecting rod, big ends and piston assembly for the Rolls-Royce Kestrel engine.

First published 2022

The History Press
97 St George's Place, Cheltenham,
Gloucestershire, GL50 3QB
www.thehistorypress.co.uk

British Library Cataloguing in Publication Data.
A catalogue record for this book is available from the British Library.

ISBN 978 0 7509 9900 7

Typesetting and origination by The History Press
Printed and bound in Great Britain by TJ Books Limited, Padstow, Cornwall.

Trees for Life

Contents

Introduction and Acknowledgements

Further detailed consideration of the renowned engineer Sir Henry Royce is surely long overdue.

It is some eighty-five years since Sir Max Pemberton's original biography, which he himself called a plain story of the man and his most able associates, notably C.S. Rolls and Claude Johnson, whom Pemberton regarded as being jointly responsible with Royce for the Silver Ghost, his famous motor car, and for the Rolls-Royce Company.

Pemberton spent time considering the lives of Rolls and Johnson (through Johnson's autobiography) as well as Royce, and made no attempt whatsoever to deal with what he referred to as 'the vast technicalities of Royce's engineering achievements'.

He sought information on Royce from some of his closest entourage, including Royce's medical friend Dr Campbell Thomson; his wife Lady Royce; his solicitor Mr G.H.R. Tildesley; another close friend, Mr G.R.N. Minchin; racing driver Captain Percy Northey; Mr A.F. Sidgreaves, Rolls-Royce's one-time Managing Director; and Royce's faithful nurse Ethel Aubin.

Reliance on the knowledge of such individuals was partly due to the fact that Royce – the most private of men – left no personal papers, a situation compounded by the decision made by Rolls-Royce during the Second World War to consign most of its historical documents to pulping during a campaign to accumulate such material.

My decision to write a second biography after so long was made in the knowledge that I could no longer consult people with personal knowledge of him, although fortunately, in the period between Royce's death and the present, a number of books and articles have been published on Rolls-Royce concerns – many through the auspices of the Rolls-Royce Heritage Trust. These include reminiscences by such individuals as Donald Bastow, Donald Eyre and H. Massac Buist. Other books that have proved of especial value from a comprehensive list are as follows:

H. Nockolds, *The Magic of a Name*,
R. Schlaifer and S.D. Heron, *The Development of Aircraft Engines and Fuels*,
Derek S. Taulbut, *Eagle: Henry Royce's First Aero-Engine*,
Peter Pugh, *The Magic of a Name: The Rolls-Royce Story, The First Forty Years*,
W.A. Robotham, *Silver Ghosts and Silver Dawn*,
Anthony Bird and Ian Hallows, *The Rolls-Royce Motor Car*,
Ralph Barker, *The Schneider Trophy Races*,
George Purvis Bulman, *An Account of Partnership: Industry, Government and the Aero Engine: The Memoirs of George Purvis Bulman*,
Ian Lloyd, *Rolls-Royce: The Growth of a Firm* and *Rolls-Royce: The Years of Endeavour*.

As with any book, I owe immense debts to both organisations and individuals. I have been most fortunate in obtaining a copy of the large number of letters and instructions which Henry Royce sent to Derby from 1914 to 1916 during the construction of his first aero-engine. (For this I am indebted to John Baker, Business Manager of the Sir Henry Royce Memorial Foundation, for having them scanned on my behalf.) These have helped me undertake a first-hand study of his methods and high technical accomplishments.

I am also much indebted to the Rolls-Royce Heritage Trust and its Chief Executive, Neil Chattle, and Sandra Freeman, Editor of *The Journal of the Rolls-Royce Heritage Trust*, for supplying me with a quite magnificent selection of pictures at such a uniquely difficult time.

With regard to learned institutions, the National Aerospace Library at Farnborough has once again played a pivotal role with its superb aviation collection. Librarians Brian Riddle and Tony Pilmer have, day in and day out, fielded my many queries, with rare thoroughness and unfailing courtesy that made it a pleasure to work there. The British Library's facilities were as magnificent as ever, especially as I was able to beat the Covid-19 shutdown. I also acknowledge the help given by the Prince Consort's Library at Aldershot with its librarian Diane Payne and the access to the aeronautical collection afforded me by the Hampshire Public lending Library at Farnborough.

I fully acknowledge invaluable support from The History Press without which the book would not appear, particularly Commissioning Editor Amy Rigg and Project Editor Jezz Palmer.

With regard to individuals, I am most grateful to Rob Cooke for his painstaking reading of the book's first draft and his valued amendments; to Mike Stanberry for his valued professional assessment and comments on it; to Paul Vickers for outstanding help with taking, identifying and processing the book's images and inspiration with its title; to Shally Lopes for her indefatigable and accurate work on the computer in producing repeated versions of the script; to Tony Pilmer for so many further significant contributions and for compiling an excellent index; to Brian Riddle for his historical assessment; to my friend Tony Hodgson for chasing up sources for the book; to Dave Evans for personal support to Barbara and myself; to my son, Martin, for his help when visiting the British Library; to Arthur Webb for his patience, humour and authoritative responses to my endless queries about aviation matters; to Rob Perry for the loan of fine books from his own collection; to my good friends among the Aerospace Library's volunteers, Katrina Sudell, Beryl James and David Potter for their support on many occasions; and to my long-standing friends at FAST (Farnborough Air Sciences Trust), notably Richard Gardner, Veronica Graham-Green, Graham Rood and Anne and David Wilson with particular thanks to Paul and Marie Collins for their continuing kindness and their amazing support at lecture times.

Every effort has been made to trace copyright holders but, in the event of any omission please contact me, care of the publishers.

Finally, as on so many occasions over the years, I thank my dear wife, Barbara, for her inestimable and lovingly given encouragement which through the trauma of Covid-19 has meant repeated feeding and watering of a pre-occupied partner and responding again and again to his partly formed ideas and early drafts.

As ever, any shortcomings are the author's responsibility.

Peter Reese,
Ash Vale

Preface

In 1866 a small boy, yet to reach his fourth birthday, stood on a hummock in a Lincolnshire field with his eyes upturned to the sky. His appointed task to assist with his family's hard-pressed budget was to wave his little arms to deter birds from eating corn in the field adjoining his home, for which service the farmer paid his diminutive bird scarer the sum of 6*d* a week (2½ new pence).

For so young a child the task was immense. The field stretched in all directions and his only accompaniment was the sounds of horse-drawn traffic moving along the nearby lane, while the opportunity to see a frail aircraft disputing the illimitable fenland skies was still half a lifetime away. The advent of both automobiles and aircraft would depend on liquid petroleum engines fired by electric ignition, technology that would not be developed until the later years of the nineteenth century.

Our young bird scarer's subsequent education was scant with just two years' formal schooling, but although he suffered ill health during his last twenty years, he was responsible for notable advances in both British automobile and aero engines. From 1906 onwards came his superlative 40/50hp Rolls-Royce Silver Ghost – long considered the best car in the world – followed in 1915 by his Eagle aero engine, which offered unrivalled levels of power and reliability for British pilots during the First World War.

Over the next two decades his contributions would continue undiminished with other first-rate cars to succeed the Silver Ghost, although his premier advances would be in aero engines. In 1926 he produced the

Kestrel, a revolutionary compact engine, whose twelve cylinders were set in a single block of aluminium alloy. This was the forerunner of the 'R' engine that in 1929 and 1931 won the final two Schneider Trophy air speed contests for Britain, during which it achieved by far the highest power-to-weight ratio of any engine so far. Its development in turn led to the brilliant V12 water-cooled engine, which became known as the Merlin, that performed spectacularly in virtually every notable British aircraft during the Second World War.

In 1933, at the age of 70, Henry Royce succumbed to the ill health that had dogged him for so much of a career spent in 'the steadfast pursuit and attainment of perfection'.[1] He had continued designing until the very eve of his death.

This book examines the glorious harvest of a premier British engineer whose achievements owed so much to his prevailing drive, uncompromising standards and extraordinary work ethic, although, as we discover, he could never have succeeded without the support of other able folk, who helped him both create and sustain his superlative contributions.

PART 1:
EMERGENT ENGINEER

Joe D'arams/Unsplash

1

Early Struggles

Like Henry Royce, a proportion of Britain's most eminent engineers came from humble, if not unpromising, backgrounds and commenced their working lives at impossibly early ages.

The great George Stephenson (1781–1848), whose father was the fireman of the colliery engine at Wylam near Newcastle upon Tyne, began his working life as a boy herding cows and leading horses at the plough. He then became a 'picker', clearing out stones from coal, before driving the horses working the gin at Black Callerton colliery.[1] At 14 he was appointed assistant fireman to his father at nearby Derby Colliery before becoming an engineman, from which point he embarked on his astounding career concerned with steam railways. Even so, he was 18 before he learned to read and write.

Likewise, entrepreneur Edward (Ted) Hillman (1889–1934) was involved in both motoring and aviation. Following the sketchiest education, at 12 years of age he enlisted as a drummer boy in the British Army. By the outbreak of the First World War he had risen to the rank of Warrant Officer and his military career seemed assured, but in 1914 he was seriously wounded during the British Army's retreat from Mons.

As a consequence, he was invalided out of the Army with a marked limp and a small gratuity, which he used to purchase a taxi. Such was his diligence and thrift that he soon bought his first motor coach, which by 1928 he had turned into a fleet of some 300. In 1934 his plans were thwarted when his coaches were compulsorily purchased as part of the Government's plans to rationalise public transport. Undaunted, Hillman used the proceeds to set up the original no-frills airline in the later tradition of Freddie Laker and Ryanair.[2]

Whatever the triumphs of such men against the odds, their early struggles could never exceed those of Henry Royce, about which, according to his early biographer, Sir Max Pemberton, he loathed to speak,[3] although Donald Bastow, who subsequently enjoyed a close working relationship with him in his final years, had no doubts about his unquestioned pride in his family's previous achievements. Henry's birth certificate shows that, in fact, he was born at Alwalton on 27 March 1863 to James Royce, a miller, and his wife Mary. The birth was registered at Peterborough, Huntingdonshire's county town.

As a result of Royce's subsequent enquiries, he came to believe he was descended from 'a Welsh master bowman called Rhys or Ryce'[4] who reputedly fought with Henry Tudor at Bosworth Field, for which he received an appropriate reward. Whatever the veracity of the legendary bowman's feats, succeeding generations of the Royce family undoubtedly prospered, and we are indebted to Donald Bastow for the following Family Tree.

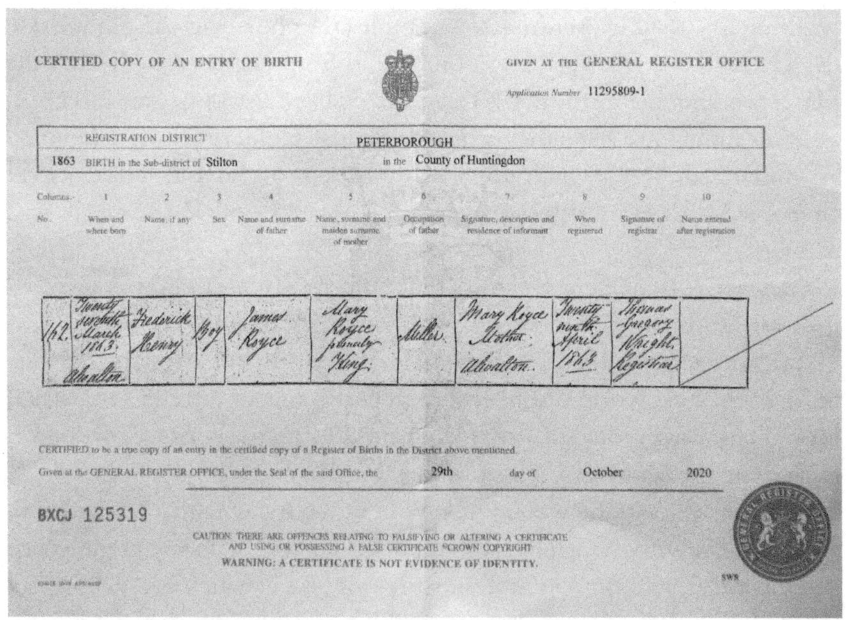

CERTIFIED COPY OF AN ENTRY OF BIRTH

GIVEN AT THE GENERAL REGISTER OFFICE

Application Number 11295809-1

REGISTRATION DISTRICT PETERBOROUGH

1863 BIRTH in the Sub-district of Stilton in the County of Huntingdon

Columns:- 1 No.	1 When and where born	2 Name, if any	3 Sex	4 Name and surname of father	5 Name, surname and maiden surname of mother	6 Occupation of father	7 Signature, description and residence of informant	8 When registered	9 Signature of registrar	10 Name entered after registration
162.	Twenty seventh March 1863. Alwalton	Frederick Henry	Boy	James Royce	Mary Royce formerly King.	Miller.	Mary Royce Mother. Alwalton.	Twenty ninth April 1863	Thomas Gregory Wright. Registrar	

CERTIFIED to be a true copy of an entry in the certified copy of a Register of Births in the District above mentioned.

Given at the GENERAL REGISTER OFFICE, under the Seal of the said Office, the 29th day of October 2020

BXCJ 125319

CAUTION: THERE ARE OFFENCES RELATING TO FALSIFYING OR ALTERING A CERTIFICATE AND USING OR POSSESSING A FALSE CERTIFICATE ©CROWN COPYRIGHT

WARNING: A CERTIFICATE IS NOT EVIDENCE OF IDENTITY.

SWS

Henry Royce's birth certificate. (Author's collection)

Royce Family Tree

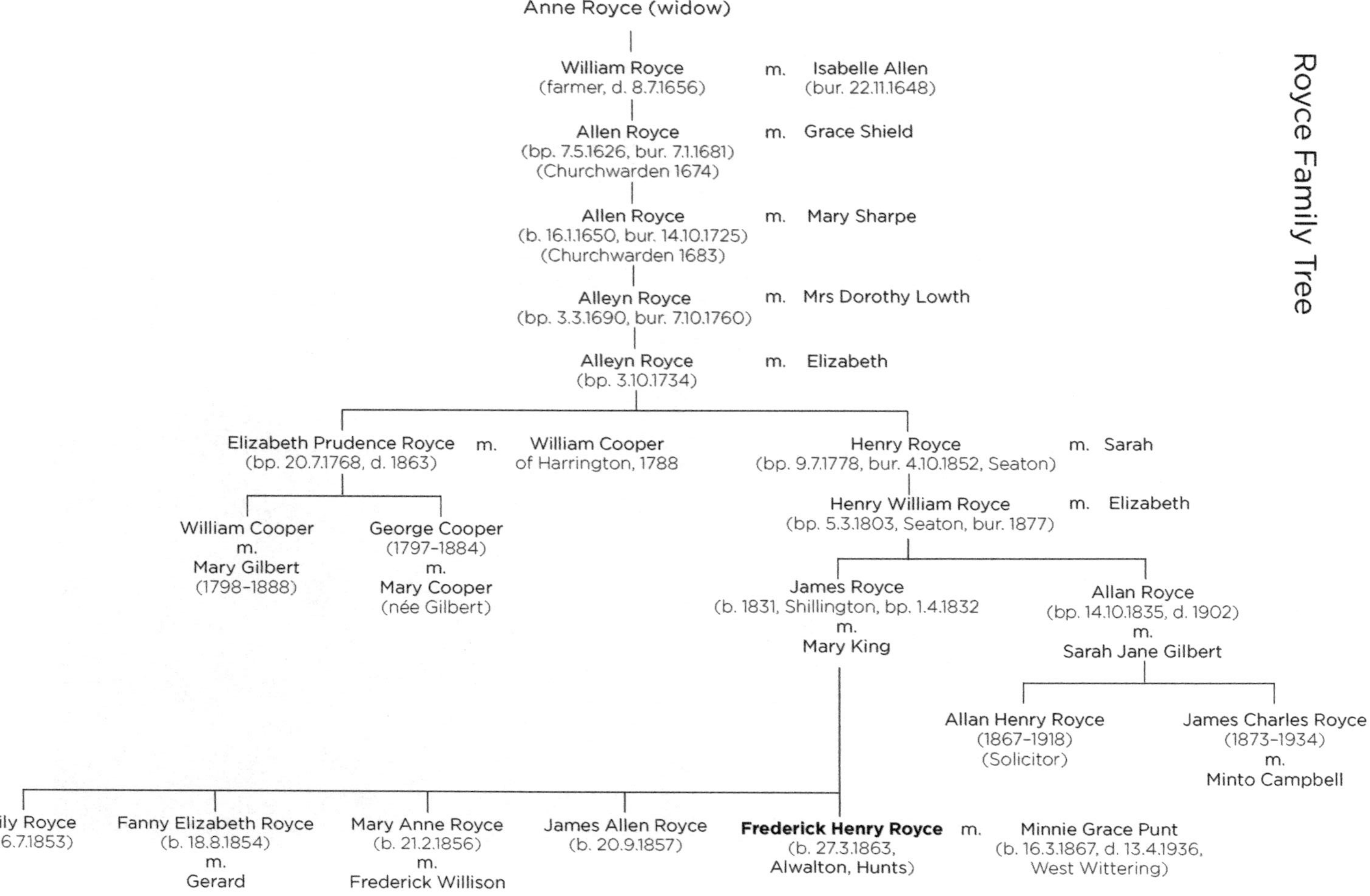

As Bastow points out, while the family tree incorporates only the essentials, the first entry of Anne Royce, a widow, was from the Elizabethan times and it shows a line of successful farmers and millers, some of whom acted as churchwardens. Henry's grandfather, Henry William Royce, was certainly a miller/engineer who pioneered the installation of steam power in water mills.

Some of the family crossed the Atlantic. Following the emigration of Robert Royce – a shoemaker – to Connecticut during the reign of Charles II, two of Robert's sons, Nehemiah and Nathaniel, became planters at Wallingford, Connecticut. Nehemiah married a member of the Morgan family that later became famous for its banking activities, while Nathaniel built a fine house at Wallingford. This was commonly called 'The Washington Elm House' due to a huge elm tree standing at its front, under whose wide branches General Washington had said farewell to the townspeople before going to war against the British.[5]

Another branch of the family under William Cooper and his wife Elizabeth (née Royce) was one of the first to be established in the West Toronto district of Canada, to where during the nineteenth century Royce's grandfather Henry William Royce – who, during a long adventurous life, married three times – would choose to emigrate.

It is feasible that he would have played a major role in his grandson's affairs had he not decided in 1866 – when Henry was only 3 – to join his cousin in Canada, where George Cooper and his brother William had been born some half a century before. William subsequently died from blood poisoning

Henry William Royce, Sir Henry's grandfather. (Rolls-Royce Heritage Trust)

following a scratch from a bear that, according to legend, was kept to entertain customers at his public house, but George bought the 400-acre plot that they had earlier decided to acquire jointly and after an interval married his brother's widow. Timber from the plot was sold to help buy a farm. This prospered and Henry William – along with most of his family – joined George on his farm.

Later, a significant connection would occur between the Rolls-Royce Company and another member of the family who had emigrated to America under the leadership of Royce's grandfather. This was professional engineer James Charles Royce (Henry's cousin). When in 1911 Henry Royce became so seriously ill that he was likely to die, Claude Johnson attempted to safeguard the Royce connection by offering James Charles work at Derby. Henry's recovery made this much less important but during the First World War, James Charles Royce became the representative engineer for Rolls-Royce in the US and Canada and was heavily involved in the campaign for the Eagle engine to be made in the US under licence.[6]

As for the Royce family's exodus from England in 1866, the only two family members who stayed behind in Britain were in fact Henry's father, James, whose business was failing and who by now was not strong enough to make the journey across the Atlantic, and Henry's great uncle, John Charles Royce, who would subsequently marry and have six children in England.

Royce's Canadian relatives. (Rolls-Royce Heritage Trust)

Whatever the positive achievements of many of Royce's ancestors, his father enjoyed no comparable successes, being referred to by Pemberton as 'bustling, hearty, florid but wholly unreliable'.[7] Royce himself devastatingly described his father as unsteady but clever, someone lacking the determination to apply himself single-mindedly to a task.[8]

Mindful of the Royce family's accomplishments, Pemberton sought other reasons for James' failure. Initially, he suspected that he might have been 'a little too fond of the bottle' but later discovered he had contracted Hodgkin's disease, which in its later stages – together with behavioural changes – was generally accompanied by anaemia and intermittent fevers, although this in no way explained his earlier failings. In fact, James followed family tradition with his agricultural training before he moved on to milling and in 1852, rented the mill at Castor, Northamptonshire.[9] In that year he appeared to make a good marriage to Mary King, whose father had a large-scale farm at Luffenham. They had three daughters, Emily (born in 1853), Fanny Elizabeth (born in 1854) and Mary Anne (born in 1856), followed by James Allen (born in 1857) and finally, more than five years later, their last child, Frederick Henry. By then James' business affairs were already taking a serious downturn following an earlier move from the family mill at Castor to another at Alwalton, in nearby Huntingdonshire, for which he took out a lease from the Ecclesiastical Commissioners. This had both steam and water power, with the former almost certainly installed by James.

James Royce, Sir Henry's father, with Sir Henry's sister Emily. (Rolls-Royce Heritage Trust)

Whatever the circumstances, by 1863 James had been compelled to mortgage his lease to the London Flour Company, but in 1867, when Henry Royce was four, the business failed completely. With most of the immediate family in Canada, no help could be expected from that quarter and there is no record of aid coming from Mary's family – with the notable exception of her sister, Miss Betsy King, whose assistance would come considerably later.

As a consequence, they faced the heartbreaking prospect of dividing the family. It was decided that the three girls, the eldest of whom was already 14, should be boarded for a time at Alwalton's Inn with a Mrs Clarke, while their mother sought employment as a housekeeper with private families, with most of her modest earnings likely to have been used to help with their keep.

As for the boys, it was agreed that they should accompany their father to London where, due to his knowledge of steam power, he had succeeded in finding work with the recently established London Steam Flour Company at its newly founded mill in Southwark.

Whatever James' employment, with his disposition and fast-deteriorating health there could be no happy outcome and when Royce turned 9, his father expired in a public poorhouse at Greenwich when just 41 years of age.

Despite the meagre details of Royce's early years, we have the strong impression not only of physical privation but of him being largely left to his own devices in a world 'which had but little use for him'.[10] A written account by L.F.R. Ramsay, for instance, maintained that due to his relative isolation as a child Royce was late to walk and speak and did not utter his first word until he was 4.[11] Whether Ramsay was correct or not, Royce's early family commission as a human scarecrow was hardly likely to help him develop social skills and during his father's final illness, money was bound to be short, although his mother Mary found work closer to him in order to help with food and shelter.

There was never any question of Henry being able to live with her, although he apparently stayed for a while at the London address of an old couple who had been with his father at Alwalton. When one of them died, this arrangement ended and his subsequent memories of lodgings were predominantly of hunger and cold. Many years later he remarked that, in one, 'My food for the day was often two thick slices of bread soaked in milk'[12] and on a particular evening, faced with the prospect of an empty, cold house, he apparently chose the greater comfort of an outside dog kennel complete with its canine occupant. (His affection for dogs would remain with him throughout his life.)

As for schooling, by the time of his father's death he had spent just one year at the Croydon British School. Between the ages of 9 and 14, Royce needed all his innate resolve and pronounced work ethic to survive the harsh environment of late Victorian London with its unforgiving attitude towards the aspiring poor. His mother was able to give only limited help, although there was a great-aunt Catherine on his mother's side who lived at Fletton near Peterborough whom he was accustomed to visit for some days at a time. At 10 he began selling newspapers for W.H. Smith at Clapton and Bishopsgate railway stations and as a result was able to attend school for a further year from 11 to 12 years of age, but in 1876, when he reached 13, he became a full-time telegraph boy. He delivered telegrams, where his favourable attitude and appearance had him selected to take them to homes in prosperous Mayfair. Even so, such work was no bed of roses. As he explained, 'I had no regular wages … They believed in payment by results in the Post Office in those days. Telegrams cost only six pence, as you know, and the boy who delivered them got a half penny, irrespective of distance, you didn't get much in a day.'[13]

Against the odds, at 14 Royce's life changed dramatically for the better. During one of his short holidays at Fletton, his great-aunt must have realised that work as a messenger was quite inadequate for him. She thereupon went to the Great Northern Railway Works at nearby Peterborough, where for the sum of '£20 per annum'[14] she arranged for him to become an indentured apprentice with hopes of becoming a skilled engineering worker. This was the equivalent of some £2,896 at today's valuation (2020) and given her limited capital, it represented a massively generous initiative. Royce's belated good fortune was further helped by the nature of his Peterborough lodgings with a Mr Yarrow and his family, including his son Havelock, who also worked at the railway works as an apprentice.

Havelock recalled being sent in 1878 to the village of Fletton to bring Fred – as Royce was always known at that time – to their house at Peterborough. 'He was a very earnest lad at that time some six years younger than myself, as interested as he could be in all that concerned the great machinery in Mr. Rouse's charge.'[15] In fact, Havelock proved far from generous about their young lodger's practical skills and he was convinced about the family's crucial contributions to Royce's subsequent successes. 'In the course of time

Frederick Henry Royce as an apprentice with the Great Northern Railway, Peterborough. (Rolls-Royce Heritage Trust)

he began to make himself quite a good mechanic, though I would not say he was over-quick at the mastery of tools. He learned by degrees, but what he learned he learned thoroughly.'[16]

Whatever the Yarrow family's contribution, Havelock did acknowledge Royce's rare intellectual appetite and industry:

> He was a very quiet lad at that time and rarely went out at night. You couldn't keep him away from books. Although he had hardly any schooling he managed to teach himself quite a lot about electricity and algebra and something also about foreign languages ... But electricity was the thing that interested him most. Not very much was known about electric currents in those days and everything was in a primitive stage, batteries and generators particularly, although electric light was beginning to be heard of and some of the companies, I believe, were actually using arc lights for the illuminations of their sidings ...[17]

Whatever additional knowledge Royce acquired through long hours of study after a full day in the workshop and continuing to sell newspapers, Havelock had absolutely no doubt about his father's contribution to his mechanical skills.

> My father, I should let you know, had quite a nice little workshop out in our back garden at Peterborough. He had a 6 inch lathe there and a carpenter's bench, a shaping machine and grindstone and it was always his idea to do every bit of work that had to be done about the house. He was a clever workman and he was very interested in Fred's first endeavours to use the tools. I think it was the instruction he received with us that made him a master at the lathe and taught him a lot about fitting and filing. When he left the works he was a very capable mechanic, and Mr. Rouse had come to think highly of him, in fact he carried away testimonials which should have got new employment anywhere.[18]

Havelock Yarrow's reference to Royce's testimonials was timely because in November 1880, after just three years' apprenticeship, his great-aunt's money was needed for another emergency and he had to leave. However glowing his testimonials at this time, British industry was suffering from one of its periodic depressions and many firms were laying off men, including fully trained ones.

His hunt for work involved him walking from Peterborough to Leeds to join his middle sister Fanny Elizabeth and her husband, where Royce's mother was by this time an additional member of the household (whom the 1881 census listed as being 52 years of age).

Although not fully qualified, within a fortnight Royce had found work – if at the parsimonious rate of 11*s* for a fifty-four-hour week – with tool-makers Greenwood and Batley, who had landed a contract with the Italian arsenal then being built to help equip the Italian Army.

At Greenwood and Batley, Royce adopted the practice of working many days from 6 a.m. till 10 p.m. and all through Friday night in a likely attempt to save some money, which after paying his board was not likely to have been that easy. In spite of such long hours, he continued to learn as much as he could about electrics and other subjects, most likely at evening classes following his 'short' days.

Within a year Royce returned to North London with the aim of using his knowledge of electrics to join what was unquestionably an aspiring industry. In 1881, when still only 18 years of age, and in spite of having no practical experience, he was accepted by the Electric Lighting and Power Generating Company as a tester at 22*s* a week (double his previous earnings). The company went on to acquire patents on incandescent lamps from the American inventor Hiram S. Maxim and on arc lamps from Edward Weston (which had earlier been used at the Peterborough Railway Works) and it accordingly changed its name to the Maxim-Weston Company. By March 1883, it had spent no less than £14,000 on patents compared with £2,000 on plant and £20,000 on stock and work in progress.[19] The results were only too predictable. In May 1884 it registered a loss of £32,000 and by 1888 the firm was in liquidation.

For its new employee such concerns were not yet a worry and he took lodgings in Kentish Town before rapidly enlisting for a course of evening studies at the City and Guilds Institute for the Advancement of Technical Education at Finsbury under legendary Professor William E. Ayrton, whom he apparently impressed. This course of study might actually have been suggested to Royce by Hiram Maxim or some of the eminent specialists associated with him,[20] although he would doubtless have needed little persuasion to take it up. Royce's work must have satisfied his employers for in late 1882 they posted him from London to Liverpool, where at the age of 19 he was appointed Chief Electrician of their subsidiary, the Lancashire Maxim-Weston Electric Company Limited at Peter's Lane Liverpool, which, in fact, was seriously undercapitalised.

In his biography, Pemberton related how the company was committed to lighting a number of streets and theatres in Liverpool, where Royce made significant investigations into the three-wire system of conducting electricity, sparkless commutation and the drum-wound armature for continuous-current dynamos. He confessed to Pemberton that at this time he used to wait in his office in as critical a state of suspense as those people in the theatre who were looking for the death of the villain or the salvation of the heroine. 'From time to time I sent a small boy round to see if the lights were still burning. Happily the tale of casualties was slight and in the main we managed to light their darkness. But it was the devil of a business.'[21]

Royce was not to enjoy such uncertain successes for long. Although on 30 October 1883, Liverpool Council accepted his company's tender for lighting the streets and theatres – and continuous lighting had actually commenced on 24 March 1884 – just two months later, on 24 May 1884, everything was brought to an end. The Lancashire Maxim-Weston Electric Company was liquidated and it was announced that 'from and after the 24 instant *(May)* the Company will cease to light the streets at present being lit by their Weston System of electric light'.[22]

Electric Lighting.

Read the following Report of the Engineer:

The Engineer begs to report that the Lancashire Maxim Weston Electric Light Company have made the necessary preparations in compliance with the terms of their Contract for the Experimental Electric Lighting in the Streets specified therein.

The continuous lighting commenced on the 24th instant.

Resolved,

That the application of Messrs. H. and J. Hughes 191, Park Road, for a renewal of their license to keep 40 gallons of Petroleum at their premises 191 Park Road be granted on the usual conditions and on the Special condition that the petroleum be stored in an Iron tank in the yard as before.

Chairman.

Council proceedings of the City of Liverpool, 25 March 1884. (Liverpool Central Library and Archives)

Due to its early successes, the parent company decided it was worth buying out their insolvent subsidiary. In May 1884 their offer was accepted, following which fresh negotiations were opened with Liverpool City Council for new lighting schemes where the Town Clerk 'expressed himself very favourably with respect to the electrician and engineer'.

In the event Royce found himself in a most difficult situation. Despite the Town Clerk's endorsement of his work, final agreement on the new contract was bound to take time, during which he would be unpaid, and he had by now apparently received encouragement from some of his colleagues about setting up on his own. The extent of his dilemma about whether he should stay with the reborn company or take the massive step of striking out on his own with his hard-earned but diminutive capital of just £20 needs no emphasis.

In favour of the latter course, he had recently become 21 – the age of majority and a significant landmark at the time. Another positive in going it alone was that although he lacked education, he had already discovered whatever information he could about electrics, supplemented by some theoretical knowledge acquired at evening classes. In fact, he later attributed his phenomenal memory to his night-school education (which was uncertain in duration and for which he had sacrificed much of his limited leisure time) that made it imperative – 'I should never forget anything worth remembering.'[23] However limited such knowledge, he had already demonstrated his ability as a practising electrical engineer.

Most important of all was his inherent sense of independence and self-assurance; he was happy in himself and never doubted his abilities. Over 6ft tall with a gaze that betokened his determination, already tempered by adversity and buoyed by his recent achievements, he drew up plans to make novel products of his own design.

To further his ambitions, Royce decided to leave Liverpool for Manchester. He was likely to have chosen Manchester over London or Liverpool, cities also well known to him, because its basic costs appeared more favourable to set up a small backstreet company. There he would shortly be joined by another young man – Ernest Claremont – in what would be a joint enterprise. However much he realised he needed a partner, it was a further measure of Royce's confidence that he decided to put the embryonic business in his own name.[24]

His early deprivations and the insecurity of working for firms that were either not well funded or unprepared to pay just rates for skilled and conscientious working men weighed on him. He sought the opportunity to see how his own skills and ferocious working practices could make commercial sense, however modest his first workplace and joint capital resources. Despite his high ambitions, dedication and rare engineering acumen, Royce could hardly have anticipated the monumental struggles the two would meet with over the next twenty years, nor when, after they were joined by a young, blue-blooded motor-car salesman, their products would come to symbolise a new standard of excellence not only for British but for world engineering. In the firm's early stages such progress must have seemed beyond belief.

2

Royce and Claremont – Branching Out

F.H. Royce and Company began its small-scale activities in Blake Street, Manchester, an unprepossessing area containing stables, a Temperance Hotel and a cabinetmaker's workshop. The Poor Rate Records for 1885 refer to F.H. Royce and Co. sharing premises with a salesman, W. Sergeant, at an annual rate of £17.[1] Royce would not have been able to pay his rent in advance and in spite of his ability to live sparely, his scant capital would never have been enough to buy the materials, along with the necessary machinery and tools, for an industrial undertaking. He required a partner and Ernest Claremont almost certainly joined him during the firm's first six months, bringing a further capital sum of £50, which he was likely to have borrowed from his father.

Although their joint application some twelve years later (in October 1897) for membership of

Ernest Alexander Claremont. (Rolls-Royce Heritage Trust)

Institution of Mechanical Engineers.
ESTABLISHED 1847.

PROPOSAL OF MEMBER, OR ASSOCIATE MEMBER, OR ASSOCIATE.

Name in full Frederick Henry Royce

Designation or Occupation Electrical & Mechanical Engineer

Business Address c/o F. H. Royce & Co Ld Hulme Manchester

being 34 years of age,* and being desirous of admission into the Institution of Mechanical Engineers, we, the undersigned proposer and seconder from our *personal knowledge*, and the three other signers from trustworthy information, propose and recommend him as a proper person to belong to the Institution.

Witness our hands, this 11th day of October 1897.

FIVE *Members' or Associate Members' Signatures are required.*

Proposed from *personal knowledge* by † (*See Note.*) J. H. Beckwith

Seconded from *personal knowledge* by [illegible]

Supported from trustworthy information by J. F. Liebert, H. N. Rowland, F. Rowe.

Signature of Candidate F. H. Royce

Served premium apprenticeship to Great Northern Railway (Loco Dept) Peterboro' from Sept 1877 to Nov 1880
Greenwood & Batley Leeds 1880 to 1881
Electric Lighting & Power Generating Co afterwards named The Maxim Weston Co 1881 to 1882 Transferred to Lancashire Maxim Weston Co 1882 to 1884
Partner in F. H. Royce & Co 1884 to 1894
Managing director in F. H. Royce & Co Ld June 4 1894 to present date

Signature of Proposer J. H. Beckwith

Royce's application for membership of the Institution of Mechanical Engineers. (Institution of Mechanical Engineers)

the Institution of Mechanical Engineers confirmed their continuing partnership, it also demonstrated that after more than a decade, the company stayed firmly in Royce's name. Even so, in Claremont, Royce found the first among a succession of colleagues who not only recognised his exceptional attributes but without whom he could never have fulfilled his ambitions.

Where Royce and Claremont met is uncertain, although author Paul Tritton believed it was likely to have been in London, possibly when attending Professor William Ayrton's evening classes in Finsbury.[2]

Like his other relationships, that with Claremont would be long-standing and it continued, in fact, until Claremont's death on 4 April 1922.

Due to their different social backgrounds, it appeared an unlikely association, for as the son of a surgeon Claremont was born into an affluent and large family of intellectually and artistically gifted individuals.[3] He was educated privately before attending University College London, although he did not graduate for during the second year of his degree course he took up an apprenticeship with the Anglo-American Brush Electric Light Corporation in London, where he was likely to have worked with the firm on lamps or dynamos. Like Royce he failed to complete his full apprenticeship, which in Claremont's case was the outcome of a major dispute with his foreman.

Although Royce and Claremont shared a common enthusiasm for electric lighting and commerce, they were very different individuals. Claremont was small and dapper with a wide number of outside interests compared with the tall undeviating Royce. Claremont prided himself on his deportment and fitness while Royce showed little interest in his appearance or even his food when he was intent on their latest engineering assignment. Claremont later became an officer in the Yeomanry with its demanding military commitments and high standards of horsemanship, although during the firm's initial development he came close to matching Royce's fearsome dedication.

By necessity their early priorities were directed towards acquiring equipment and materials rather than meeting their personal needs, and being unable to afford lodgings they shared a room over the works where they both ate and slept (in hammocks). Their staple food was sandwiches and any cooking – often of sausages – was carried out in an enamelling oven, which Claremont held responsible for their later digestive problems. Apparently their main diversion from the grinding regimen of work was a wild card game called 'grab' that culminated into a form of all-in wrestling, which often ended with them rolling round the floor in their boiler suits.

With such limited resources, their early output was bound to be modest. In fact, Royce's first successful product was a domestic electric bell consisting of a bell and push, with wire and a Le Clanché cell battery, that apparently sold for just 7*s* 6*d*. Royce drew up the plans, made the simple jigs required and set about producing it while Claremont was responsible for everything else: sales, contracts, payments and deliveries – although if needed he would also help at the bench.[4]

Their firm at this time was described as electrical and mechanical engineers for, to make ends meet, they apparently accepted any engineering task placed before them, including the repair of sewing machines. In the electrical field it manufactured lamps, filaments (for Edison–Swan) and holders for incandescent bulbs, with the early employees remembering broken glass lying everywhere.

Throughout the first three years, things remained on a knife edge as the partners took on their first employees. They started by engaging a freelance worker with sales experience, Thomas Weston Searle (whose employment could easily be terminated), and then six young women, before in 1887 'Old Tom' Jones, their first journeyman, arrived.[5] He received the doubtful honour of being allocated a vice next to the irascible perfectionist Royce. The young women assembled the bells and the filaments for light sockets, while the rest undertook all the other commitments.

Even so, with his unmatched ability and drive for perfection, no one else approached Royce's work rate. It was customary at this time for him to frequently work through the night and when the others came in the next morning they would find him catnapping at his bench. As he commented in later years to the *News Chronicle*:

> For many years I worked hard to keep the company going through its very difficult days of pioneering, personally working on Saturday afternoons when men did not want to work and I remember many times our position was so precarious that it seemed hopeless to continue. Then owing to the great demand for the lighting dynamos we made for cotton mills, ships, and other lighting plants, we enjoyed a period of prosperity.[6]

Along with his bench work, Royce was responsible for designing all the firm's products, including the dynamos made to his own specification and his first patent, the bayonet-cap lamp socket, which was granted on

Blake Street Premises in 1852

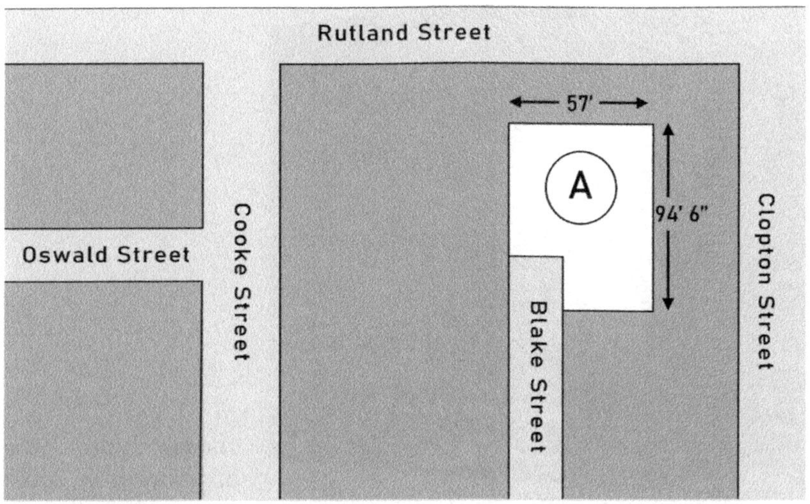

Area A: 1,346 Square yards. Land bought by Lawrence McKenna, owned by Oswald Milne, E. C. Milne and Lawrence McKenna. Rent £33 . 14s . 0d.

Blake Street and Cooke Street Premises in 1863

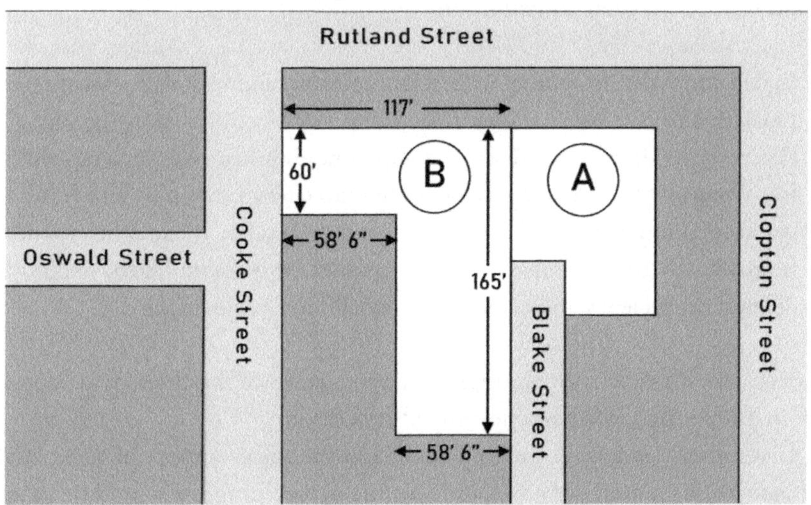

Area B: 1,462 Square yards. Land owned by Oswald Milne, E. C. Milne and George Shorland. Rent £36 . 11s . 3d.

Blake Street premises. (P.H. Vickers)

The last photo of the doorway of 1A Cooke Street. (Rolls-Royce Heritage Trust)

24 July 1897. His dynamos were superlative and he was subsequently to acknowledge his own contributions:

> In dynamo work, in spite of insufficient ordinary and technical education, I managed to conceive the importance of sparkless commutation, the superiority of the drum-wound armature for continuous current dynamos and [the company] became famous for continuous current dynamos which had sparkless commutation in the days before carbon brushes. While at Liverpool from 1882 to 1883, I conceived the value of the three-wire system of conduction in efficiency and economy of distribution of electricity …[7]

Royce was, however, not alone in his appreciation of the three-wire system for in 1882 it had also been developed by Edison.

Given their leaders' vision and skills, and the loyal support of their small workforce, it seemed only a matter of time before progress would be made. Sure enough, at some time before 1888 the partners felt able to take lodgings with John and Elizabeth Pollard at 24 Talbot Street, Moss Side, although there was no question of them easing the throttle, for they were accustomed to continue discussing current problems as they walked together between their lodgings and Blake Street after finishing work.[8] They were certainly

Memorial stone in Hulme Park, Manchester, with a red plaque marking the site of the Cooke Street factory. (P.H. Vickers)

with John and Elizabeth in 1888 when the business moved into larger premises in Cooke Street, where Royce still refused to consider reducing production space by accepting an office of his own. It was his custom to be seated at a small table in the corner of the busy and noisy workshop where he produced a steady stream of sketches while Claremont, together with the firm's secretaries and typists, shared a separate room. This practice continued into the 1890s before Royce finally agreed to have an office, which he shared with Claremont and his Secretary but rarely occupied.

Even so, by the late 1880s much-needed advances in their living conditions occurred as their domestic responsibilities increased. By the end of 1888, both had quit the Talbot Street lodgings to acquire separate houses. Claremont, who was due to be married to Edith Punt, the daughter of a licensed victualler, moved into 246 Moss Lane East and on 19 January 1889, he engaged a young servant girl, Mary Walters. In the same year Royce occupied a house at 45 Barton Street, Moss Side, where his mother joined him, for whom he engaged the services of a 15-year-old servant girl, Patricia Brady.

Claremont introduced Royce to Edith's younger sister, Minnie Grace, a former governess in Scotland. Predictably the relationship prospered and Minnie married the 29-year-old Royce on 16 March 1893. Following the recent death of their father, both sisters were well provided for financially and between them they invested £1,500 in the firm[9] before subsequently purchasing a further number of shares in it. In 1893 Claremont moved into a fine house in the Manchester suburb of Chorlton-cum-Hardy, which he proudly named 'Electron', with Royce moving his new wife into a substantial semi-detached house called 'Easthome', around the corner from the Claremonts.

Prior to his marriage, Royce, who always held his mother in high regard, found her separate accommodation at 21 Warwick Road, Chorlton-cum-Hardy, where it became his practice to visit her most days on his way home from work, although he was usually so late that he would find her propped up in bed knitting him endless pairs of socks. When Royce moved, he found his mother new accommodation at nearby Chapman Street, in Hulme, where he continued to visit her until her death in 1904.

Apart from the partners' high professionalism and rare commitment, their growing prosperity reflected a major boom that was taking place in the provision of electricity, where from 1889 onwards a number of power generating stations were being built in London. By 1893 they were planning significant expansion, for which during March 1894 they had the business valued as a going concern. On 31 March, its assets were set at £2,721 18*s* 4*d* (compared with its original capital of £70), while its workers now

Summary

	Page			
Turning and Fitting Shop	21	1063	12	·
Monitor Shop	30	652	9	6
Lamp Store Room	31	8	11	6
Brass Finishing Room	36	203	12	6
Store Room	38	40	8	6
Boiler House, Packing Shop and Yard	40	91	19	6
Pattern Room	42	33	18	6
Dynamo Room	43	125	1	·
Girls' Workroom	46	73	15	6
Cook House	48	13	4	·
Instrument Room	53	169	17	9
General Office	55	75	19	5
Private Office	56	61	0	8
Show Room	57	29	8	9
Staircase and Entrance	58	34	14	·
Plant at Manchester Ship Canal Contract	60	44	5	3
	£	2721	18	4

Inventory of business F.H. Royce carried out in 1894. (Rolls-Royce Heritage Trust)

numbered 100 or more, compared with the nine of five years before. These were exhorted by written instructions from Royce that hung in the shops 'to work to a model'.

During the same year they established the business as a limited liability company called F.H. Royce and Company Ltd, owned by its shareholders and described as 'Electrical and Mechanical Engineers and Manufacturers of Dynamos, Motors and Kindred Articles'. A young accountant, John De Looze, was engaged as Company Secretary. He turned out to be a strong disciplinarian with limited humour and a natural parsimony, although he was also extremely hard working. Like so many others who joined Royce, his acquaintanceship proved long-standing for he stayed with the firm for fifty years until his retirement in 1943. Although it was Royce's custom to mock De Looze for his quaint sayings and mannerisms, he never doubted

John De Looze, who joined F.H. Royce and Co., became Company Secretary in 1884 and retired in 1943. (Rolls-Royce Heritage Trust)

his loyalty and value to the company.[10] In his turn, De Looze ensured that Royce, who neglected to eat, was supplied with regular glasses of milk by a boy who was told not to come back until Royce had drunk it.

Royce was appointed Managing Director of the new company and he subscribed for 5,349 shares, with Claremont becoming Chairman and taking an identical number. Further capital was raised when their friend and neighbour James Whitehead became a large shareholder and was made a Director. As already mentioned, the two wives also participated, Minnie Grace bought a total of 1,131 shares, with Edith close behind with 1,101. In contrast, Claremont's brother Albert and John De Looze purchased just one share each.

During the rest of the 1890s, the firm continued to grow strongly due largely to a major contract with the Manchester Ship Canal that led to opportunities for general engineering work in addition to its electrical projects. Its premises were extended from Blake Street into Cooke Street with a further major expansion occurring during 1895 (to facilitate the manufacture of Royce's large-span electric cranes), followed in 1898 by an additional three-storey building.[11]

By now the product range included arc lamps and dynamos, electric motors and a wide range of switchgear, together with Royce's cranes, which rapidly became legendary for their lightness, strength, longevity and dependability. His high sense of responsibility was demonstrated by his insistence on instituting centrifugal braking among their controls to avoid any slippage of ladles containing molten metal when in the foundries. Although the company built large varieties of cranes for a countrywide and ultimately international market, Royce produced as many standard components for them as possible.

By October 1897, the firm had book orders worth £6,000; by the following March they had risen to £9,000.[12] With such demonstrable success even Royce felt able to relax the frugality of their early years. During 1898, for instance, he commissioned Manchester architect and surveyor Paul Ogden to draw up plans for 'Brae Cottage', a comfortable villa that he proposed building in the most fashionable thoroughfare of well-to-do Knutsford some 15 miles from Manchester. The spacious dwelling was not just for Royce and Minnie but for Minnie's niece, Violet 'Vi' Helena, an outdoor-loving tomboy whom they adopted after her mother died and with whom Royce apparently had a very close relationship. In later years, following subsequent serious domestic crises, she still referred to his sense of humour and his fondness for children.[13] Vi was joined by her brother Errol, for, although the Claremonts had agreed to care for him, the reception provided by Edith, whom Tom Clarke described as 'a rather Victorian figure with little sense of humour, no warmth and as somewhat unsociable',[14] was such that he came to spend much of his time with the Royces and was even reported as coming to worship Royce. Michael Evans' research came to a rather less rapturous picture about Errol and Royce's relationship. Although Royce was undoubtedly generous in taking Errol on permanently, Evans believed he gave him something of a hard time – although he might well have believed it was for the best reasons. Even so, Errol lived with them until the beginning

Brae Cottage, Legh Road, Knutsford, which Henry and Minnie built in 1898 and (inset) gable showing plaque of initials of Frederick Henry and Minnie Grace. (Rolls-Royce Heritage Trust)

of the First World War, when he joined the Army. After the war he stayed in France, where with Royce's probable assistance he worked in Paris for Franco Britannic Autos.[15]

The arrival of Vi and Errol was likely to have given Royce – who undoubtedly possessed a deep regard for children – some measure of compensation for the children he could never expect due to the Punt sisters' mutual horror about the physical side of life, including illness and the possibility of becoming pregnant. This appeared to have been corroborated by a family photograph taken when Royce was 33, in the prime of life, with both arms round his adopted children. Despite such restrictions, C.W. Morton, for one, believed that for some years Minnie and Royce were pretty devoted,

Henry Royce, aged 33, with his adopted niece and nephew Violet and Errol Punt. (Rolls-Royce Heritage Trust)

with Minnie a supremely loyal, if slightly staid, wife whom he described as 'a portly lady with fine hair which went grey rather early, [who] … dressed well but soberly and wore steel-rimmed reading glasses'.[16]

Minnie's deep admiration for Royce's accomplishments at work led her to willingly forgive his frequent lateness for meals and other appointments. On Royce's side, during 1898 he publicly showed his regard, or his deference, to Minnie's likely capital contribution by having a plaque constructed on the gable of Brae Cottage with the joint initials of Frederick Henry and Minnie Grace Royce.[17]

Although Royce's life would always be dominated by his encompassing interest in engineering projects, while at Brae Cottage he found some time for relaxation. His favourite leisure activity was gardening, particularly fruit growing and the cultivation of roses – which he often carried out under his patent floodlights that were needed due to his customary late return home. To a lesser extent he also enjoyed music, particularly that of Gilbert and Sullivan, whose songs he would hum to himself while working, and he was reputedly an occasional visitor to the Hallé Concerts in Manchester.[18]

The Claremonts matched the Royces' more comfortable circumstances when, even before Brae Cottage was ready for the Royces, they had occupied 'Endsleigh', a large seven-bedroom house also in Legh Road, Knutsford.

Notwithstanding the advancements in their material circumstances, the emotional limitations of the Punt sisters were only too likely to affect the quality of both marriages. With the Claremonts marrying three years earlier, their marriage was the first to face serious challenges – which makes one bound to wonder whether or not Claremont had warned Royce about the sisters – and if so whether their financial assets might indeed have been a powerful factor for the second marriage taking place. The causes of the Claremonts' difficulties were not hard to see. Ethel was less outgoing than her sister and Claremont was a far more sociable individual than Royce. As we know, in 1896 he became an officer in the Yeomanry (4th Volunteer Battalion, the Manchester Regiment), which brought powerful diversions. He also played a variety of sports, including polo, and so determined was he about the need to keep fit that – when he could afford it – he even employed the services of a professional wrestling partner.[19] Unlike Royce, Claremont enjoyed nightlife pursuits not shared with his wife and while at home he proved to be something of an obsessive and martinet. Vi recalled that he required his toast to be just right, along with his vigorous complaints to his wife if it fell below his standards.[20] Claremont had very soon sought consolation elsewhere and finally found his home life – with Edith's formidable nagging – intolerable. In 1906 they began to live apart when he found more peaceful accommodation at the works of W.T. Glover.

However, by this time he had already enjoyed a relationship with a Miss Jane McKnight that had begun as early as 1899 and was to last for the rest of his life.[21]

Royce showed far greater loyalty to his wife and niece, although by 1911 he too would find comfort in the appointment of nurse Ethel Aubin, who would assist in his convalescence from serious illnesses and steadily take command of his household until he finally separated from Minnie and Vi in 1917.

In the meanwhile, the company's progress continued. By February 1899, its orders had risen to £20,000 and in March of the same year a new prospectus was issued with the aim of doubling its capital to £30,000, of which £20,000 was required for a new factory. Following a successful flotation, the name of the firm was changed again, this time to Royce Ltd with Claremont continuing as Chairman and Royce as Managing Director.

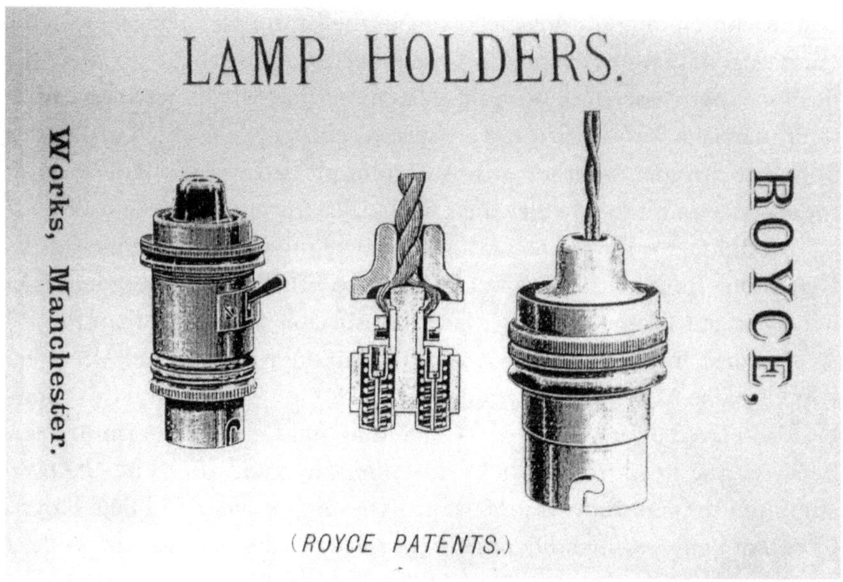

Royce's patent bayonet socket for light bulbs. (Rolls-Royce Heritage Trust)

D 133 (36) (RF 844 20.7.03)

TIME SHEET.

TRAVELLING BY TRAIN.

ROYCE, LIMITED,

MANCHESTER.

Time of Departure } ....

Time of Arrival } ....

Name of Workman......W. Grove......

At......Major Machell...... *Week ending Thursday*......31/12/1903

	MORNING. FROM	MORNING. TO	FORENOON. FROM	FORENOON. TO	AFTERNOON. FROM	AFTERNOON. TO	NIGHT. FROM	NIGHT. TO	TOTAL HOURS.	STATE IF CONTRACT OPEN ORDER OR EXTRA.
FRIDAY ...	6.30	8	8.30	12	1	4	4.30	11	14½	Open order
SATURDAY	6	8	8.30	12	1	4	4.30	11	15	
Sunday			8	12	1	4	4.30	11	13½	
MONDAY ...	6.0	8	8.30	12	1	4	4.30	11	15	
TUESDAY ...	6	8	8.30	12	1	4	4.30	6	10	
WEDNESDAY										
THURSDAY										✓

TOTAL...... 68

THIS HALF TO BE RETAINED BY TIMEKEEPER.

(E.P. 12848) ☞ See Over.

Specimen time sheet for the installation of electric lighting at Penny Bridge Hall near Ulverston. (Rolls-Royce Heritage Trust)

The site chosen for the proposed factory was in the newly established Trafford Park industrial estate, comprising 1,200 acres alongside the Manchester Ship Canal, for which they acquired land on 8 June 1901. Royce agreed to take on the additional responsibility of designing a purpose-built factory capable of significant expansion opposite a factory owned by the cable maker, W.T. Glover, whose products Royce Ltd used. Following its own flotation of 200,000 of its £1 shares, W.T. Glover had moved to the Trafford Park Site during 1901, a year before Royce Ltd. In fact, its proprietor, Walter Glover, had died in 1893 and electrical inventor and entrepreneur Henry Edmunds took over the company before, in 1899, he also became a Director of Royce Ltd following the exchange of shares in Glover for a block of shares in Royce.[22]

The two companies' close association also offered particular benefits for Claremont, who in 1899 became a Director of W.T. Glover at a salary of £500 per annum. From now onwards author Tom Clarke believed Claremont recognised his 'strength and interest in financial management and began to diversify his working life beyond Royce Ltd.'[23] In 1902 his remuneration at Glovers increased to £1,000 a year and in 1903 he took over from Edmunds as its Managing Director and began spending a larger proportion of his time there than at 'Royces'. He also assumed directorships of other companies like the Trafford Park Power and Light Supply Co. and Howard Conduit Co. on sites adjacent to Royce Ltd.

At W.T. Glover's, Claremont gained the reputation of being a strict disciplinarian and its factory's corridors became festooned with his printed instructions – although under such firm and close direction it continued to prosper. Whatever his major new responsibilities, there was never any question of Claremont relinquishing his executive role at Royce, even if his approach could be expected to be somewhat less hands-on than in the past.

Whatever the possible effects of such management changes, the endeavours by Royce Ltd to raise more capital for its proposed new factory at Trafford Park relied on further strong commercial growth. Unfortunately, they coincided with a rapid and sharp recession in the electricity industry, which by 1901 had caused the collapse of the German home market and that country's goods being exported to Britain at very low prices (for products on which Royce had neglected to take out his own patents). At the same time, large American companies like Westinghouse, BTH and GEC entered the British electrical market, leading to the prices of electric motors falling sharply with 'a Crompton 10hp motor that sold for £65 in 1901 down to £30 by 1905'.[24]

Royce Ltd responded by making every effort to reduce its costs of manufacture without compromising the quality of its products. Inevitably the company's order book fell sharply, but far more seriously, Henry Royce, the lynchpin of the company's fortunes whose experience included several important fields of engineering and whose reserves of energy and endurance had always been legendary, began to show alarming signs of strain.[25]

Along with the multifarious responsibilities he had, of course, undertaken the planning of an additional factory in which to house the firm's latest equipment and provide a new site for its crane work and iron foundry without jeopardising production. Yet undoubtedly the most daunting of his problems was to maintain his own superlative standards in a fast-diminishing and ever more competitive market where his competitors appeared to recognise no code of conduct in their attempts to gain superiority. In near desperation Royce came to issue a plaintive caution to his customers: 'Owing to the inexperience of the public upon electrical matters in consequence of the industry having been created comparatively recently, it is an easy matter for unscrupulous contractors to undercut us by omitting important items, without attracting attention until the work is finished.'[26]

Claremont recognised Royce's growing problems and consulted Knutsford's general practitioner, Dr Theodore Fennell. In 1901 they arrived at the somewhat simplistic solution of trying to get Royce into the fresh air, while continuing to stimulate his engineering interests by purchasing a De Dion quadricycle for him to travel more effectively from the factory to his home in Knutsford. The chosen solution might well have been influenced by the fact that the doctor already owned a De Dion-Bouton quadricycle. Another quadricycle was ordered for Claremont.

The De Dion was far from being an advanced vehicle. It is best described as being like two bicycles side by side with a single-cylinder engine between them geared directly to their driving wheels. It had no clutch and its brakes were inefficient; to start you had either to pedal furiously or run and jump on. The problems of starting were matched by those of stopping, since the engine would habitually run for a short time even after the throttle was closed. Maurice Olley, who later worked closely with Royce, told Michael Evans about one of Royce's reminiscences about his 'quad'. Apparently, its brakes were so inefficient that he felt forced to build a rockery at the end of his driveway so that when turning into the house he could be sure of coming to a halt without descending into the spinney below.[27]

Whatever Royce's solutions, Claremont never got on with his quad and left its maintenance to Connor, his odd job man, who proved a failure. However far the quad might have helped awaken Royce's interest in motorised vehicles, it failed utterly to relieve him from the deep concerns caused by the threats to his company's core products.

The threatened nervous collapse duly took place and, despite Royce's fierce protests in 1902, his fellow Directors insisted on him taking his wife on a prolonged sea trip to South Africa to visit her relations there.

For ten weeks, Royce was cut off from all contact with the works,[28] following which he returned apparently physically and mentally refreshed. Even so, Dr Fennell and Claremont apparently persisted in their original aim of getting him into the fresh air by suggesting that instead of the crude De Dion quadricycle he should (along with Claremont) buy a motor car to travel more satisfactorily between the works and his home at Knutsford and to take his wife and niece out at weekends.[29]

What neither of them anticipated was that, regardless of its possible effects on Royce's health, his purchase of a motor car would transform his aspirations for the firm and lead to most far-reaching results.

3

Royce and His Motor Car

Royce's enforced break gave him an unforeseen but golden chance to reconsider his core business objectives.

Following years of unremitting application with protracted working hours filled to capacity, the ten-week interval – including extended sea journeys to and from South Africa – not only relieved him of his everyday responsibilities but gave him a unique opportunity for reflection, including some reading of trade journals and other publications.

In this regard, a book of 1902 entitled *The Automobile: Its Construction and Management*, based on a French textbook by Gerard Lavergne, was later found in the South of France with Henry Royce's signature on its fly leaf, along with the handwritten date of September 1902. The Royces did not return to the UK until late 1902 and there is a very strong chance that he had read the book.

Whether he did or not, the break gave the 39-year-old Royce undoubted time to consider whether the relatively untapped potential of automobile construction might offer new business opportunities akin to those in the electrical industry during its early days.

The last half century had certainly seen remarkable developments in this field. In 1876, the German Nicolaus Otto had produced the four-cycle gas engine, although it was not until 1889 that an internal combustion engine working on the four-cycle system – suction, compression, explosion and exhaust – began its rapid development. However, by the commencement of the twentieth century a new industry was in being with firms like Panhard,

Levassor, De Dion and Peugeot in France and Daimler, Napier, Wolseley and Lanchester in Britain producing motor cars. In 1895, M. Levassor won a Paris to Bordeaux race at the then amazing speed of 19.91mph and the new industry was given further recognition with the founding of the Automobile Club of Great Britain in 1897.

Intriguingly, whether, in fact, Royce was persuaded by Claremont or his doctor to buy a motor car, or, as Tom Clarke believes, he had 'bought it before his South African trip'[1] is not clear, although he had already shown a lively interest in the internal combustion engine when, for instance, he travelled by car through Hyde Park on an earlier business trip.[2] What was more, during 1900, he had undoubtedly constructed the motor for an electric car designed by Pritchetts and Gold – the company who acted as agents for Royce's dynamos in the South of England. Such was its quality that, following its removal from the car in 1914 and its transference to powering an acid pump, it was still working in the 1930s when Max Pemberton wrote his life of Royce.[3] Royce's chosen car was a Decauville, built by a French locomotive company that began producing automobiles in 1898. It had a

A Decauville similar to that acquired by Henry Royce. (Rolls-Royce Heritage Trust)

two-cylinder side-valve engine of 2,090cc, with the engine, gearbox and clutch as a single unit. However uncertain the events behind Royce's ordering of it, we are in no doubt about the circumstances of its collection. Here things began unpromisingly. When Royce went to pick it up at Manchester's Goods Station the engine obdurately refused to start. Master engineer or not, he had to hire four strong men to push it through the streets to the Cooke Street Factory while he sat at the wheel enduring the taunts of the city's urchins and other wags.

Despite its unfortunate debut, the Decauville was one of the better makes of car at the time, being reasonably reliable and speedy, if undoubtedly noisy by modern standards.

On the following day the fault was fixed and that evening he drove it home to Knutsford, but on the next Sunday morning its caprices again became apparent, although this time it ran out of petrol during a run due to its previous owner's over-optimism about its fuel consumption.

Royce used the car extensively and it soon experienced further problems, if of a relatively minor nature, including an overheating engine, ineffective brakes and oiled-up plugs. These were remedied, but when its flywheel worked loose more fundamental repairs were needed. Author Ian Lloyd believed that, at this point, Royce was not actually thinking of changing the whole car and still had no intention of manufacturing one. 'But in bringing the Decauville up to his own high standards he virtually redesigned the whole car and eventually produced a completely different, and in a number of important aspects, superior product.'[4]

It was therefore through such modifications, allied with Royce's aim for a car with unrivalled qualities of 'silence, lightness, durability and reliability',[5] that he came to believe he could make a better one himself.

Fortunately, Royce's new ambitions coincided with the removal of the firm's crane division to Trafford Park, thereby freeing up capacity at Cooke Street, a circumstance that enabled him to approach his fellow Directors about making not one, but three experimental motor cars, to a broadly similar specification as the Decauville, with prospects for further manufacture.

The conservative Claremont, for one, proved far from enthusiastic, even advising young Ernie Wooler that in the circumstances he should leave the firm and join W.T. Glover instead.[6] Claremont's opposition was shared by R.D. Hulley, a fellow Director and Royce's Works Manager, but Royce was determined to go ahead, if in a relatively modest way. He set up a small car

Car drawing office at Cooke Street. (Rolls-Royce Heritage Trust)

drawing office under experienced draughtsman A.J. Adams who was assisted by another called Shipley, with Ernie Wooler acting as their junior assistant.

On the construction side, Royce appointed Ernie Mills as his foreman over two electrical apprentices, Eric Platford and Tommy Haldenby.

Ernie Wooler subsequently related how he became involved from the beginning in Royce's plans:

> I started in the Drawing Office of Royce Limited in 1903 where I ran errands and mashed tea for the draughtsmen, made and delivered blueprints, learned to 'read' them and to know mechanical and electrical terms. Looking back, it seems that quite a lot of my time was spent 'visiting', asking questions and in the absence of the draughtsmen, scribbling comic sketches in the corners of their boards. One morning [in May 1903] soon after Mr. Royce arrived, George Bagnell, the shop general foreman, came up to me and said, 'Mr. Royce wants to see you in the Drawing Office.' His voice was ominous, and I went quickly. Mr. Royce gave me a severe dressing down for casual 'visiting' and scribbling sketches on the draughtsmen's

boards. Then he said, 'Now go along to the storeroom and get a typist's note pad.' I departed, at the double, returned with the pad and offered it to Mr. Royce. He waved it away saying, 'You hold on to that and follow me.'[7]

The nature of Wooler's admonishment revealed Royce's close knowledge of his staff, even juniors, and his shrewdness in selecting someone, however inexperienced, whose skill at sketching would play a crucial part in his plans.

As for Wooler, his use of the term 'Pa Royce' showed a measure of affection rather than fear for his outwardly stern and undoubtedly demanding chief.

After collecting Ernie Mills the three went to the small building housing Royce's car, where Royce straightaway took off his jacket and along with Mills set about stripping it down, piece by piece.

Ernie Wooler was told to sit on a box and make a sketch of each part as it was removed and measure it to capture its principal dimensions. It was a long and painstaking process, but Ernie's sketches became vital reference points for Royce and the two draughtsmen as they began to design the new car. The work did not enjoy priority over current contracts and it was general operative Florrie Austen, for instance, who had the task of winding the car's ignition coils on her modified Singer Sewing machine, while a tug of war developed over putting various machines to work on Royce's cars rather than on their regular assignments.

Under Royce's guidance, Ernie Mills, supported by apprentices Tommy Haldenby and Eric Platford, who together with Ernie Wooler would eventually come to hold senior positions in the company, worked assiduously on his new project.

Caricature showing Royce's temperament. (Rolls-Royce Heritage Trust)

As the drawings emerged they were sent to the shops for casting and, under Royce's rigorous demands, the car soon reached a level of mechanical development unattained by the Decauville or many others produced at the time. Royce's advances were seen in such things as the car's improved electrics, its carburettor, his choice of a differential rather than chain drive, a well-planned manifold system with a large silencer and clear run for the exhaust, a more effective radiator, a large-capacity water tank and single gear lever for the three-speed gearbox.

Royce, the electrician, made his own commutator, distributor and contacts, which functioned with the evenness of a chronometer. His carburettor, based on the Krebs system used in France, was so improved that truly automatic carburation was achieved – by shutting the throttle the engine speed was reduced to a tickover and on opening it the engine picked up smoothly (unlike most cars of 1904).

Major tasks like heavy forging and works on springing had to be done elsewhere, and when the parts were returned they had to pass the critical eye

First Royce two-cylinder 10hp car on test in the open stable yard at the Blake Street rear entrance to the Manchester Factory, 1903. (Rolls-Royce Heritage Trust)

of Royce, who had early on developed considerable knowledge about the composition and qualities of metals. In this regard he also came to insist on using expensive nickel steel for the car's components, which led Claremont to refer sarcastically to 'the guinea an ounce job'.

With Royce, the team's working hours were never short. On Monday they started at 8 a.m.; on the other days it was an hour and a half earlier and they uniformly worked right through Friday night until Saturday lunchtime, for which the apprentices earned just five shillings a week. Under such conditions, food could present a problem. When one of the apprentices became faint from hunger, he might suggest they got something to eat. Royce would agree and tell him to buy some food – although he would not always offer any money. The apprentice would return with a loaf of bread and some eggs. The eggs would be boiled on a furnace in the workshop and the bread torn apart in untidy hunks, which were passed round them. Royce worked equally hard as the others and at the weekend he often took home an experimental chassis to see if he could break anything or cause it to malfunction. During the process, the car's engine was subjected to long hours of bench running where it was coupled to a dynamo and run at full power for some hours, the results of which were meticulously observed in a log kept by Platford and Haldenby that began on 16 September 1903.

Following such intense application, by 1 April 1904 the first car was finally ready for its road run. This commenced with a couple of turns of the starting handle that brought the engine to life[8] with a gentle 'phuf, phuf, phuf' and, with Royce at the wheel, it moved through the doors of the workshop towards the factory's main gates and onto Blake Street. As it went out, the excited workforce paid their ultimate acclaim to its constructor by enthusiastically hammering on 'bench tops, metal sheets, castings – anything to hand to raise a din in honour of the occasion'[9] – a custom fully appreciated by the quietly smiling Royce.

As a precaution, Platford followed in the Decauville, but the 30-mile journey to Knutsford and back was incident free. All had been tested so thoroughly that within a week the chassis was sent to a local coachbuilder to have a two-seater body fitted. The other two chassis were finished and bodied soon afterwards. The application of the Royce principles of engineering, developed in his electrical works, had helped to 'transform the [relatively] unreliable, fussy, noisy, motor car into a reliable, smoothly functioning machine'.[10]

The first Royce car on the road. (Rolls-Royce Heritage Trust)

The first car was initially given to Claremont as a test vehicle, but it was soon used for other purposes. Claremont was subsequently given the long-term use of Royce's second car, where he demonstrated his early lack of faith, if not impatience, with Royce's near perfect car by routinely briefing a hansom cab to follow his intended route in case of 'failures to proceed'. He revealed his dour humour by having a plate attached to the dashboard on which were engraved the words, 'If the car breaks down please do not ask a lot of silly questions'. Even so, his regard for Royce was immense. On one occasion Royce told his tester, Eric Platford, to take Claremont in the second car to keep an important appointment. Having discovered the front axle pivot had cracked, he told the Chairman of the occurrence and said he could not take him that day. Claremont was very insistent, but nothing would induce Platford to go against Royce's teaching. On seeing the fault, Royce, realising what he must have gone through, praised him and later Claremont sent for him, thanked him for saving his life and praised him for his grasp of Royce's principles and his loyalty to them.[11]

While understandably at this time virtually all Royce's concern was with the development and construction of his three prototype vehicles, he was shortly to receive unforeseen, but unrivalled, opportunities to market them from three men who played prominent roles in early British motoring. They were Henry Edmunds, the Honourable Charles Rolls and Claude Johnson, who in their different ways came to recognise Royce's exceptional engineering skills and unceasing quest for perfection.

Royce's relationship with Henry Edmunds was by far the most fleeting of them, but as the catalyst who brought about the groundbreaking meeting between Royce and Charles Rolls, Edmunds' role proved fundamental.

Henry Edmunds, who introduced Rolls to Royce in May 1904. (Rolls-Royce Heritage Trust)

Born in 1853, Edmunds was the son of a successful ironmonger and Methodist preacher who enjoyed a private education, during which time he made a particular study of scientific books, before entering the engineering works of Edmunds and Hookway, where his father was senior partner.

He was soon to make an impact when at the age of 20, along with Joseph Arthur Wood and David Pitcairn Wright, he submitted a patent application in the new field of electricity for 'certain improvements in lighting and heating by the combustion of hydrocarbons or other volatile fuels'.[12] Within four years, after travelling to America where he met the inventors Dr Graham Bell and Thomas Edison, he returned to the UK with the Swan incandescent lamp as one of Britain's pioneers in electric lighting. By 1880, Edmunds was involved with what would become the British Electrical Engineering Company and by 1881 was responsible for the introduction of electric lighting in the Royal Navy.[13]

Edmunds' acquaintance with Royce came about after he had joined businessman Walter Glover in the formation of W.T. Glover and Co., which manufactured cables used by Royce for his cranes. In 1893, on W.T. Glover's death, Edmunds took over the company and a closeness developed between the two firms, which was seen in 1899 when Edmunds became a Director of Royce Ltd and in the following year when Royce's partner Ernest Claremont became a Director in W.T. Glover. Along with their joint business interests, by 1901 Edmunds, Royce and Claremont shared an enthusiasm for early motoring. All three owned De Dion motor cycles, although Edmunds was undoubtedly ahead of the other two for he had acquired his tricycle as opposed to their quadricycles some two years before theirs. In 1899 he went on to buy a motor car at the Paris Motor Show, before later in the year progressing to a second and superior model in the shape of a 4hp Daimler. That year he also joined the exclusive Automobile Club and took part in its epic 1,000 Mile Trial of 1900, before in 1902 sponsoring what became known as the Henry Edmunds Hill Climbing Trophy, which was put up for competition in 1903.[14]

Yet whatever Edmunds' undoubted energy and eagerness to throw himself into what he believed were exciting new scientific developments, he seemed destined to experience setbacks. In 1900 alone he submitted eight patent applications for electrical contrivances, despite failing to obtain a financial return on several earlier inventions that might have made him a rich man.[15] From now on, however, with his increased motor activities he came to devote more time to the engineering problems associated with mechanical transport and less to those of electrical generation and distribution.[16]

In spite of his undoubted business achievements so far and his prominence in the Automobile Club, Edmunds' mercurial temperament made it most unlikely that he could ever match Royce's exceptional sense of commitment nor Ernest Claremont's brand of micro-management. Edmunds' biographer Paul Tritton tellingly described him as someone never committed to any one person or idea to the exclusion of others, a friend and confidant of all the great inventors of the day, an effective public speaker, always ready for a new adventure or idea, which would usually be dropped as the next one caught his attention, and a genuine zest for life's curiosity and variety.

Such gadfly tendencies and inconsistencies would, however, be left behind by what became a steadfast determination to bring Royce and Rolls together.

In pursuit of his aim Edmunds was able to adopt an avuncular role with Royce, where as the much more experienced motorist he could offer advice and encouragement.[17] Although much older, he could never adopt a similar attitude with the aloof young aristocrat Charles Rolls, who by 1902 had not only established a reputation as a leading driver and motoring propagandist but had set up in business selling superior motor cars.

Notwithstanding, a relationship developed between them through their joint activities as committee members of the Automobile Club. Both took part in its 1,000 Miles Motor Vehicle Trial in 1900 and Rolls competed for Edmunds' Hill Climbing Trophy.

Evidence of their association came in an invitation from Lord Llangattock for Edmunds to dine at the Rolls' palatial family home in South Lodge, Knightsbridge. In fact, the dinner took place a week after the Automobile Club's 1,000 Mile Trial and during it 'the guests received news about the relief of Mafeking'.[18]

According to Edmunds, it was Rolls who, in 1903, made the initial contact about the possibility of finding a British car constructor, due to his business arrangements with Panhard cars losing their allure and his intention to look for alternative producers, saying, 'I wish you would give me any information you may get hold of relative to improvements in the building of motor cars.'[19]

By this time, or shortly afterwards, Edmunds was likely to have learned from his friend, Ernest Claremont, that contrary to Royce and Co.'s activities in electric crane work, 'Royce had been building a motor car according to his own ideas which he wished me to see.'[20]

Strong circumstantial evidence points to Edmunds having seen and been much impressed by Royce's new car, even to the extent of thinking Royce was a genius as a car designer and, by the spring of 1904, he had not only told Rolls about it but Rolls had responded by saying that 'he would like to have an opportunity of meeting Mr. Royce and trying it for himself'.[21]

At this point, Edmunds seems to have believed that Rolls was still only moderately interested and he attempted to place the onus on Royce – whose car it was – to come to a meeting with Rolls, saying it would be much more convenient 'if you could see him in London as he was so very much occupied and further that several other houses are in negotiation with him wishing to do the whole or part of his work'.[22] Edmunds, however, ended on a positive note by offering to do everything he could to bring about such an arrangement as he thought Royce's car deserved well and ought to take its place once it was recognised by the public on its merits.[23]

True to his word, on the same day, Edmunds wrote to Rolls sending him photographs and specifications of the Royce car along with the reassurance that, 'Knowing as I do, the skill of Mr. Royce as a practical mechanical engineer, I feel one is very safe in taking up any work his firm may produce.'[24] Edmunds ended his communication with the hope that 'a meeting might lead to business to our mutual interest in the future'.[25]

Despite Edmunds' encouragement Rolls' response was less than he had hoped, for not only were there other options but he harboured a definite dislike of two-cylinder cars.

Equally frustrating, Edmunds received no help from Royce, who remained in Manchester engrossed on getting his first car ready for its road test and working on the second, whose engine was ready for fitting onto its chassis.

At this point Edmunds, determined to end the impasse, created a situation whereby the car's outstanding qualities could be seen and his own commercial interests furthered. Edmunds was currently Chairman of the Parson's Non-Skid Company, dedicated to preventing cars from side-slipping on the hazardous roads of the day by attaching a series of chains to their tyres, and he recommended that Royce should release his prototype car to take part in the non-skid road tests.

As a consequence, it took part in a series of tests held by the Automobile Club between 18 and 25 April 1904. On Day One it travelled to Margate and back, where one of its passengers on behalf of the Automobile Club was the noted Rolls-Royce observer Massac Buist. It covered a total of 145.5 miles, during which it performed splendidly in tests that Edmunds knew would be performed in front of the Club's Organising Committee – including Charles Rolls.

This time the bait was swiftly taken for on 29 April, as the cars gathered for their final tests in North London, Rolls sent Edmunds the following succinct letter:

> Dear Edmunds, can you come to Manchester any time next week?'
>
> Yours Truly,
> Chas S. Rolls[26]

Rolls and Edmunds travelled to Manchester by train, where in the dining car Edmunds must have been delighted to hear Rolls acknowledging his ambition to have a motor car connected with his name so that in future it might be a household word 'as much as Broadwood or Steinway in connection with pianos; or Chubbs in connection with safes'.[27]

Edmunds recalled that they went to the Midland Hotel in Manchester, where the three dined together; Rolls and Royce apparently took to each other at first sight and Rolls went to see the Royce car.[28]

According to author Wilton Oldham, following this meeting, Rolls returned to London full of enthusiasm and went straight to his partner, Claude Johnson, to tell him all about his trip to Manchester, saying, 'I have found the greatest engineer in the world.'[29] Whether the story is apocryphal or not, it is hard to think of a more fortunate match for Royce and his laboriously produced and yet unproven cars than with such a well-connected young entrepreneur and established car salesman, along with Claude Johnson, his inspirational partner and one time Secretary of the Automobile Club.

After Johnson met Royce and inspected the 10hp car, he was as enthusiastic as Rolls and it was quickly arranged that the firm of C.S. Rolls and Co. would have the sole selling rights of the marque, one of the conditions being that the car would be sold under the name of Rolls-Royce.[30]

Some three months later, on 8 August 1904, Henry Edmunds received a communication about a forthcoming formal agreement between Rolls and Royce – which he had done so much to bring about – written in Royce's measured language.

> Dear Mr. Edmunds,
>
> With reference to Mr. Rolls taking our manufactures, he has at present in his possession an agreement we have got out on these lines, and with reference to his suggestion that you should be named as umpire, I should be most happy to agree to this, as I know your anxiety would be for everything to be quite fair on each side.
>
> I must thank you for your introduction which is promising well, and I think we ought to be of great service to each other.
>
> Yours faithfully,
> F.H. Royce[31]

The Midland Hotel, Manchester, where the first meeting took place. (P.H. Vickers)

Forecourt of the Midland Hotel, showing the brass plaque commemorating the meeting of Rolls and Royce. (P.H. Vickers)

Through an uncharacteristic combination of persistence and high personal skills, Edmunds could be certain he had achieved the objective he so richly deserved – one that would be destined to lead to momentous results.

Relief sculpture by Lynda Addison in the forecourt of the Midland Hotel, depicting the first meeting between Rolls and Royce. (P.H. Vickers)

PART 2:
OF WHEELS AND WINGS

4

Rolls and Royce

It was an undoubted fact that Henry Royce's prospects of marketing his meticulously constructed cars were transformed by his commercial union with the Honourable Charles Rolls.

Rolls launched his motor business in London during January 1902 with the aid of a £6,500 loan from his father Lord Llangattock. C.S. Rolls & Co. offered a sales agency for petrol-driven cars from premises containing a spacious repair shop of some 30,000sq. ft at Lillie Hall, a garage at West Brompton and subsequently a showroom in Conduit Street in London's West End. Its aim was to sell high-class motor cars, most of which would come from France, and under its young gentleman salesman it soon flourished. In late 1903, due to its growing complexity and size (its Mayfair showrooms opened at 28 Brook Street in December), Rolls took on noted events organiser Claude Johnson as his partner, to help with the marketing and assist in running the business as a whole.

Tall, singular and austere, in spite of his privileged background Rolls did not initially seem destined for distinction. From early childhood he had been something of a natural solitary with few acquaintances and his short temper, somewhat crude public-school sense of humour and monumental meanness did not appeal to many. On the other hand, he was a natural and committed proselytizer for powered transport whose social position gave him an influence disproportionate to his age. During his somewhat undistinguished time at Eton, he began to find himself and displayed a strong interest in practical engineering, which along with his high self-confidence involved him in surprising undertakings. In his school holidays, for instance, he wired the servants' quarters at 'The Hendre', his father's stately home in Monmouthshire, to run off the electricity produced by a steam generator he had talked his father into buying – although, unsurprisingly, he was not permitted to wire the main house.[1]

The Honourable Charles Rolls. (Rolls-Royce Heritage Trust)

While not academic, following supplementary coaching he was admitted to read engineering at Trinity College, Cambridge, from where following a three-year course he graduated in 1898 in the new discipline of Mechanism and Applied Science, a feat that helped determine the future pattern of his life. At Cambridge he quickly became known as a cyclist and for his love of speed. By 1896 he had graduated to four wheels – the very year the maximum speed limit in Britain had been raised from 4 to 12mph – after spending a weekend with Sir David Salamons, who owned a Peugeot motor car in which Rolls travelled at up to an amazing 20mph. Rolls thereupon took a shopping trip to Paris, where he bought a 3.75hp Peugeot costing £225, towards which his father contributed £140.

At Cambridge, Rolls was the first undergraduate to own a motor car and he became accustomed to repairing it in the university workshops, where he was supervised by Professor J.A. Ewing. He soon became a dedicated propagandist for the horseless carriage[2] and went on to try out all manner of automobiles, including Panhard racing cars. Yet, while he was always looking for new motoring challenges and in 1899 installed his own workshop in South Lodge, the family's home in Kensington, he was no mechanical originator and his activities there were limited to repair work.

Predictably Rolls, who throughout his life always liked to win, was soon attracted by early motoring competitions, where the competitors struggled against multiple mechanical malfunctions and the weather. While at Cambridge he attempted to take part in the original London to Brighton Emancipation Run of November 1896, but on his way to London he broke an axle and ended up in a ditch, from where he and his passengers continued their journey by train. As one of the youngest members of the Automobile Club of Great Britain and Ireland – where he served as a loyal committee member until 1908 – Rolls quickly became renowned for making long-distance journeys in a variety of cars along the hazardous roads of the time, in both Britain and Europe, including at night time and in winter. These included the Automobile Club's epic 1,000 Mile Motor Vehicle Trial during April–May 1900 over a journey between London and Edinburgh designed to demonstrate the fast-growing power of motor cars. As he solemnly explained to his father in a letter asking for financial assistance, he attended the Trial as a sort of duty. During it he drove a 12hp French Panhard and duly won the Club's medal for the best amateur performance.

Writing in the *Motor Car Journal* prior to the Trial, Rolls explained his firm belief in racing and trials, for, 'The maker who can produce a vehicle to stand the strain of a great race is best able to build one for ordinary touring or pleasure.'[3] He believed that racing improved the breed and that a motor car needed selling as a tried and dependable vehicle – not just as a temperamental toy for the leisured classes. He would only race, however, if he considered the event was sufficiently important to the project that most interested him at the time. By the beginning of 1902, the time allocated by him for competitions both in Britain and in Europe (he was the first British driver to race on the Continent) was having to give way to his prime business interests.

At first glance, entering the motor trade might have seemed rather odd behaviour for the son of a peer but, as with Rolls' other activities, selling motor cars represented a logical step in converting the British public to their use and to meet his need for more than his father's allowance of £500 a year to support his competitive motor expenses and his ballooning. In spite of his personality shortcomings, his success as a demonstrator owed something to his title but probably far more to him offering hire-purchase terms of 25 per cent down, with the balance to be paid in four quarterly payments at 5 per cent interest. His acuteness was also evident when he kept his large garage at Lillie Hall going by undertaking insurance repair work and hiring cars out with chauffeurs.

Rolls confirmed his business' success in a peculiarly formal letter to his father on 5 December 1903, telling him that he had got 100 cars on order for the next year, 'which shall be able to sell (in London) as cheap as can be bought in Paris owing to getting much better terms for 1904'. He ended by saying:

> … my business has turned out so enormous with so many different departments that it has really been too much for me and I have had to leave far too much to others, who unfortunately have not always turned out to be the best men for the job.
> However, am gradually getting it right.
>
> Yours ever,
>
> Chas S. Rolls[4]

The first Royce car being demonstrated by Rolls on manoeuvres at Folkestone in the uniform of the Motor Volunteer Corps. At his side is HRH the Duke of Connaught. (Rolls-Royce Heritage Trust)

The letter demonstrated cool confidence for someone not yet 27 years of age who fully recognised the importance of his business in his wider campaign for publicising the motor car. We see the same reasoning applied to his competitive driving. Following his agreement to sell Henry Royce's cars and the subsequent establishment of Rolls-Royce, the aim of Rolls' driving was to emphasise their mechanical superiority. Following his successes, his abandonment of competitive racing was fully in keeping with his wider ambitions and he believed, in accordance with Claude Johnson's policy at Rolls-Royce, that once a race had been won there was no point going to the great expense of repeating the process.

While this proved a stellar period for Rolls' driving, it also served to demonstrate that even Royce's cars could suffer malfunctions. Rolls was, for instance, entered to drive Royce's 'Light Twenty' – with its comparatively modest four-cylinder 20hp engine – in the first ever Isle of Man International Tourist Trophy Race held on 14 September 1905,[5] where to his extreme anger, during the race's early stages his car suffered a fatal gearbox failure. At first Rolls raised wild accusations of sabotage but fortunately the firm's second car, driven by Percy Northey, gained a very creditable second place. If on this occasion Rolls did not distinguish himself as a driver, he could at least come forward as a public speaker. When, on 3 November 1905, the Rolls-Royce Company held a dinner in London to celebrate Northey's success, Rolls used his after-dinner speech to announce the firm's production of an outstanding new car, a six-cylinder 40/50hp model (subsequently called the Silver Ghost). During the course of the dinner, he also paid remarkable and genuine tribute to Henry Royce, telling his audience that he was no ordinary designer,

> ... but a man of exceptional ingenuity and power of overcoming difficulties – his extraordinary genius had enabled him to effect clever improvements in general and in detail which have been possessed by no other make of car. The result is the vehicle which you now know under the joint name of Mr. Royce and myself and which I think I may go as far as to say has now to be reckoned amongst the first rank of automobile manufacturers in the world, having established for itself in a very brief period an honest reputation for silence, simplicity and high quality.[6]

During 1906, it was back to driving: Rolls was once more involved in most meticulous preparations with Royce's 'Light Twenty' in which he went on to break the Monte Carlo to London record, taking twenty-eight hours fourteen minutes to drive the 771 miles from Monte Carlo to Boulogne. Later in the month he succeeded in winning the Isle of Man TT Race at his second attempt.

This victory crowned Rolls' driving career, although in 1907 he shared in driving the Silver Ghost during the 15,000 Mile Trial held by the Automobile Club in which the car gained its reputation for unparalleled reliability.

The inspiration for such a spectacular endurance test came from Claude Johnson, although Rolls enthusiastically took it up. By the terms of the competition, the Automobile Club was invited to appoint officials to observe – under the strictest conditions – a non-stop run of 'no less than 15,000 miles to be accomplished on set journeys between England and Scotland',[7] the equal of three years' normal wear in an owner-driver's hands. The Trial was run day and night on weekdays without stopping the engine. On Sundays,

The first Rolls-Royce logo. (Rolls-Royce Heritage Trust)

THE COMPANIES ACTS, 1862 TO 1900.

COMPANY LIMITED BY SHARES.

MEMORANDUM OF ASSOCIATION OF ROLLS-ROYCE, LIMITED.

1. The name of the Company is Rolls-Royce, Limited.
2. The registered office of the Company will be situate in England.
3. The objects for which the Company is established are:—

(1) To manufacture, sell, or let on hire, or in any manner dispose of or turn to account, motor vehicles for use on land or water or in the air, and any parts of or accessories to the same, and internal combustion engines for stationary use, and to carry on all or any businesses directly or indirectly relating to or connected with any object or thing which the Company is authorized to manufacture.

(2) To purchase or otherwise acquire from Royce, Limited, their factory at Cooke Street, Hulme, Manchester, with the machinery, plant, and stock-in-trade therein, and the goodwill of their business of motor car and motor chassis manufacturers, together with book debts and other assets as a going concern, and to that end to enter into the Contract, draft of which is already prepared and is referred to in the Articles of Association of the Company, with such modifications (if any) as may be thought desirable.

(3) To manufacture all or any machinery, tools or things for the purpose, directly or indirectly, of the manufacturing of any vehicles or other objects which the Company is authorized to manufacture.

(4) To buy or otherwise acquire, sell, let, trade with, or otherwise deal in, or with all or any motor vehicles, machinery, tools and things as aforesaid.

(5) To carry on any other business, whether manufacturing or otherwise, which may seem to the Company capable of being conveniently carried on in connection with any of the above objects, or calculated, directly or indirectly, to advance any of the above objects, or add to the value of any of the Company's property or rights.

(6) To purchase, sell, take, or let on lease, or otherwise acquire or dispose of any land or buildings or personal property, or rights or privileges, for the purpose of the Company, or of advancing the Company's interest.

(17) To lend money to persons and on terms as may seem expedient, and in particular to customers and persons having dealings with the Company, and to give any guarantee or indemnity which may be or may be thought to be desirable.

(18) To raise or borrow or secure payment of money in such manner and on such terms as may seem expedient, and in particular by the issue of debentures or debenture stock, perpetual or otherwise, charged on the whole or any part of the Company's assets, present and future, including its uncalled capital, and to redeem, purchase, and pay up any such securities.

(19) To draw, accept, indorse, discount, and otherwise deal with promissory notes bills of exchange, and other negotiable instruments or securities.

(20) To remunerate (subject always so far as necessary to compliance with the Companies Acts and the Company's Articles of Association) any persons for services rendered or to be rendered in placing or assisting to place or guaranteeing the placing of any shares in the Company's capital, or any debentures or debenture stock or other securities of the Company, or in or about the formation or promotion of the Company.

(21) To do all or any of the above things as agents or trustees, or by or through agents or trustees.

(22) To divide any of the profits of the Company in specie among the members.

(23) To do all such other things as are incidental to the attainment of the above objects.

The objects specified in the several paragraphs of this clause shall (except where otherwise expressed in such paragraphs) not be restricted by reference to, or by inference from the terms of any other paragraph or the name of the Company.

4. The liability of the members is limited.
5. The capital of the Company is £60,000, divided into 60,000 shares

1. The name of the Company is Rolls-Royce, Limited.
2. The registered office of the Company will be situate in England.
3. The objects for which the Company is established are:—

(1) To manufacture, sell, or let on hire, or in any manner dispose of or turn to account, motor vehicles for use on land or water or in the air, and any parts of or accessories to the same, and internal combustion engines for stationary use, and to carry on all or any businesses directly or indirectly relating to or connected with any object or thing which the Company is authorized to manufacture.

or indirectly to conduce to the interests of the Company, or of its | R. D. Hulley, Albert Road, Levenshulme, Manchester, | One Preference Share.

Memorandum of Association of Rolls-Royce Ltd. (Rolls-Royce Heritage Trust) the car was locked in a garage until the next day. Claude Johnson drove the first 4,000 miles and Rolls during the final leg. For Johnson, Rolls and the car's other two drivers, Reg Macready and Eric Platford, the test's main feature was its monotony. Between June and mid-August, the Silver Ghost covered some 400 miles a day without giving the slightest trouble. There was one exception: after 629 miles, when bumping along a very rough track, its petrol cap was shaken into the shut position and the car stopped for a minute before the problem was identified. At the end of the run, the Automobile Club's mechanics were invited to strip the car down in order to give every part a thorough examination and replace it at the sign of wear so that the car would be as new. They reported that the only wear ascertainable was less than one-thousandth of an inch in part of the steering and universal joints, that the valves needed regrinding and the water pump could do with repacking – at a total cost of £2 2*s* 7*d*.[8] Never before had a car been submitted to so searching a test and, as Rolls and Johnson anticipated, the result gave precious publicity to a company whose relative anonymity had recently brought about major problems in getting itself established. On 15 March 1906, Rolls-Royce Ltd was registered with a capital of £60,000 prior to its official flotation on the Birmingham Stock Exchange, due in December of the same year.[9] By this time it had been decided to increase the firm's capital to £200,000 and 'a public issue of preferred and ordinary shares to the value of £100,000 to acquire the business of C.S. Rolls & Co. was made on 11 December 1906'.[10] In spite of inspired publicity by Rolls and Johnson in particular, the excellence of the cars emerging from what remained a small firm was still not yet widely appreciated (the Silver Ghost did not go on a public road until April 1907) and the response to the issue proved disappointing. A minimum subscription was set at £50,000 on the understanding that unless this was received, the flotation would have to be abandoned. This caused a crisis for, on the day before the flotation closed, only £41,000 had been subscribed – far short of the minimum needed. At this point, the Company Secretary, John De Looze, had a flash of inspiration. He decided to appeal for help from Arthur Briggs, a wealthy textile manufacturer who had bought the firm's first 'Light Twenty' car. De Looze boarded the earliest available train from Manchester to Harrogate and returned triumphant, waving a cheque for £10,000. Briggs was rewarded with a seat on the Board and on 9 January 1907 it was announced that £63,000 in all had been subscribed, thus ensuring the firm's continued existence.[11]

The first Royce chassis completed and ready for the body. (Rolls-Royce Heritage Trust)

It had been a near-run thing and by the end of 1906, the firm faced a longer-term threat in that the interests of its two key figures, Rolls and Royce, were already beginning to diverge. For Rolls the success of the firm's public share issue and the advent of the outstanding Silver Ghost meant its affairs were taking on a steadier evolutionary pattern where the thrills and alarms of the initial years – including his headlong racing – had for the most part been supplanted by seemingly endless demands to demonstrate the firm's cars to would-be buyers. As a consequence, the man who had long been an ardent balloonist felt able to pay increased attention to this activity and to the novel and highly dangerous field of powered flight.

In contrast, Royce's commitment remained totally with the company, where he continued to shoulder an immense workload dominated by the production of the Silver Ghost. Here, he experienced unprecedented problems with its crankshaft, which he originally based on the dimensions used in his smaller cars. He eventually solved the issues with the design of 'a robust seven bearing crank shaft much stiffer in torsion located in a [new] rigid aluminium crankcase providing massive front centre and rear main bearings'.[12] There was also the pressing requirement for him to plan a new factory, due to be opened by 9 June 1908, which had to be equipped with a proportion

The first six-cylinder (30hp) crankshaft nearing completion. (Rolls-Royce Heritage Trust)

of high-specification machine tools needed to produce the Silver Ghost in the numbers required. With further growth expected, Royce's factory design had to anticipate 'the likelihood of a further large extension [to it] should the need arise without involving disorganisation'.[13] In the event he showed surprising skill in this regard for his proposed buildings proved as spacious, airy and well-appointed as most factories half a century later. Under his direction, 'the company acquired or had firm options on sufficient land to serve the needs of the company's war and post war expansions'.[14] He also developed many special tools and even automatic machines for use in the factory intended for the production of six-cylinder chassis.

In contrast, Rolls' restless daemon was looking elsewhere, with the pull of aviation proving so strong that within three years his hands-on role with Rolls-Royce would be largely over and during April 1910 he would sever all his remaining responsibilities with the company.

Since the beginning of the twentieth century Rolls had developed a special interest in ballooning. While other pioneering car drivers like John Moore-Brabazon – who had served as a gentleman mechanic to Rolls – and early car racer, aviator and future industrial leader, Tommy Sopwith, also took part in balloon flights, neither felt the same rapport as Rolls. Away from his normal bustling existence, Rolls – like aviation pioneer Frank Hedges Butler who found rare peace floating silently 'among the ever-changing panorama of clouds, sometimes [resembling] glaciers and snow mountains, sometimes the rolling billows of the sea'[15] – loved the skyscapes and became a connoisseur of aerial photography.

To Rolls ballooning went even further, representing a carefree experience away from the frequent police interference that plagued early motorists and away from the company of ordinary people who could be burdensome for a solitary like himself. Yet in spite of ballooning's detachment and serenity, it was essentially a recreation that, while giving him rare opportunities for reflection, could never match his subsequent enthusiasm for powered flight.

During one of his many ascents with Frank Butler's daughter, Vera, they made plans to launch the Aero Club[16] to help govern aerial sport in Britain, which although primarily concerned with balloons, included the conduct of power-assisted vehicles. As Rolls remarked proudly 'in a week or ten days, we had a hundred applicants for membership'.[17]

By 1906, it was apparent that Rolls' aviation interests were competing fiercely with those concerned with automobiles. While closely involved in his preparations for the Isle of Man's Tourist Trophy Race, he still found time to represent Britain (with distinction) in the Gordon Bennett Cup for the International Balloon Race. After starting in Paris, he crossed the Channel, for which feat he received a gold medal for the length of time spent in the air.

During the same year, when Rolls went to America on a sales tour to promote the 40/50 Silver Ghost and set up a motor agency in New York, his aviation interests were again apparent when, after taking part in experiments with gliders based on the Wrights' designs, he succeeded in interviewing the elusive brothers in their home town.

During January 1907, Rolls was back in America exhibiting Rolls-Royce cars in New York's Madison Square Garden and his enthusiasm for motoring matters appeared to have been rekindled. He complained vigorously, for instance, about British car makers being apathetic about exports, including those to America, and demonstrated he had not lost his enthusiasm for competitive driving when, in a five-mile race at the Empire City Track in New York, he won the Silver Trophy in an obsolescent 'Light Twenty'. Confident in its robustness, he cornered savagely to keep the American drivers from jockeying him out of the way, defeating far more powerful cars in the process, like a 30hp Packard, 45hp Peerless and Westinghouse models and a 60hp Renault.[18] This proved something of a false dawn for back in England, although he was still committed to a succession of sales meetings and demonstrations, it was apparent his interest in motoring affairs was flagging. As his Secretary Florence Caswell recalled, while he had always been accustomed to keep irregular hours, this had increased with his additional interests, and he forgot appointments and would appear without warning. Rolls' last public appearance in the world of motoring came during 1908 in Paris when he took part in the International Roads Congress, where he gave a thoughtful paper on the effects of road surfaces on vehicles 'in the course of which he proposed the proper balancing of engines, the use of longer springs and wheel bases and the provision of shock absorbers'[19] – which at the time were still uncommon. However, following the event in Paris, Rolls showed intense interest in watching Wilbur Wright demonstrate his advanced flying skills, following which he took up various members of the French Bollée family of carmakers. During the second week of October, Rolls, along with six others, was able to fly with Wilbur Wright. His enthusiastic summary of the flight included a detailed observation of the atmosphere near the earth's surface, '[which] even in what we call calm weather – is made up of spiral movements of varying diameter, sometimes vertical and sometimes horizontal, undulations of all sorts, little hills and valleys and streams of air, in fact, one might call it a new world conquered by man.'[20]

His extraordinary but reasoned passion was evident in a magazine article, where he wrote about the exceptional thrill of flying: 'The power of flight is a fresh gift from the Creator, the greatest treasure yet given to man, and one, I believe destined to work changes in human life as we know it today.'[21]

During a Board meeting in 1909, Rolls attempted to interest his fellow Directors at Rolls-Royce in aircraft construction with the proposal 'that this Company should acquire the right for the British Isles to manufacture the Wright Aeroplane'. Despite the proposer's high status, it was turned down without further consideration.[22] Although in fairness, apart from the other Directors' lack of imagination where aircraft were concerned, the decision could have been influenced by a shortage of working capital together with the fear that by becoming involved with aero engines, Henry Royce might further overtax himself. Their negative attitude was also likely to have been influenced by a personal initiative taken by Rolls during 1907 when the Army's airship 'Nulli Secundus' was being built by Colonel Capper at Farnborough. On his own authority, Rolls ordered the mechanics at Lillie

Hall to make shafting and drives for it, along with forging its aluminium casing. This predictably aroused the wrath of Ernest Claremont, who moved a resolution 'that this company not be allowed to depart from its standard work and manufactures without first obtaining the consent of the Board'.[23]

At the same time, Rolls decided to order for himself one of a batch of six Wright-type aeroplanes being built by Horace Short and his brothers at Leysdown on the Isle of Sheppey and to spend much of his time learning about their controls by practising on a glider that Shorts supplied. In May, when the Wrights came to England, Rolls assumed the role of host. He took them down to Sheppey in his Silver Ghost, gaining undoubted publicity for the car in the process, where he introduced them to Horace Short.

Henry Royce in 1907. (Rolls-Royce Heritage Trust)

Rolls driving the Wright brothers in a Silver Ghost at Sheppey, May 1907. (Rolls-Royce Heritage Trust)

At a dinner given by Frank Butler in the Wrights' honour, Rolls talked both about the likely future popularity of aviation and its place in warfare when he presciently warned them that the dropping of bombs from airships was already practical and would be resorted to in the next war.[24] By this time, Rolls' determination to develop his flying skills had seen him make a growing number of glider flights prior to receiving his Short-Wright biplane. On its delivery he increased his efforts further and by the end of the year had succeeded in making a powered flight lasting some forty-eight minutes.

By 1910 flying had come to dominate Rolls' life. His appearances at Conduit Street became steadily fewer, and at a Board Meeting in January he asked his co-Directors to be relieved of some of his motor-car demonstrations, although at that time he still wished to retain his seat on the Board. However, in April he finally resigned from the Board to relieve himself of duties that he had come to consider 'irksome' compared with aviation, and in the following months he discussed plans to set up as an aircraft manufacturer[25] with young aviator Mr E. Keith-Davies.

In April, at Nice, he took part in his first flying competition, where his sixth place in general classification showed him the equal of any foreign aviator, and on 2 June 1910 he became the first flyer to make a non-stop cross-Channel flight in his Short-Wright biplane to Sangatte and back. This lasted some ninety minutes, although his average speed of 30mph was slower than Blériot's original one-way journey. For this achievement he received a gold medal from the Royal Aero Club, a distinction only so far given to Wilbur and Orville Wright, and to his genuine surprise found himself becoming something of a national hero – an achievement not possible with car driving at the time.

Rolls' final involvement with Rolls-Royce was on 8 July when he attended a gathering of its Directors at Derby. Just five days later, he and his aeroplane attended the Bournemouth International Aviation Meeting, attended by nineteen entrants from Britain and France. Rolls was experiencing particular problems with his aircraft over its longitudinal control. He had ordered a new elevator that did not arrive until 7 July and he fitted it three days later, giving him no time to conduct flight tests before the meeting commenced. On 12 July, in wind gusting up to 25mph, he was making a sharp descent when parts of his tailplane gave way, causing him to dive straight into the ground. He was thrown clear but died within a few seconds from concussion of the brain. Pioneer aviator Samuel Cody

Rolls in the French Wright Flyer at Bournemouth. (Rolls-Royce Heritage Trust)

was the first to reach the stricken airman, who at just 33 years of age became the first air show fatality.

On hearing the news, Henry Royce was much affected by the loss of someone who in his own fashion mirrored his single-mindedness, although Rolls' mind ranged beyond Royce's consuming interest in the mechanics of engines and vehicles to the future of powered transportation as a whole.

Of Rolls-Royce's three early giants, Royce, Rolls and Johnson, Charles Rolls had by far the shortest connection with the firm.

It was an association lasting just four years and four months. compared with Claude Johnson who, after becoming Rolls-Royce's outstanding Managing Director, died in 1926 while still serving the company and its founder, Henry Royce, who would continue into the 1930s.

Even so, Rolls' contribution was indispensable. Without his agency for superior motor cars, Royce's peerless models would not have been acclaimed nearly so quickly – if at all – for there were other formidable rivals and still relatively few potential sales. Unlike Royce and Johnson, the Honourable Charles Rolls did not have the same imperative to make a living from manufacturing or selling cars; he did so to help finance his long-held vision for the future development of automobiles and aircraft, including their roles in war,[26] hence his work with the Motor Volunteer Corps. More than the other two he remained a restive, questing adventurer, for although he energetically supported Royce's superb vehicles he also envisaged a far broader transport revolution and the coming of small cheap runabout cars[27] for ordinary motorists that would inevitably relegate the role of Rolls-Royces. In helping to point his generation to the growing applications of aircraft, he also helped spearhead another of the most momentous developments of twentieth-century society and gave a lead to Royce in this direction, which he would subsequently pursue to the great benefit of the company.

5

Johnson, Royce and the Silver Ghost

Although Charles Rolls' allegiance to Rolls-Royce slackened within a relatively short time, the same could never be said of his one-time partner Claude Johnson, whose energy, people skills and unswerving belief in Royce's unique talents were offered unconditionally to the company throughout his life.

Claude Johnson was born in 1864, a year after Henry Royce and eleven years before Charles Rolls. As the sixth child and fourth son of William Goodman Johnson and Sophia Fanny Adams, his circumstances were immeasurably better than those of young Henry Royce, although his family was by no means well off. Following a number of false starts his father secured a modest post in the

Claude Goodman Johnson. (Rolls-Royce)

Department of Science and Art at the South Kensington Museum, which he held for thirty years. Even so, with his large family he had to supplement his income by acting as a watchman to the Museum of Bethnal Green. During his career William acquired a wide knowledge of art, and this allied with a strong religious faith led him to teach his children to love church and organ music. Claude came to have a passionate regard not only for music and art but for the physical world as a whole that subsequently led his admiring daughter Betty to declare that nothing beautiful or lovely went unnoticed by him or unworshipped[1] – which, of course, included superlative motor cars.

He attended St Paul's School in London, which was likely to have been by way of a scholarship for he was a gifted boy. His father had high ambitions for him and subsequently enrolled him at the Royal College of Art, where before long Claude soon realised that he possessed little genuine artistic talent, although while there he became acquainted with Sir Philip Cunliffe-Owen, the influential Deputy General Superintendent of the South Kensington Museum. Cunliffe-Owen was impressed enough by the qualities of the 19-year-old that he offered him the post of clerk at the Imperial Institute. This proved a sound decision for under Cunliffe-Owen's tutelage, Johnson soon revealed exceptional organising ability and between 1883 and 1886 he became associated with a number of successful exhibitions.

In the case of the Colonial and Indian Exhibition of 1886, Johnson had charge of 200 men, some of whom were double his age. He fully earned their respect for he not only cut an impressive figure due to his good looks, height, broad shoulders and immaculate dress but, whatever his requests, he was ever courteous and always accompanied them with the trace of a smile. Although naturally a rapid worker he schooled himself to hear out a problem before coming to what was usually an assured and authoritative judgement. Johnson's brain teemed with ideas and his physical vigour led to an enthusiastic pursuit of outdoor activities that included swimming, golf and fishing. He also had a lifelong ability to relate with children and was popular with women, although his precipitate elopement at 19 years of age with a girl he had known from childhood served to arouse the fury of both set of parents. Against expectations the marriage held, although it came to be much affected by the fact that although the couple would have seven children, only one daughter survived to adulthood. Johnson later married Evelyn Maud Mill and had a second daughter, Claudia, whom he nicknamed 'Tink'.

Another of Johnson's strengths was his marked ability to establish affable relationships with people from all backgrounds, which quickly bore fruit because a key component of his responsibilities at the Imperial Institute was the handling of highly influential individuals, including the Royal Family and other senior representatives from both Britain and the Commonwealth.

Johnson acquired his initial experience of motor vehicles when the Prince of Wales appointed him to organise the First International Exhibition of Motors and their Appliances – in the course of which the Prince rode in a motor car.

With the exhibition proving a considerable success, Johnson came into contact with a number of leading figures in early motoring, including Frederick Simms. In 1896, Simms founded the Automobile Club of Great Britain for gentleman who were also practical pioneers in that revolutionary form of transport. In December of that same year, he offered Johnson the position of Club Secretary. Johnson was an obvious candidate for, in addition to running the First International Exhibition of Motors, he had already shown an active interest in motor cars by attending the original London to Brighton Emancipation Run held in November 1896. This went from the Metrpole Hotel in the Northumberland Avenue, near Charing Cross, to the Metropole Hotel in Brighton and Johnson covered half the course on his bicycle, during which time he came to appreciate the tremendous potential of motor cars.

The Automobile Club had yet to flourish and Johnson's initial salary was just £5 a week with a 10*s* commission for any new member he attracted. As for aspiring new applicants, as Johnson suavely expressed it, 'Anyone interested in automobilism is eligible for membership, though naturally enough we observe some social restrictions.'[2] In other words, those lacking the right background could be blackballed, although any such decision would be up to the Club's full committee rather than its Secretary alone. Johnson was soon responsible for a number of unprecedented initiatives, such as the Club's epic 1,000 Miles Motor Vehicle Trial Run held during the summer of 1899, which apart from publicising individual motor cars, endeavoured to give intending purchasers unbiased and authentic information about them.

During the Run, Johnson planned to visit practically every major town and city in Britain and when the Club's committee expressed doubts about his high aspirations, he swiftly sought the invaluable help of outstanding young journalist Alfred Harmsworth (Later Lord Northcliffe), who undertook to publicise the Run in his *Daily Mail* by featuring a series of articles on motor cars. More importantly, he agreed to guarantee its viability by offering £450 in prizes. To Johnson's advantage, Harmsworth not only remained a great supporter of such initiatives but a valued and lifelong friend.

Another founding member of the Club soon to have a massive influence on Johnson was, of course, Charles Rolls, who entered and won Johnson's 1,000 Miles Motor Vehicle Trial and who at 23 years of age was already one of the country's leading authorities on motoring with plans to set up a sales organisation of his own.

Under Johnson's skilful promptings, the Automobile Club prospered. In January 1899, it had 380 members, but by the turn of the century this had increased to 540, when Johnson's salary was raised to £1,000 a year along with his continuing 10*s* commission for each new member.

By the end of 1901, the magic figure of 1,000 was reached, with Johnson instituting a system of vetting and licensing of hotels for motorists who displayed the Club's sign. He also set up an Engineers' Department to help turn coachmen into chauffeurs and to assist members, especially those buying cars, from falling victim to the new breed of repairing sharks.[3]

In October 1901, Johnson had commemorated the fifth anniversary of the original London to Brighton Emancipation Run by holding one from London to Southsea where no fewer than 111 cars took part. These included Charles Rolls in his 20hp Panhard Levassor and Johnson, who as Secretary to the Judges Committee drove his 7hp New Orleans under his usual alias of Mr William Exe.[4]

In the following year, the Club moved into larger and grander premises at 119 Piccadilly and Johnson founded its Touring Department to provide members with detailed information about possible routes and places of interest.

By 1903, when its membership exceeded 2,000, and with Johnson believing he had moved the Club on as far as he could, he submitted his resignation and started looking for new challenges. Some idea of his prodigious work rate became evident when in April 1903, the Club felt it had to appoint three officials to replace him.

In June, he joined his friend Paris Singer to help promote Singer's Electric Brougham car that was unique in being absolutely silent, although its range of operations was severely limited due to its short battery life. Johnson was not destined to stay with Singer for long for Charles Rolls' car agency was expanding rapidly (with plans for a showroom at 28 Brooke Street, Mayfair, London W1), and Rolls decided he would make an ideal right-hand man.

Whether flattered or not, Johnson took the precaution of discussing Rolls' offer with his close friend Alfred Harmsworth before, in late 1903, he agreed to join as a partner.

Predictably, the combination proved an immediate success due to Rolls' valuable contacts and what has been described as Johnson's gift of making every client feel that they were the only person that mattered.

By far their most important decision, however, came in May 1904 when Rolls discovered Royce's new car and Johnson proved equally enthusiastic. As a result, on 23 December 1904 it was agreed that Royce Ltd would exclusively supply C.S. Rolls and Co. with four different types of superior car chassis: a 10hp two-cylinder to sell at £395 (over £48,000 at 2020 prices), a 15hp three-cylinder to sell at £500 (over £61,000 at 2020 prices), a 20hp four-cylinder to sell at £650 (over £79,000 at 2020 prices) and a 30hp six-cylinder at £890 (over £108,000 at 2020 prices), all of which would bear the name Rolls-Royce,[5] although the company was not officially established until March 1906.

Rolls and Johnson immediately set about publicising the cars. In early December 1904, they booked a stand at the Paris Salon de l'Automobile – which at the time was the most influential motor show in the world – and made arrangements to send two of Royce's 10hp twin-cylinder models by steamer to Le Havre and have them driven to Paris.

Early the next year both men manned the show stand, where they put one of the two-cylinder cars on view and helped emphasise the comprehensive nature of their products with 'partly finished' four-cylinder and three-cylinder models and a six-cylinder 30hp engine.[6] The second two-cylinder car was kept outside to give practice runs to would-be customers, where it received a very favourable reception and was awarded a special medal for 'elegance and comfort'.

Competition was keen between the early motor firms, who used the races and long-distance trials of the day to publicise their cars' qualities, with Rolls-Royce deciding that in all competitions they would never enter any vehicle except a standard model. Rolls and Johnson decided to compete with the 'Light Twenty', Royce's four-cylinder 20hp car, equipped with a four-speed gearbox, which by now was earning high praise. Johnson christened it 'The Grey Ghost' and such was their confidence that they took two 'Light Twenties' over to the Isle of Man to compete in the International TT Race of September 1905. In the event their second entrant, driven by Percy

C.S. Rolls and Co. stand at The Third International Motor Exhibition at Olympia, February 1905. (Rolls-Royce)

Northey, gained a magnificent second place. At the subsequent celebration dinner given for Henry Royce and Percy Northey, the imaginative Johnson provided the guests with place names engraved on cardboard goggles with the menu printed on cardboard motor cars.

In the meanwhile, Royce produced two further cars, both with advanced V8 engines. Both, however, suffered distinct handicaps: one was burdened by its cumbersome landaulette coachwork while the other was deliberately geared down to a maximum speed of 20mph, to be within the legal speed limit at the time. As a result, neither captured the public's admiration.

In contrast, the lively 'Light Twenty' went on to achieve further competition successes. In May 1906, Rolls drove it for his Monte Carlo to Bologne record and followed this with victory at the 1906 Isle of Man TT Race. This time it was Percy Northey who had to retire and his explanatory telegram to Royce said it all: 'Spring Broken, heartbroken.'

Not to be outdone, during the following year Johnson, who was himself a very fine driver, drove a six-cylinder 30hp Rolls-Royce over the formidable Scottish Reliability Trials Course of some 1,660 miles, held under

Cutaway drawing of the 1906 Silver Ghost engine. (Rolls-Royce)

Automobile Club Observation, to repel the challenge of Captain Deasy in what became known as 'the battle of the cylinders'.[7] Johnson's was the only six-cylinder car to lose no marks at all and its only unscheduled stop was one of forty seconds to adjust the foot brake.

Such imaginative and skilful publicity undoubtedly helped put the Rolls-Royce company on the map and Johnson achieved a further triumphant breakthrough at the London Motor Show at Olympia during November 1906, for which Royce built a magnificent chassis for a new 40/50hp six-cylinder car. Johnson succeeded in accentuating its chief attributes by having it highly polished, its sump removed and placing a mirror beneath the engine to reveal its big ends and bearings.

This caused it to steal the show and the firm received orders for far more 40/50 cars than they could possibly produce. In fact, the car was not seen on the road until April 1907 after Royce had experienced water seepage into its cylinders. As a result, he suffered the indignity of having his test car towed to his home at Knutsford by a horse. The following Monday he stormed into the factory, and seizing a sledgehammer, demolished brand-new six-cylinder blocks, shouting out that 'We must start again.' The fault was quickly solved by a new type of casting, and when Johnson tried out a chassis he was so certain it would be a sensation that he entered it for an ultra-gruelling 15,000-mile trial round Scotland, to be held in July 1907.

For this he arranged with coachbuilders Barkers to build a beautiful open touring body finished in aluminium paint. He then had all its fittings, internal and external, silver-plated, including its wheel hubs, headlamps, windscreen and door handles. To complete the effect, he had a silver plaque made for the scuttle inscribed with the words, 'The Silver Ghost'.[8]

Apart from its breathtaking appearance, when the 40/50 was made available to the general public its incredible smoothness, flexibility and silent running were quickly recognised as outstanding.

By March 1908, Johnson had become the firm's dominant managerial figure and he instituted the courageous decision that the company should drop all Royce's other models in favour of the 40/50 in order to market it as the finest car in the world, 'thereby lowering costs, leading to a more competitive selling price, better profit margins and simplifying problems for spares and servicing'.[9] Another great advantage was that it left Royce to concentrate on making improvements to his ideal conception of the motor car,[10] which at the time were being carried out right up to the time they entered competitions. Such were his standards that every profiling, turning, milling and grinding operation had to be carried out to the exact limits he set down. Many of the tolerances decided upon – some as close as one ten-thousandth of an inch – had never been considered necessary in motor car work up to that time[11] but were only to be expected from someone who could file a hub cap so perfectly that it was better than if it had been done by machinery.

Johnson's advertising flair and concern to preserve the dignity and beauty of the Silver Ghost at all times are to be seen in his efforts towards having an appropriate mascot made for it. Early in 1909 he met the well-known artist Charles Sykes and commissioned him to paint a variety of pictures of Rolls-Royce cars to help keep them in the public eye. At the time Johnson deplored the number of comic mascots and figurines then circulating, which he thought unbecoming for a Rolls-Royce. He went on to give Charles Sykes a further commission to design an exclusive mascot that would be worthy of the car. Legend has it that Lord Montagu of Beaulieu, who was a great friend of Johnson, had subsequently taken Sykes out for a ride in his 40/50 Silver Ghost. The artist had been so charmed by the

16 THE AUTOCAR. ADVERTISEMENTS. MARCH 30TH, 1907.

THE BEST SIX-CYLINDER CAR IN THE WORLD.

THE SIX-CYLINDER

ROLLS-ROYCE

THE MOST GRACEFUL, THE MOST ATTRACTIVE,
THE MOST SILENT, THE MOST RELIABLE.
THE MOST FLEXIBLE, THE MOST SMOOTH RUNNING,
in fact,

The best six-cylinder car yet produced.

You are invited to take a trial run to prove the above.

ROLLS-ROYCE, Ltd.,

14 & 15, CONDUIT STREET, LONDON, W.

AGENTS for LEICESTER, NOTTINGHAM, RUTLAND, AND DERBYSHIRE .. .. .. The Midland Counties Motor Garage Co., Granby Street, Leicester.
AGENTS for NORTH RIDING OF YORKSHIRE AND DURHAM .. .. .. The Cleveland Car Co., Cleveland Bridge Works, Darlington.
AGENTS, FRANCE .. .. .. La Societé Anonyme "L'Eclaire," 59, Rue la Boëtie, Paris.
AGENTS, UNITED STATES of AMERICA .. .. .. The Rolls-Royce Import Co., Broadway New York.

Telegrams: "Rolhead, London." Telephones: 1497 / 1498 Gerrard.

The first *Autocar* advertisement of the new 40/50 in the issue of 30 March 1907. (Rolls-Royce Heritage Trust) experience that he asked Eleanor Thornton (Lord Montagu's beautiful Secretary and fellow passenger) to pose for the mascot there and then. The artist's creation for Lord Montagu depicted a graceful young woman leaning into the wind with the scantiest of clothing clingily tightly to her body and her finger to her lips, which came to be named 'The Whisper'. The mascot commissioned by Johnson for Rolls-Royce was without the whispering but Eleanor Thornton in flowing robes again acted as its model. Sykes named it 'The Spirit of Speed', although in a Deed of Conveyance of 16 March 1911 to Rolls-Royce Ltd, the signatories Lord Herbert Scott and E.A. Claremont (along with John De Looze, the Company Secretary) obviously felt that a Rolls-Royce represented far more than speed for they renamed it 'The Spirit of Ecstasy'.[12]

Henry Royce himself would never have had a mascot, preferring the plain radiator cap as he believed the mascot spoilt the line of the bonnet. However, Johnson's early initiative bore further fruit when, some twenty years later and five years after his death, the cars' body contours began to be lowered. Henry Royce suggested a smaller version to ensure optimum visibility for the driver. Artist Charles Sykes was again commissioned and he responded by designing a figure of a woman with draperies flowing. This version of 'The Spirit of Ecstasy' – as the mascot is now universally known – became the most famous motor car mascot in the world, being carried on the great majority of Rolls-Royce cars, with unique examples prior to 1951 bearing the artist's signature.

Johnson not only enthused about the Silver Ghost but used it for his personal transport, during which time, as a born showman, he delighted in giving dramatic demonstrations of its smooth running by placing three tumblers on the bonnet, each filled to the brim with water coloured with red, green and black ink. The engine was then started, a revolution counter was placed on the front of the crank shaft and a photograph was taken. The engine revolved 4,600 times at 1,150rpm during the four minutes required to take the attendant picture. Throughout the time the liquid remained absolutely steady in the glasses and not a drop was spilt. He varied this by balancing a penny on its edge on top of the radiator cap while the car's engine was running.[13]

As Harold Nockolds rightly observed, 'The complex nature of motorcar manufacture and marketing gave full play to Johnson's outstanding talent for organisation while the superlative quality of [the company's] products gratified his artistic sensibilities.'[14]

Proof of the high regard for Johnson's abilities became apparent at the setting up of Rolls-Royce Ltd when it was agreed that he should be entitled to the same remuneration as Charles Rolls, namely £750 a year plus 4 per cent of the profits. For Johnson this might have seemed by no means generous compared with his earlier salary at the Automobile Club, but Rolls-Royce was an exclusive firm and the percentage of the profits represented a potentially valuable addition.

His importance to the firm rapidly became evident when, prior to the Board's agreement to his proposal that production should be concentrated on the Silver Ghost, he (along with Royce) had also come to believe that its anticipated level of production could never be met from the firm's current facilities and he became involved in negotiations for acquiring land for a new works, financed through the money raised from the 1906 public share issue.

Rolls' chauffeur Tom Smith related how, in early 1907, he drove Johnson, Royce and Rolls to Derby, where on the south side of the town they viewed a site where a recently made road ran through absolutely flat and barren countryside. They gazed at it and without a word re-entered the car. Some days later Rolls told Smith that they were thinking of opening a new factory and had gone to inspect the site.[15] By 6 April 1907, the *Autocar* reported that the 'location of the new works has now been indisputably settled, Rolls-Royce Ltd having acquired a considerable tract of land on the Ormaston Estate, Derby'.[16] Not only were large economies anticipated by tooling up the Derby factory exclusively for the Ghost but by enabling Royce to concentrate his design skills on the one car, Johnson was sure it could keep well ahead of its contemporaries and enhance the name of Rolls-Royce with its mechanical excellence. In fact, no year passed without some detail or refinement being added.

When in March 1909 Johnson moved on from Commercial Managing Director to General Managing Director, he went on to undertake a major reorganisation involving both the role of Henry Royce and arrangements for the immediate and longer-term production of the Silver Ghost.

For some time Johnson had been painfully aware – as were Ernest Claremont and other Board members – that the company's reputation for outstanding design relied on the continuing good health of the inspirational and seemingly irreplaceable Henry Royce. However, in recent years, the exceptional problems he experienced with developing the Silver Ghost and setting up the Derby factory had appeared to exacerbate his long-standing custom of overworking to perfect his designs. Royce's overworking was, of course, legendary:

> At Manchester, it had not been extraordinary for him to work a day, a night and a second day without stopping, being accompanied by Wormald, Platford and a few others all the time. In fact from the time he turned his attention to designing motorcars, time and meals seemed to have no apparent meaning. A colleague said he looked upon them as a confounded nuisance. Every time a hasty meal was snatched the problem was 'How soon could they get back to the Works'. Sometimes Royce would ignore all regular hours for feeding for weeks at a spell and he would treat the hours usually devoted to sleeping in the same way.
>
> So utterly oblivious did he become to the mere passage of time that one day he was quite astonished when told that work was to be discontinued on the morrow because it would be Christmas Day.
>
> At Manchester, De Looze had made it the duty of a small boy to approach Royce with a glass of milk. The child considered himself lucky if he could succeed in passing it to his employer's hand by noon, only to be rewarded by the observation that the milk was too cold to drink.
>
> Royce would often reach the office in a state of over-stimulation, with ideas that he was eager to put into practice without a moment's delay. Characteristically he would not even take his overcoat off before plunging on his back under a car. When he emerged someone might succeed in tearing the garment off him, probably only to be rewarded by his request for the loan of the man's overalls.[17]

During September 1907 he had fallen sick, although after missing a number of Directors' meetings, he was present at the Derby Factory's official opening on Thursday, 9 July 1908.

Johnson faced the dual problem of maintaining Royce's health and possibly relieving him of his responsibilities as Works Director. This appeared necessary because, from his earliest days with Royce and Co., he had always considered administration subordinate to production and production subordinate to improvements in design. Along with this, 'after years of strain his sternness appeared to have taken an irascible and autocratic turn'.[18] It had on occasion become Royce's practice that when an employee's work failed to satisfy him – even in a single case – he would dismiss him summarily.

The Derby factory opens, 9 July 1908. (Rolls-Royce Heritage Trust)

An early view of the Derby works from Nightingale Road. (Rolls-Royce Heritage Trust)

Entrance to the factory in Nightingale Road, Derby. (P.H. Vickers)

A blue plaque located to left of the entrance. (P.H. Vickers)

In practice, when Royce left the operative was usually reinstated by his local works foreman, but despite Royce's great reputation it was his behaviour that brought obvious problems for the Works Managers in maintaining production. The way Johnson attempted to solve the problem was by creating the post of Engineer-in-Chief so that Royce might devote 'all his time and energies to design and to affording such technical assistance to the works as may be asked of him'.[19] While it was Johnson's genuine intention to take some of the burden off Royce, he also aimed to persuade him to relinquish his role as Works Director, which it was his custom to conduct from a tiny office in the erecting shop.

It was a big ask for Royce, who, along with his wife Minnie and their niece Vi, had rented a property called 'The Knoll' at Quarndon, just north of Derby, because he felt it important to live close to the factory when it was engaged on specific tasks like replacing the Silver Ghost's rear springs and the concentric braking drums for both its foot and hand brakes. Notwithstanding, Royce recognised Johnson's undoubted planning ability and genuine appreciation of his own powers, together with the undoubted burden of his own wide-ranging workload, and agreed to limit himself to design and development.

With this core issue seemingly resolved by 1910, Johnson's other concern as newly appointed General Managing Director was the rate of production for the Silver Ghost, Rolls-Royce's single, if sublime, product. In May 1909, an endeavour had been made to raise output to twenty-five chassis per month but its production was still under 300 per annum[20]

Royce's home in 1908–11. (P.H. Vickers)

because, although the Board was fully aware that deliveries remained six months behind orders, the thinking was that if production increased beyond a certain point then demand could diminish rather than increase. However, by 24 June 1910, with the Manchester premises released, the move to Derby was expected to show a steady increase in production. (In later years Henry Royce actually came to believe that it would have been better to have moved further south, nearer the classic London market with its more congenial climate and superior transport facilities.) Yet whatever Johnson's ultimate ambitions, financial prudence was the spirit of the day, with the firm's finance sub-committee made up of himself and his fellow Board member Lord Herbert Scott, younger son of the Duke of Buccleuch. This worked on the principle that the capital expenditure in any year 'should not exceed half the balance of the estimated profits after deducting a sufficient sum for the distribution of dividends, the remaining half of such balance to be invested outside the company in First Class Securities'.[21]

Under Johnson's strong but cautious eye, the firm's financial prospects seemed favourable, with continuing strong demand for the Silver Ghost, whose output would be increased in a deliberate and controlled fashion, with further expansion planned in the shape of future industrial units in France and India.

All such projections were thrown into confusion by a crisis that literally came out of the sky when, on 12 July 1910, Charles Rolls was killed while performing at the Bournemouth air show. While Rolls had already severed himself from direct contact with the firm, his sudden death had an unexpectedly profound effect on Henry Royce, resulting in a physical collapse that brought most serious concerns for his life.

As a result, Claude Johnson's management skills faced a defining moment with the future of the company, that depended so heavily on its matchless designer, hanging in the balance.

The *Temple 2000* sculpture in Hulme Park, Manchester, marking the site of the original factory. (P.H. Vickers)

Plaque on the *Temple 2000* sculpture. (P.H. Vickers)

6

The Silver Ghost in Peace and War

With Royce near death, Johnson moved with characteristic speed and urgency and he arranged for him to be brought to London with its world-renowned medical facilities. There the specialists carried out a major operation likely to have been for cancer of the bowel, following which they gave Royce three months to live. Knowing Royce's legendary determination, Johnson believed they were being over-pessimistic and, as he showed signs of recovery, he had him taken to Overstrand, a small Norfolk village near Cromer where Johnson hoped he could recuperate further.

Johnson's next move was to appoint a nurse to institute and oversee Royce's care. His selection of Ethel Aubin proved brilliant for she not only turned out to be highly dedicated but rapidly came to appreciate her patient's extreme work ethic. In consequence she was taken on permanently and came to enjoy the closest relations with Royce over the rest of his life, which she undoubtedly extended by her regulated and devoted approach. Faced with a rather more optimistic outcome, the doctors advised Johnson to take Royce to a warm climate, which they hoped would lead to him continuing his remarkable recovery.

Johnson accepted their advice and took the extraordinary decision of handing over control of the company to fellow Director and aristocratic ex-soldier Lord Herbert Scott – while he accompanied Royce on an extended furlough. He left responsibility for the Derby factory to Tommy Haldenby, who as an apprentice in 1903 had shown outstanding loyalty to Royce throughout the construction of his first motor car, and Arthur Wormald,

Captain Lord Herbert Scott, DSO. (Rolls-Royce)

whom Johnson recruited in 1904 to act as joint Works Managers. In addition, he made Eric Platford, who in 1903 had carried out prolonged testing of Royce's two-cylinder 10hp engine and had later driven the Silver Ghost during its 15,000-mile endurance run, responsible for the quality control of new cars leaving the factory.

With the firm in what he believed were loyal and capable hands, Johnson took Royce to Egypt, sparing no expense. Nurse Aubin took him to London and on to Dover, then by boat and train to Tours, during which time he had a whole carriage seat on which to lie.[1] Johnson met them at Tours in an elegant Silver Ghost, with a closed body that cost £1,365 and which Johnson had named 'The Charmer'.

They drove across France and Italy to winter in Egypt before returning in the spring to the Cote d'Azur, where by Johnson's careful design they came to the remote village of Le Canadel. There he owned a spacious house called 'Villa Jaune' high on a hill overlooking the sea. As anticipated, Royce was enchanted with the view and expressed a wish to live there.

Johnson thereupon purchased land below his own villa and 'La Villa Mimosa' – named after the predominant flowers of the region – was built to Royce's own design. Royce seemed invigorated by planning the house along with its challenging landscaping and this encouraged Johnson to consider a unique change to the firm's management structure. This not only meant keeping Royce away from Derby's bustling factory, which he had both planned and built, but enabling him to work in a simple, near monastic, environment amid rural surroundings that in summer could be at a peaceful location along Britain's South Coast or in winter at sun-kissed Le Canadel.

There, in the company of his closest draughtsmen, Johnson hoped Royce could continue to produce his incomparable design schemes for dispatch to the firm's main drawing offices at Derby, where blueprints could be made and incorporated into experimental cars that would subsequently be returned to Royce for approval.

Through this unorthodox and seemingly laborious system Johnson believed he could maximise Royce's unique gifts and maintain the amazing workrate of someone who in reality was never off duty. To facilitate the system, Johnson arranged for another villa to be built below Villa Mimosa for Royce's design team.

With such plans in train, during the early summer of 1912 Royce and Johnson returned to England. Royce went to 'Westwood' near Crowborough in Sussex while Johnson resumed the reins of management, including Royce's earlier factory responsibilities.

At Westwood Royce – accompanied of course by Nurse Aubin – rejoined his wife Minnie and niece Vi. Unsurprisingly, it proved a far from happy household where, to the fury of young Vi, the nurse firmly restricted access to her patient. In October, with the approach of cold weather, Royce and his nurse left for Le Canadel, although once there an unexpected recurrence of Royce's bowel cancer threatened to ruin all Johnson's careful planning and led to him being rushed back to London for a colostomy operation.[2]

Johnson arranged for him to be brought home in a Silver Ghost that was converted into an ambulance and the story goes that as the car was speeding along the long and straight French roads, Royce became aware of another car following them. Raising himself from his pillows he murmured, 'Faster, faster. They must not overtake us,' but the chauffeur, being aware of Royce's condition, was afraid to go too fast and the pursuing car slowly gained on them. To the chauffeur's relief, Royce then gasped, 'It's all right, it's one of ours'[3] as another 40/50 sped past.

In London, following the operation, Royce was transferred to a nursing home, where Nurse Aubin took twenty-four-hour charge, even sleeping on a camp bed in his room. Royce eventually made a fair recovery and he and his nurse were able to return to Westwood, where the domestic situation would prove intolerable.

With his marriage at an end, Royce, accompanied by Nurse Aubin, soon returned to Le Canadel, leaving Minnie and Vi to stay on at Westwood where they would remain until 1921. Royce saw to it that Minnie would be provided for until her death by buying a house called 'Woodside' at Boxhill for her and Vi to live in, and later made partial amends to Vi by giving her a handsome wedding present of £100.[4]

The final years before the First World War saw Johnson's devolved system working well. Royce returned to an acceptable state of health and continued his improvements to the Silver Ghost where he strictly supervised each new modification, thereby enabling the car to remain in the public eye and excel in the competitions that Johnson chose to enter.

Such an opportunity arose in 1911 due to suggestions by the Napier Company that Rolls-Royce cars were for old ladies, which they followed with a demonstration of mechanical excellence when a 65hp car travelled in top gear from London to Edinburgh at a maximum speed of 76.42mph with a favourable petrol consumption of 19.35mpg. In the obligatory response, a Silver Ghost driven by Ernest Hives performed the same run at a higher maximum speed of 78.26mph with a superior fuel consumption of 24.32mpg. Johnson followed this up with a demonstration of how fast the car could go. Just before Christmas of the same year, with Hives once more its driver, a model fitted with a light 'bath-tub' body and a high gear ratio reached an incredible 101mph at Brooklands over the quarter mile. This was astonishing for a side-valved engine designed before the First World War, but by this time

The 1911 London–Edinburgh Silver Ghost (chassis 1701E). (Rolls-Royce Heritage Trust)

Royce's improvements, including flexible front engine mountings, had helped to make it a distinctly faster, livelier and more comfortable vehicle than the original. Earlier in the year, another Rolls-Royce driven by N.C. Neill had excelled on the Prinz-Heinzrich-Fahrt, a tour named after H.R.H. Prince Henry of Prussia that followed chosen routes across Germany and Britain.

During the following year, however, proof that the company could never rest on its laurels came when, due to its high gearing, a Silver Ghost embarrassingly failed to climb one of the appointed hills during 1912's Austrian Alpine Trial. As a consequence, Johnson decided to enter three cars for the 1913 Trial, for which thorough preparations were made after Eric Platford had been sent to discover the percentage rise and fall of the Austrian hills. Royce made a number of significant modifications to what became the Continental model of the Silver Ghost, including changing to cantilever springing, installing a four-speed gearbox, increasing the radiator capacity and creating greater ground clearance.[5]

Count Salamanca, Claude Johnson's wife, Claude Johnson, Royce and Lord Northcliffe.

The chosen drivers for the Trial were C.C. Friese, Hives and Jock Sinclair, with James Radley in his private Silver Ghost acting in support. Although a crash prevented them from winning the team prize, the four Rolls-Royces entirely dominated the event. They were by far the largest cars, which brought problems over the narrow and twisting Alpine roads, but they proved much faster during both the ascents and descents of the nineteen passes involved, and covered the 1,645 miles without replenishment of the radiators.[6] They swept up the demanding ascents with ease and with a silence and smoothness that amazed the onlookers as they easily kept ahead of the other competitors.

Whether from Le Canadel or England's South Coast, Royce and his personal team of designers continued to work hard to keep the successes coming, while Rolls-Royce executives from Derby or London regularly visited him to discuss technical developments, sometimes taking with them a chassis in the process of modification. Among the impressive range of improvements that sprang from Royce's fertile brain were 'variable lubrication of the pistons and cylinders in accordance with the throttle opening; a torque tube propeller shaft; a new type of rear spring anchorage; a live axle adjustment; a hydraulic shock absorber; a spring coupling between the clutch and the gearbox; an epicyclic gearbox; a flexible engine mounting; and a new brake design'.[7]

The final months before the war saw additional successes for the Silver Ghost with the irrepressible James Radley driving his car in a private capacity. In February 1914, he he made the fastest time yet of twenty-six hours four minutes on the London to Monte Carlo run and in the 1914 Austrian Trial beat the other seventy-seven starters, some of whom were either works teams or had larger engine capacities, without incurring any penalty points and winning both its timed tests.

During the years before the First World War, Royce's continued innovations therefore helped to confirm his cars as the finest in the world, although the Rolls-Royce company failed to set up new satellite branches overseas. In 1911, a public subscription aimed at establishing a separate company in France failed to reach its anticipated levels and, although during the year new departments for the repair and assembly of Silver Ghosts were actually set up in France and India, both were destined to make considerable losses. In early 1914,Claude Johnson followed Charles Rolls' example by crossing the Atlantic to sound out the American market, although he apparently achieved relatively little beyond discovering there were just eighty-one Rolls-Royces in the country.

In spite of disappointing progress with its overseas ventures, under Johnson's direction the company's balance sheets showed steady if not spectacular increases in profits. In 1910 these totalled £37,760, in 1911 £50,713, in 1912 £71,062 and in 1913 £91,183.[8]

The advances continued until the summer of 1914, when major political storm clouds heralded the likelihood of a war that was expected to have the profoundest effect on the company and the country as a whole. In the circumstances, Johnson decided that Royce and his staff must return at once to England, where he installed them in 'Seaton', a large house at St Margaret's Bay, midway between Dover and Deal. Even so, when war actually broke out on 4 August, Rolls-Royce, along with the majority of British industrial enterprises, proved amazingly unprepared for its economic and social consequences.

The company's Board of Directors literally had no idea about the likely outcome of the war. Initially they believed that war would bring ruin for a company devoted to the manufacture of luxury motor cars because it would have to shut down after it had fulfilled its contracts.

At an emergency meeting, Claude Johnson was authorised 'to reduce the Works' wages to about one-fourth, by discharging about half the hands and allowing the remainder to work only half time'.[9] The Directors decided 'that the company would not avail itself of the opportunity that was possibly arising'[10] of the firm making and assembling aero engines for the British Government. The question of undertaking aero-engine design was, of course, by no means new for in 1909, after Charles Rolls had bought his Wright aircraft, he suggested that Royce's 20hp four-cylinder car engine would make a much better power unit for it.

The topic was revisited on 10 August 1914, just two days after the company's emergency meeting, when James Radley, now a reserve officer in the Royal Naval Air Service (RNAS), accompanied Royce to watch RNAS airships struggling to make progress against a headwind and begged him to provide a suitably modified 40/50 engine for them.

On both occasions Royce refused, on the perfectly reasonable grounds that car engines were not suitable for aircraft.

Meanwhile, with the factory's closure in prospect Johnson advised all his employees to exercise stringent economy. He even went as far as to say that those with no reserve funds should stop paying their rent and save their cash for food, and he floated the idea that in the event of their eviction he would consider providing accommodation at the works for men and their families.

Another piece of advice offered was for men with wives and children to consider enlisting in the armed services, as then their wives would qualify for a government separation allowance.

Fortunately, as early as 13 August, such wild ideas were giving way to a growing belief in the firm's survival through likely wartime orders. Johnson took Royce with him on a visit to the Royal Aircraft Factory at Farnborough, which at this time had authority to design and construct aircraft and their engines in addition to its traditional experimental and inspectional duties. What Johnson had in mind was the possible assembly of French Renault engines and constructing others to the Royal Aircraft Factory's designs. He also took pains to contact the military authorities about the 100 car chassis in Rolls-Royce's hands that with their great strength might be suitable for armoured versions, and even explored the possible manufacture of shell cases, ambulance wagons and other munitions. His tender to the War Office for manufacturing shells was refused, as was an offer to make machine guns[11] because policy at the time was only to use well-known munitions firms. Johnson rightly believed that work on aero engines appeared a much more likely prospect for during the first months of the war, dependence on French aero engines had been total. Although by 1914 Britain's private aircraft firms were building some 100 aircraft per annum, less than a year had passed since Farnborough obtained authority to design its own engines with just £5,000 allocated for the purpose. Although a naval and military competition for aero engines 'that could run for 6 hours or more under complete power' saw a 100hp six-cylinder Green engine declared the winner and awarded a £5,000 prize from the War Office, it saw little service with military aircraft and none of the other contenders would have engines in production until 1915.[12]

During their visit to Farnborough on 13 August, Johnson and Royce met Superintendent Mervyn O' Gorman, who favoured his own constructors at the Royal Aircraft Factory and much preferred to view Rolls-Royce as subcontractors rather than possible engine designers. It was agreed that the firm should construct fifty air-cooled Renault engines, which in many ways offended Royce's engineering principles, although the much-needed work for Rolls-Royce employees could, of course, not be refused. Rolls-Royce ultimately built 220 Renault 80hp engines during 1915–16.

O' Gorman subsequently asked both Rolls-Royce and Napier to consider the development of a new Royal Aircraft Factory air-cooled 200hp engine for installation in an intended large military aircraft. Napier built a twelve-cylinder air-cooled engine (RAF3), which was produced before it had been proved and suffered from major crankshaft weaknesses, along with a twelve-cylinder version of the factory's own RAF1. Royce was not involved in this project for, by 19 August, he had decided he should undertake the design of his own water-cooled aero engine. This represented a monumental decision on his part that would require the utmost commitment of both his own team and the firm's construction facilities in Derby. In the national interest he substantially cut down his own salary, although he faced the prospect of spending extremely long hours over a matter of months in formulating, calculating and honing detailed plans that would be sent to Derby, from where components would be returned to St Margaret's Bay for them to come under his unique scrutiny.

Official reaction to his decision was likely to have proved mixed for, prior to the establishment of the Royal Air Force in 1918, it was the custom to place individual aircraft firms under the aegis of one or other of the traditional armed services, with the Royal Flying Corps and the Royal Aircraft Factory representing one viewpoint and the Admiralty's RNAS another.

Under this arrangement, Rolls-Royce came under the Admiralty's sponsorship where, unlike the War Office with its partial dependence on aeroplanes built at the Royal Aircraft Factory, their policy was to buy aircraft, engines and spares in any available market. A most important development here was a meeting between 19 and 26 August involving Royce, Johnson and Lieutenant-Commander Wilfred Briggs, liaison officer to the RNAS, where Royce accepted Briggs' request to consider building a major aero engine of some 200hp.

At this time the RNAS was commanded by the confident and aggressive Commodore Murray Sueter, whose ambition was to obtain a power unit suitable for a large Handley Page bomber that he hoped would be 'a bloody paralyser of an aeroplane' and would attack the German High Seas Fleet. As a consequence, on 3 January 1915 a firm order for twenty-five 200hp Rolls-Royce engines – soon to be called Eagles – was received from the Admiralty with another for a further seventy-five on 19 April. These were followed by a final order that year for 300 Eagles and 100 Hawks, smaller 75hp engines for use in anti-submarine operations. The total cost for these orders was £453,000.[13] Following the short period at the beginning of the war when it was feared the Rolls-Royce factory would have no work, at the end of 1914 Ernest Claremont wrote to Johnson acknowledging that the volume of orders had become 'quite bewildering'.[14] By far the most important product was, of course, Royce's projected 200hp aero engine, the design and construction of which will be described in detail in the following chapter.

In the meanwhile, a number of warlike roles were about to be found for his magnificent and long-proven motor car, the Silver Ghost, for which Claude Johnson tendered to the War Office for a further batch of 100. Their chassis were considered so robust that they offered the military authorities the opportunity to equip them with some type of armoured body.

Even so, for some Rolls-Royce owners this was too long to wait. Twenty-five of them decided to form themselves into the Royal Automobile Club Corps and, led by the Duke of Westminster, they immediately offered their cars and their own services to the common cause in the belief that vehicles that had made little of the hazardous roads of the Austrian Alpine Trials were capable of traversing the notably straight roads of France and Germany with unrivalled speed and reliability. Although he was, in fact, a reserve Army Officer in the Royal Horse Guards, the Duke straightway took his car over to France, where in early November he attached himself to the RNAS. The RNAS had already been in Flanders since 27 August 1914 and within days had supplemented its air operations with road patrols.[15] The Duke was accompanied by other owners such as Lord Dalmeny, Captain Frederick Guest, James Radley, Oscar Morrison and Barrington Stopford. Stopford was accustomed to keeping a couple of rifles in his car, which apparently came in useful on the occasions he ran into small groups of German calvary roving ahead of the advancing German main armies.

Many of these skilled drivers, in their peerless motor cars, came to drive VIPs around what was still a fluid battlefield: Captain Guest became Field Marshal Sir John French's ADC and driver, while Lord Dalmeny drove Colonel (later General) Seely.[16] On meeting with road blocks, their cars had to take to the fields, where they encountered swamps, ditches, broken bridges, streams and shell holes,[17] apparently without a single breakdown.

Another role that came to be exclusively carried out by the Silver Ghosts was to maintain a regular daily service for the King's Messengers, who carried official documents between French ports and the British Headquarters. For two years four selected cars operated this service with notable regularity, although the location of the Headquarters was accustomed to change with the varying battlefield situations. Even so, not one mechanical breakdown was reported.

HRH the Prince of Wales en route for GHQ at St Omer. (Rolls-Royce)

A King's Messenger car in 1914. (Rolls-Royce Heritage Trust)

Ghost ambulance, chassis no. 1766. (Rolls-Royce)

Another unusual task for the cars was to be converted into ambulances, for which their smooth-running qualities made them particularly suitable. One such vehicle was sent out to France in 1914 by the American Ambulance Unit and it continued in daily use for the next three years. It carried over 5,000 wounded French soldiers and never enjoyed the protection of a garage.[18]

However imaginative and effective these roles might have been in the early stages, some military commanders were already considering further, more aggressive, ones after the cars were given armament and armour protection.

By September 1914, Commander Charles Samson, leader of the Eastchurch section of the RNAS, stationed at Dunkirk, was actively fitting some of his cars with armour and arming them with either Lewis or Maxim guns, while also contacting his superior, Commodore Murray Sueter, about whether standard armoured cars could be built.

Authority was accordingly given for sixty chassis to be converted, of which eighteen would be for Rolls-Royces with two other batches of twenty-one each using Wolseley and Clement Talbot ones. In fact, plans for a design based on a Rolls-Royce chassis had already been drawn up by the Admiralty Air Department and approved by Winston Churchill (then First Lord of the Admiralty), who did so without consulting Samson. In the event, the pattern did not prove popular with Samson's unit, for it offered no protection above waist height and its armour was just 4mm thick, although it was lined on the inside with oak planks, and the driver the only crew member to have a seat. For armament a Maxim gun was mounted on top of the driver's headcover and there were rifles for the crew. Such cars were organised into four squadrons of fifteen cars each, the first of which was commanded by Charles Samson's brother, Felix, and reputedly equipped with Rolls-Royce chassis that were considered to be the most reliable and suitable.[19]

By October 1914, all four squadrons were operational, although the design proved a short-term stopgap when the Admiralty began considering a more advanced one, involving a turreted car on a Rolls-Royce chassis with armour 8mm thick, thus rendering it impervious to German armour-piercing rounds. The first to be built to this specification was despatched to the headquarters of the Royal Naval Armoured Car Division at Kensington on 15 November 1914.

In official language, the marque came to be called 'Turreted Rolls-Royce of RNAS UK, 1915', which by providing end, side and overhead protection for the whole crew, together with a revolving turret carrying a machine gun, was an altogether more successful design.[20]

Although primarily designed for the Silver Ghost's chassis, with its strong side girders braced by five cross members and the firm's iconic radiator at the front, it also came to be carried (in lesser numbers) by Lanchester, Talbot and Delaunay-Belleville chassis. The Rolls-Royce version had extra leaves inserted in its springs to cope with the increased weight, although its gears were still unsynchronised and the driver needed to double-declutch during gear changes. The engine continued to be started on a crank handle (electric start motors were not introduced until 1919) and for braking, the foot brake operated on the propshaft, with the handbrake acting on the rear wheels only.

For its main armament, a water-cooled Maxim gun of 0.303 calibre was carried in the turret (later to be replaced by a Vickers weapon); elevation, depression and rotation of the turret were carried out by the driver, who sat on a leather cushion.

This pattern of armoured car would continue to be used by the British Army for decades, although opportunities for it on the Western Front rapidly dried up after it coalesced into unbroken lines of trenches faced by thick belts of barbed wire. By the spring of 1915, most armoured cars were recalled from the RNAS, although in March the Admiralty actually established a division made up of seventy-eight Rolls-Royce, thirty-six Lanchester and three Talbot models under the command of Commander E.L. Boothby, RN.[21]

Winston Churchill subsequently described the adverse situation for them on the Western Front: 'Just as they became numerous and efficient the Trench lines on both sides reached the sea and there was no longer any open ground for manoeuvre or any flanks to turn.'[22]

Towards the end of 1915, the RNAS handed the cars over to the British War Office, who formed them into a special section of the Machine Gun Corps (Motors). By March 1916 they had been reformed again into so-called Light Armoured Batteries, each made up of four cars, but few opportunities were found for their use and they were finally withdrawn from France by October 1917. This stopped them from taking any part in the first major tank battle during the following month at Cambrai, and the full co-ordination of armoured cars with the emergent tanks would have to wait until another war.

With the main theatre of operations barred to them, their sponsors had no option but to consider other opportunities 'in isolated areas of warfare in distant countries'.[23]

In 1915 an abortive attempt had been made to use them at Gallipoli, where eight cars from the Nos. 3 & 4 Squadrons RNAS were landed on the peninsula. Only one engagement was recorded where they were mistakenly used as tanks and came under so much fire that they had to be extricated and removed from this theatre of war.

Also during 1915 they had a similarly short employment in the jungle conditions of German South West Africa, where No. 1 Squadron RNAS experienced immense difficulties with its supporting transport before the Germans surrendered and the Squadron was ordered home.

Another most challenging use for such vehicles was in the vast deserts stretching across North Africa, Arabia, Iran and Mesopotamia.

The first group to capture wide public interest during operations in the Western Desert was the Army's Light Armoured Car Brigade of three batteries commanded by the indomitable Duke of Westminster – who was now a major in the Cheshire Yeomanry – based at Mersa Matruh. In March 1916, he dramatically rescued the crew of HMS *Tara*, a small cargo ship sunk by a submarine in the Mediterranean, who were being kept prisoners at the inland oasis of Bir Hakeim. This involved a 300-mile round trip into the desert to save ninety-one British sailors, who by this time were half-starved.[24]

By far the most famous of the desert operations was achieved by the Hedjaz Section of Rolls-Royce armoured cars that operated with Lawrence of Arabia in support of Sharif Hussein Ibn Ali and the Great Arab Revolt.[25] Lawrence succeeded in gathering together a fleet of nine, along with tenders and in a series of ingenious and daring operations – made possible by his utter faith in his cars – the armoured version of the Silver Ghost came into its own. During one of Lawrence's desert reconnaissances the heavily burdened cars sped across a vast mudflat at 65mph, which as he himself wrote was 'not bad for cars which had been months ploughing the desert with only such running repairs as the drivers had time and tools to give them'.[26] With Lawrence there was very little of that. On one occasion, according to his driver S.C. Rolls (no relation of Charles Rolls), 'Lawrence took three of them and captured two Turkish Ports, blew up a bridge, wiped out a Kurdish cavalry regiment, blew up another bridge and ripped up six hundred pairs of rails – thereby throwing the whole Turkish supply system into chaos – all in one day.'[27]

On another occasion, Lawrence was returning at speed from a bridge demolition operation when the car in which he was riding broke a rear

T.E. Lawrence with driver Cpl McKechnie of the Army Service Corps, Damascus, 2 October 1917, in Silver Ghost 'Blue Mist'. (Rolls-Royce Heritage Trust)

spring bracket. As he wrote, 'A Rolls in the desert was above rubies and though we had been driving in them for 18 months, not upon the polished roads of their makers' intentions, but across country of the vilest, at speed, day or night, carrying a ton of goods and four or five men up, yet this was our first structural accident in the team of nine.'[28]

They improvised by binding the spring to the chassis and running board by using wooden blocks and captured telegraph wire. So strong was the running board that the car was able to resume its punishing duties for the next three weeks before being taken to Damascus at the end of their operations. In Lawrence's words, 'Great was Rolls, and great was Royce! They were worth hundreds of men to us in these deserts.'[29]

In such ways Henry Royce's magnificent car demonstrated its robustness and excellence of design during the war's initial stages and later, when burdened by armoured plate, in special operations over the most hazardous terrain. Fortunately for his country, these qualities would be equally evident with Royce's iconic aero engines with his Eagle, in particular, becoming renowned for its durability in all weather conditions and in long-distance operations.

Specifications for the Silver Ghost 1906–25

Chassis Details

	1907		1914	1923	
	Short	Long		Short	Long
Overall Length	180in	187¼in	190¼in	190¼in	196¾in
Width of Frame	36in	36in	36in	36in	36in
Wheel Base	135½in	143½in	143½in	144in	150½in
Track	56in	56in	56in	56in	56in
Weight	18½cwt	19½cwt	25½cwt		
	(without tyres)		(with tyres)		

Engine: Six cylinders in two groups of three, 4½in bore x 4½in stroke, capacity 7,036cc (1909: 4½in x 4¾in, 7,428cc), cast-iron pistons. By 1919 aluminium alloy standard.

Valves: Side valves, operated by single camshaft through rocking levers, carrying friction roller lying between valve spindle and cam.

Crankcase: Cast aluminium.

Crankshaft: Hollow supported by bearing between each crank (1911: vibration damper flywheel fitted to forward end).

Lubrication: Oil supplied by gear-type pump; pressure capable of regulation from 1lb to 20lb/in^2. Oil delivered under pressure to crankshaft, big ends and gudgeon pins. Oil capacity 8 pints, with 11 pints in reserve tank.

Ignition: Two independent systems, with separate plugs for each system. One system high tension with trembler coil and accumulators coupled to coil and commutator. Other system high-tension magneto driven through gears to crankshaft.

Cooling system: Centrifugal water pump driven from crankshaft through spur gears and belt-driven fan. Radiator of vertical thin solid-drawn copper tubes, with horizontal copper plates for cooling surface (1921: thermostat installed).

Carburettor: Two-jet type with dash control and automatic air valve.

Engine control: By hand lever on steering wheel but can be overridden by accelerator pedal.

Starter: Standard fitting from 1919.

Transmission: Gearbox four-speed with direct drive on third. Clutch cone type.

Brakes: Foot brake: external contracting type acting on propeller shaft. Handbrake: internal expanding type in brake drums on rear hub. 1924: front brake system operated by mechanical servo.

Suspension: Semi-elliptic front springs and platform rear spring suspension. 1912: cantilever springs mounted over the axle made standard. 1908: friction-type shock absorbers.

Steering: Worm and nut.

Wheels: Normally artillery pattern with wooden spokes. 1913: wire wheels prevail but wooden artillery wheels available until 1921.

Lighting: By acetylene lamps. 1914: electric lighting optional extra. 1919: electric lighting as standard.

(Information obtained from *The Rolls-Royce Motor Car*, 1975, pp. 226–230.)

7

Royce's Move to Aero Engines

The importance of Henry Royce's decision to design his first aero engine and its succeeding family can hardly be exaggerated. Whereas in August 1914 his luxurious motor cars had been for the wealthy few, by 1918 his engines effectively provided over 1,500,000hp for the country's warplanes and the Rolls-Royce company was transformed from its former exclusive role into a national asset.

Royce's resolve to construct a major aero engine (and its derivatives) for Rolls-Royce, rather than building the French Renault 80hp engine on contract for the Royal Aircraft Factory, committed him to working immensely long hours from his home at St Margaret's Bay, where he was assisted by his two personal designers, Albert Elliott and Maurice Olley. Its design and construction took him eighteen months from August 1914 until February 1916, the early stages of which were spent planning, calculating and then drawing up plans for a highly advanced machine of twelve cylinders designed to produce 200hp or more.

Throughout the project, Henry Royce would despatch a stream of both detailed and demanding instructions to his construction staff at Derby. Fortunately, due to Royce's separation from the factory since 1911, he and his designers were already well practised in sending draft plans of car components for manufacture at Derby. It was destined to be a similar process with his aero engine, with Maurice Olley and Albert Elliott working under his direct supervision to draw up the mechanical design schemes, while, at Derby, designer Robert Harvey-Bailey would supervise the detailed drawing of every part, specifying the dimensions, tolerances and materials to be used. General Manager Claude Johnson placed himself at Derby to oversee the assembly and construction of the engine, where he was supported by Works Manager Arthur Wormald and the redoubtable Ernest Hives (who headed the Experimental Department). Although an experienced and capable team, they had, of course, never before been responsible for launching such a complicated and strategically important product.

Good communication between St Margaret's Bay and the factory was essential and this was achieved through the assistance of the efficient postal services of the time, where a letter despatched on the afternoon of one day could be confidently expected to arrive promptly the next morning, while a telegram was, of course, faster still.

Royce would despatch 541 letters over the eighteen-month period – chiefly to the Derby factory and his General Manager but also to his potential customers at the Admiralty and in the initial stages to the Royal Aircraft Factory. Author Harold Nockolds subsequently praised them highly for their perpetual freshness of outlook (along with their writer's extraordinary ability to improve on existing theories and principles) and his refusal to be content with easily found results.[1] It was therefore fully understandable that at the time Claude Johnson felt inclined to publish them (in chronological order) in a book that subsequently became known as the Rolls-Royce Bible, or the 'Blue Book' from its dark blue leather binding. This was titled *The First Aero Engine made by Rolls-Royce Ltd* and it was printed under confidential cover because it was the intention not to show it to anyone without the authority of the Directors. Its preface stated that 'In the opinion of the Board of Directors the Memoranda and letters written by Mr. F.H. Royce, the Engineer-in-Chief, in connection with the design, testing and manufacture of these Engines are so admirable as evidence of extreme care, foresight and analytical thought, that the Directors decided to have them printed and bound in order that copies may be available for study and as an example to all grades of Rolls-Royce Engineers present and future.'[2]

As such, it provides an invaluable source where, over almost 300 pages, it shows Royce wrestling with a monumental construction project, which not only presented innumerable engineering problems but required him to manage strong-minded and diverse individuals from a distance. While in no way affecting its importance, there are major frustrations for the researcher because the book's typed pages lack Royce's original hand-drawn sketches and his accompanying notes. The letters were also censored by Johnson and the names of their recipients removed. Addressees are referred to in general fashion either as W (standing for the Derby Works) or GMD (standing for the General Manager's Department). The letters Royce sent to the Armed Services are either addressed to the Royal Aircraft Factory or to the Admiralty. It is also unfortunate that two of the typed pages are missing: pp. 199 and 200 of 20/22 April 1915. These apparently featured Royce's immoderate criticisms of a jig – which was unusual for, however devastating his criticisms might be, they were usually fully justified. The designer concerned with the jig seems to have convinced Johnson that Royce had subsequently withdrawn his remarks and the pages were therefore extracted. In spite of such defects, the letters provide an amazing insight into the breadth of knowledge, driving force and the clarity of language used by a quite exceptional designer at the height of his powers.

To better appreciate Royce's achievements one needs to have some idea of the immense task in conceiving such a power unit at a time when Britain was almost entirely without home-built engines.

Even so, despite Royce's undoubted capacity for original thought – so well appreciated, for instance, by Charles Rolls – there was never any question of him starting from a blank canvas. In any case, in 1903 he had set a clear precedent with his careful examination of an existing Decauville two-cylinder car before going on to construct his own model.

In any event, Britain's acute shortage of aero engines at the beginning of the First World War meant it was never feasible to put aside what had already been accomplished elsewhere. Consequently, Royce began by considering the best contemporary aero engines before deciding on the construction of a superior model that he could subject to demanding trial and experimentation to bring it to a level of unrivalled efficiency.

Royce's earlier expertise in water cooling for motor cars undoubtedly affected his attitude to an air-cooled engine initially suggested for the Royal Flying Corps by Mervyn O'Gorman, Superintendent of the Royal Aircraft Factory. O'Gorman anticipated great advantages from its relatively low maintenance during a war of rapid movement, which, in fact, never materialised. At the time, virtually all contemporary motor cars, including the Silver Ghost, used water cooling and the system was already widely used in contemporary aero engines, including those entered for the Naval and Military Engine competition for best British aero engines held at Farnborough in May 1914. This was won by a six-cylinder water-cooled engine built by Gustavus Green.[3] It was a similar story with the Kaiserpreis competition held in Germany during 1913 for the best aero engine, which was won by the four-cylinder water-cooled Benz, with second prize going to a water-cooled six-cylinder Daimler-Mercedes DF80 engine. This became the preferred option for the German Air Service and by 1914, it had already gone into wide production. (By March 1913 Claude Johnson had actually purchased a German Mercedes car, powered by a 7¼-litre DF80 water-cooled aero engine, for his company.)

Despite Royce's strong inclination towards tried and tested water-cooled systems, he respected O'Gorman's preferences for air cooling, but on receiving no outright request from him for such an engine and with the RNAS appearing a more likely customer, he went ahead with plans for a water-cooled system of his own, which he considered best for the high horsepower and swept-volume engine he had in mind.

Royce's preference for water cooling proved utterly sound. Although W.O. Bentley's BR2 rotary of 1918 was the most powerful air-cooled engine

Daimler-Mercedes D1 six-cylinder aero engine, exhibited in March 1914 at the International Aero and Marine Exhibition, Olympia. (Rolls-Royce Heritage Trust)

of the First World War, during manoeuvres it experienced serious trouble with its torque and high gyroscopic reactions, while in the following year an attempt to obtain 350hp from another air-cooled radial, the ABC Dragonfly, proved an utter failure, due among other things to its inadequate cooling.

Royce was fully aware of the Daimler-Mercedes DF80's engine that was held by Rolls-Royce at Derby and on 19 August 1914 felt obliged to make the 200-mile journey from St Margaret's Bay to Derby for the first time since 1911, to assure himself that if he adopted it – including its water cooling – his staff would be capable of carrying out the advanced welding required and to confirm that its built-up steel cylinder construction would be likely to give him the much higher power-to-weight ratio he required.

In the process he came up against his formidable nurse, Ethel Aubin, who, anxious that he did not tire himself too much, allowed him one hour to examine it. Her influence over him became apparent when, after two hours finding him still surrounded by some of his staff, she insisted he leave.[4]

By this time his inspection had left him sure it was within the competence of Rolls-Royce to do the necessary welding, and he left Derby convinced that by incorporating the pattern of the Mercedes DF80's upper engine works with its overhead valves and compact combustion chamber, he could obtain the relative light weight and high compression for the power pack he had in mind. He also planned to improve the engine by using separate cylinders instead of paired ones and by installing a seven-bearing crankshaft with which he aimed to achieve high-bearing rigidly.

It said much for Royce's pragmatism that he was not only prepared to incorporate features of what he considered the best current system but in doing so to rely on the technology of Britain's wartime opponent.

As a result, in 1916 an English Mercedes-Daimler syndicate actually made a claim on Rolls-Royce for the infringement of two particular Daimler patents, although by this time Royce had made significant changes and in 1918, the company learned that the cylinder construction patents had been revoked and costs granted against the German company.

For his engine Royce rejected the DF80's weak crankshaft and his proposed bottom layout was closest to that of the Silver Ghost. He also proposed to incorporate the articulated master and slave connecting rod from the 1912 Renault 80 while rejecting its other features, especially the air-cooling system. Finally, he intended to make use of the 1913 Peugeot's double valve springs while rejecting its double-overhead-camshaft system.

With the vital elements of his proposed engine decided upon, the Blue Book's letters of instruction not only reveal his detailed directives but the overall patterns of the construction process.

Table of the letters dispatched by Henry Royce during his construction of the Eagle engine and their recipients
(A total of 537 letters have been identified as opposed to the official total of 541. It is assumed that the outstanding four letters were on pages 199 and 200 of the book.)

	Admiralty	Royal Aircraft Factory	Derby Works	General Manager's Dept	TOTAL
August 1914	–	–	–	2	**2**
September 1914	1	–	1	13	**15**
October 1914	–	–	5	7	**12**
November 1914	–	1	34	6	**41**
December 1914	1	5	32	6	**44**
January 1915	1	2	33	9	**45**
February 1915	2	–	39	6	**47**
March 1915	6	–	67	6	**79**
April 1915	5	–	49	9	**63**
May 1915	8	–	30	1	**39**
June 1915	11	–	10	–	**21**
July 1915	4	–	17	1	**22**
August 1915	8	–	5	–	**13**
September 1915	3	–	4	1	**8**
October 1915	7	–	20	–	**27**
November 1915	6	–	15	2	**23**
December 1915	–	–	11	–	**11**
January 1916	2	–	12	2	**16**
February 1916	2	–	6	–	**8**
March 1916	–	–	1	–	**1**
TOTAL	**67**	**8**	**391**	**71**	**= 537**

As for his intentions, from August 1914 to late September of the same year Royce's aim was to have his plans for a new aero engine or engines approved by Rolls-Royce's General Manager, Claude Johnson. During September and October he sent fifteen letters to Johnson where, in authoritative and convincing fashion, he outlined both the nature and capability of the proposed engines (compared with just single letters to the company's Derby Works and the Admiralty, their most likely customer.)

Following Johnson's approval, during October the bulk of Royce's letters – some thirty-four in all – were to the Derby factory and contained his detailed requirements and questions regarding production techniques, while a further six kept Claude Johnson fully informed about progress.

As the programme gathered momentum, their frequency rose to some forty a month – more than one every day. Although most were to the Derby Works expressing Royce's concerns about such things as jigs and tools for the construction of cylinders, epicyclic gears to control propeller speeds and engine connecting rods, some still went to brief General Manager Claude Johnson.

The frequency of forty or more letters a month continued through December 1914 and January and February 1915, by means of which a host of constructional problems were considered and overcome.

By now the Admiralty rather than the Royal Aircraft Factory had emerged as definite customers and letters began to be sent to them concerning their specific needs. By the end of February, the Eagle engine performed its first run on a test bed at Derby, and the problems that were identified led to the number of letters rising to an amazing seventy-nine during March, sixty-seven of which were destined for Derby.

A total of sixty-three were sent during April, forty-nine of which went to the Derby Works with the remaining fourteen going to the General Manager and the Admiralty. In May the level dropped somewhat with thirty to the Derby Works and eight to the Admiralty, with the latter concerned about equipment for their operational needs, including propeller designs, control wires for the aircraft's instruments, safety devices and cranking gear, and just one to Claude Johnson.

By June 1915, the programme was entering a more mature stage with some forty-three letters sent during the whole of June and July, while throughout August and September the total dropped to twenty-one before rising to twenty-seven and twenty-three in the lead-up to the engine's first flight during October and November – of which thirteen were to the Admiralty about their concerns regarding extra equipment and malfunctions. On 17, 18 and 31 December, the engine's initial flights took place in a Handley Page O/100 bomber and in 1916, with the engine proving an undoubted success, just twenty-five were despatched during the first three months of the year. By now their main concerns were with the plane's enhancements, like improving the engine's hand-starting system, increasing its horsepower and correcting a previous pump failure.

During the autumn of 1914, Claude Johnson felt the full force of the letters' firepower. Things began with the second one of 26 August, in which Royce wrote:

> We are working at the new 200hp engine to find out the space required. We propose to fit it with wrought steel jackets. Each cylinder is to be separate. The arrangement appears to be very sound and straightforward. Each line of cylinders would have an overhead camshaft which would permit the engine running at very high speeds with less risk of the valves leaving the cams.[5]

By now he had plainly inclined to water cooling: 'Altogether I am much more satisfied that we shall be able to make something more creditable in this water-cooled design.'[6]

By 1 September, Johnson was informed about the need for its 'valve to be in the [piston] head so as to obtain an excellent combustion chamber and also to meet the requirements of light construction by making the cylinders in wrought steel'.[7] This letter also assured him that the Royal Aircraft Factory engineers were of the same opinion and asked him to satisfy the Admiralty about the proposal that made the removal of the exhaust valve seat impracticable.

In yet another letter of the same date Royce made the bold claim that, 'We hope to have an engine running in twelve weeks from this date i.e. by the end of October, so that we answer the question of whether the 200hp engine is "to be" in the affirmative, as far as Rolls-Royce are concerned.'[8] In fact, he was not fully aware about the range of major problems that would arise and its first run did not take place until the end of February, although this still marked a remarkable rate of progress and justified his positive stance to Johnson.

Although by 5 September Royce was to build two specific varieties of engine for his potential clients, by 8 September, after sleeping on the subject, he decided that for practical reasons he should produce just 'one engine of rather larger size than that suggested by the Royal Aircraft Factory which would be lower stressed having its object rather more than 200hp at less than 2,000rpm.'[9]

He assured Johnson that he was prepared to design a scheme of epicyclic gearing in order to meet the Admiralty's required propeller speeds, which he was arranging to float on the crankshaft in order to cause no out-of-balance pressure in any way on the bearings, for which he would make blueprints available.[10] By 22 September, Royce had produced blueprints for his proposed engine whose drive would have a universal joint for Royal Aircraft Factory purposes and an epicyclic system of gearing for the Admiralty, upon which he was currently working. Over some twenty-seven days, his letters also revealed his plans to incorporate what he believed were the best features of design then in existence.

However important it was to convince Claude Johnson, his central task was to inspire and cajole his own staff at Derby into achieving his ambitious and complex construction programme. It is therefore through the series of instructions to his staff at Derby that we have a first-hand opportunity of evaluating his pronounced skills as a master designer and motivator.

His second letter to the works during the autumn of 1914 left no one in any doubt about both his sense of urgency and high expectations. It read:

> I am very surprised to hear there was any difficulty about finding machines to work on the aero engine cylinders. I am afraid the position is that we must find machines. We have worried the R.A.F. and the Admiralty. We have also worried and worked continually on the designs for this and there must be no delays put in the way of the progress of the engine, because we must either do the work promptly or abandon the idea of doing it altogether. We cannot possibly have it hanging about, otherwise it will only be a disgrace to us.[11]

After communicating his uncompromising commitment, five days later he was demonstrating his concern with detail:

> With reference to the aero engines it might be advantageous for there to be a scraper ring above the piston pin, the object being to keep the surface

> subject to the pressure due to the angularity of the connecting rod, well lubricated … I should be glad to receive a copy of any detailed prints which you have already made for any parts that are issued to the shop.[12]

His sense of urgency was again evident in a letter despatched at the end of November: 'I presume that the trial cylinders are progressing and not waiting for the tools, because even if they should turn out to be wasters, for want of tools, it would be better to make this trial trip rather than find out that we have to make changes later on.'[13]

Another letter of the same day emphasises his complete authority: 'With reference to the rig for testing the connecting rods, I do not quite know how this is used but it seems to be not the best for the purpose. If it is found desirable to make a new one, let us proceed in the following way …'[14]

Early the next month this is again apparent through a seemingly gentle admonition that left no chance of escape. 'I hope these so-called improvements will not cause you any serious delay.'[15] He followed it a week later with an acknowledgement of their joint responsibility without considering any compromise: 'It is a pity we did not foresee this when we were getting out the design but that is no use now.'[16]

Towards the end of the month Royce shows he is willing to give undoubted praise, although with him it often comes with a further condition. 'I certainly do not approve of this and think your modifications of it very much better … A point occurs to me, however, that the teeth are hardly suitable for squaring up the wheel, and I am inclined to think that there should be …'[17]

The technique was repeated in January 1915: 'You have evidently got it right this time but I think you can improve it in the following way …'[18]

The design of the engine's cylinders was one of his most important concerns and it was the subject of many letters, some of which revealed his principles of working at speed without jeopardising his overall aim:

> My suggestions are intended always to be taken in parallel rather than in series and not in any way stopping something which is good with the hope of finding something which is better: let the good and the better proceed together. It is often taken otherwise in the Drawing Office and the work is stopped.[19]

His next letter actually referred to always keeping the main aim in mind and retaining a sense of proportion:

> We are not people that put a high finish on parts unless it is necessary and I quite agree that on this work no money should be spent on unnecessary finish but spend all the money and time necessary to make a good and reliable working job of the highest possible efficiency.[20]

In this regard while he was undoubtedly prepared to recognise when someone was working under undue strain and needed relief, he still insisted that additional arrangements needed to be instituted for the work to proceed satisfactorily: 'Thank you for your remarks with reference to the 200hp engine. Please get somebody else to work on it when you are tired and want a rest so as to keep the testing going or the necessary alterations made while you are away resting.'[21]

If seven months into a most strenuous programme anyone imagined that Royce might have relaxed his requirements somewhat, he was sure to have been disabused by two letters during April 1915 when he sharply brought his staff up to the mark, chiding them for shortcomings in their work. With regard to blueprints he told them that, 'They do not get the attention that is possible because they send me [ones] which are insufficiently distinct for rapid perusal, moreover anything that is really urgent should be brought to me by the draughtsmen responsible for the original drawings'.[22] He continued, 'With reference to the drawing of the trestles for assembly and dissembling engines, I do not know who is the author of this tackle but it does not appear to me to be very suitable for any purpose that I can call to mind.'[23]

In fairness Royce undoubtedly recognised the contributions of his staff to the development process, although in his continuing hunt for improvement he is determined to retain the initiative:

> I think the arrangement you show of the crankshaft is very ingenious, but I do not think it is quite the best for the purpose. I am not sure whether my scheme is practical for the space at disposal and whether it is really better than the one suggested but it appears to me as being more orthodox, simpler in case of any changes of diameter and to some extent self-setting ...[24]

First Rolls-Royce aero engine on bench test. (Rolls-Royce Heritage Trust)

And no one was left in any doubt when he was displeased: 'I have written about the [operations for the aero cylinders] before and it is quite evident my instructions have not been followed.'[25]

By October, with the engine giving satisfaction, Royce showed himself gracious and willing to express his gratitude: 'Thank you for your report on the first two engines tested under the supervision of the Admiralty. Thank you very much for the trouble you have taken to make this job a success.'[26]

Despite their joint efforts there would always be a chance of malfunctioning, but this would never be due to inattention on his part for it was his custom to sift and re-sift through the systems adopted to discover any potential problem. On one occasion he wrote:

> I find from looking over the tools, that a water regulator has been introduced so as to partly cut off the water heating up the [cylinder] jacket. It is a mistake that this fitting has been made without my knowledge and it should really have been drawn by … It is scarcely of the pattern I should have recommended because if wrongly fitted up it would probably stop the water altogether and might be capable of causing frozen or burst pipes without anyone knowing it.[27]

From his instructions relating to the construction of the Eagle engine, Royce comes across as a wholly capable and dedicated leader with universally high expectations who was prepared to apply himself as hard or harder than anyone else. Throughout the programme he combined a high level of energy with mastery of detail and a positive relish for repeated problem solving. As particular systems caused him major concerns, he paid them his undivided attention and, when work pleased him, he could be generous.

He also showed he could keep his customers at the Admiralty fully in the Rolls-Royce camp by his unfailing courtesy and patience, however sharp and strong their criticisms might be. Whenever possible he endeavoured to give them a degree of choice where the engine's components were concerned.

During December 1914, for instance, he took particular pains to familiarise them with his proposed engine by sending blueprints to illustrate the arrangement of its carburettor and the inlet and exhaust pipes that he considered would give the best results.

However, he soon found himself involved in an interchange of letters about electric self-starters, on which the Admiralty were very keen while he tended to give them a somewhat lower priority. In March 1915, he wrote saying, 'We are sorry we have not yet made progress with the electric starters, and shall be obliged to write to you later.'[28] However, having probably felt he might have been too dismissive, three days later he was offering to explain a proposed scheme, with accompanying rough drawings, that he would describe during a projected visit to London the following Wednesday.[29]

In spite of such efforts on his part there remained differences between the Admiralty's concept of the starter they required and that which Royce felt best able to provide. Some four months later the question had still not been resolved and we find Royce telling Johnson that: 'I am really quite tired of drawing starting gears for these engines which are afterwards condemned.'[30]

Whatever his irritation over the question, he was careful not to let the Admiralty become aware of it.

In early 1915, Royce became much concerned about the likely damage that could occur to the engine shaft by the two-bladed propellers that the Admiralty proposed to use with their engines. At the beginning of May he wrote: 'We are rather persistent on this subject of two-bladed propeller types as we are anxious to avoid any possible source of vibration.'[31]

Notwithstanding, the Admiralty continued to be reluctant to commit themselves to four-bladed propellers. By October Royce was certain four-bladed propellers were required and that he had to resolve the problem. While studiously cautious, he forcibly conveyed his feelings of urgency: 'We have now all come to one understanding that the two-bladed propeller is a serious source of high gyrostatic forces … liable to set up a destructive vibration … We therefore persistently beg of you to use in all cases, where possible, a four-bladed propeller.'[32]

Royce also needed all of his diplomatic qualities with regard to an engine connecting rod that broke down during testing, which was understandably of high interest to the Admiralty.

At the end of October 1915, he was required to explain what exactly happened. This he did in some detail, blaming in part the fact that it was a left-hand engine where the stress on the main rod was apparently much greater than a right-hand one.

> You have no doubt been informed of the breakage of the connecting rod in one of our left hand engines and we understand you wish us to explain for the good of other similar engines our views on the cause of the breakage. The rod in question was the main rod, which was broken by the bending stress put upon it by the articulated rod being off centre with the crank pin during the period of greatest explosive pressure within the cylinder … that was accentuated by the fact that it was a left hand engine where the strain on the main rod was much greater.

He followed by proposing a range of necessary improvements, including increasing the section of the rod at the position where it broke.[33]

The Admiralty responded by demanding to see the broken rod. In early November Royce sent it together with an explanation for the breakage, which he had omitted earlier. He was quite candid. 'You will notice that the section has been badly cut into by the lightening process. This is not in accordance with the design and was a works error.' He explained that the necessary improvements undertaken included condemning undercutting and ended by emphasising his own good faith.

'We hope therefore you will realise that we have taken the matter up seriously and made sufficient changes to avoid the trouble in future, irrespective of whether it was caused by running the engine in the reverse direction.'[34]

This appeared to resolve things but the need to keep the Admiralty fully in the picture undoubtedly took up a considerable amount of Royce's time, although things were much helped by his excellent relations with the Admiralty's co-ordinator, Engineer Lieutenant-Commander Wilfred Briggs.

As a designer Royce was identifiable for a number of passionate beliefs. Essentially, he was an empiricist who took nothing for granted unless it had been subject to the most demanding testing. In the case of the gearing for the Eagle's propellers, during May 1915 he specifically congratulated his team for their detailed testing but still needed to be satisfied about its actual effectiveness:

> I was very pleased indeed to hear that the gear had completed a ten hours test. We presume that you are getting on with this test for some hours, then stripping it and carefully measuring the part to see what the wear is likely to be over a fairly long period.[35]

His same concern for testing related to the engine's carburettors and connecting rods, where he told his designers that 'you might send us a sketch of the gauze protector, and where it is applied, and a note further to yours of 20 May and also any further reports of carburettor experiments'[36] and, on 27 May, 'With reference to the connecting rod work, no one can tell better than by experimental experience which is the best way of treating connecting rods prior to white metalling them.'[37]

A day later he revealed his belief that the only way his doubts about an engine foot bracket could be resolved was to test it extensively – even to destruction:

> Should this bracket succeed in withstanding three times the load given we think it is subject to, I think we had better go on and find out in what way it breaks, by continually increasing the vertical and horizontal load in both directions. It is just possible our fears are unfounded and that the bracket is quite suitable for the work.[38]

With Royce there could never be any half-measures with testing. In fact, he believed in the opposite. He wrote approvingly, 'In fact all our testing was done on the lines of making the engine break down, if possible, even by unreasonable handling.'[39] On 9 June 1915, in a letter to the Admiralty, Royce summarised his high belief in testing, admittedly using it as a partial excuse for the engine's late delivery:

> You may think we are keeping the aero engine under test for a long time but some large and smaller defects have occurred from time to time due to our attempting perhaps more than is wise. We believe now that all the troubles have been weeded out and pieces made to replace the ones which we have managed to prove the weakest on test and we are now busy manufacturing the engines and designing the controls in accordance with your wishes …[40]

Another characteristic of Royce as a designer was his deep interest in the materials used and the need to maximise their performance.

In September 1914, he wrote to the Works about an aero cylinder's metal components:

> My impression is that it should contain about 0.4 to 0.6% carbon, something like tyre steel. Great care will have to be taken that it is not too high in carbon to be brittle, but it must be of such a quality as not to be very liable to seize with the piston rings or to hammer out the valve face. We could heat-treat it after it has been roughed out to about ½ inch thick in the usual way; oil quenching and re-heating are recommended for whatever steel we are able to get.[41]

In November 1914, he wrote to the Royal Aircraft Factory for comparative evidence over the composition of a valve:

> We have just had a German valve analysed and we enclose herewith a copy of the analysis … You will notice also that there is a surprising amount of chromium in the steel, which one would have thought would have made it brittle. Will you kindly let me know if this bears any comparison to any analysis you have had of tungsten steel for a similar purpose.[42]

In the spring of 1915, his concern was drawn to the metallic composition of the engine's vital connecting rods and the need for their adjacent liners to be of the same material, the elements of which he most carefully specified:

> The steel liners to be used in the connecting rods are to be of the same metal as the rod is forged from and the same heat treatment, so that they will not be likely to be crushed by the pressure of the bolts. The nuts were [*sic*]

> to be of K.E.805, and were [*sic*] to be heat-treated and left rather stiff, say, B450/500, so that the threads do not collapse with the load or the corners rub off the spanners. The bolts themselves must be tougher, say, B-350.[43]

Two months later, he was writing about another faulty connecting rod and its bolt: 'If you cannot get any explanation of this, it would appear that the material was not as good as the nickel chrome of K.E. 805 steel. These bolts, being ordinary bar and not drop forgings, can be made in any of the high class materials.'[44]

With Royce, it was not just a question of identifying the final causes of metal breakages, he wanted to reduce any stresses caused by manufacturing as far as possible in an early attempt to avoid or delay possible metal fatigue:

> I think it will be advisable if we make an attempt at boring these [valves] in an annealed state, afterwards normalising them, that is just heating them to a red heat and permitting them to cool in the air. This hardness is entirely a question of the chemical contents of the steel and the temperature and the rate of cooling, and if we cannot do the work fairly easily in an annealed state, it might also be advisable to try the effect of a boring tool, like that used for the gun barrels, which probably can be made very hard at the point ...

As far as valves were concerned, he wrote: 'It would also be instructive if you would send me the process sheets for the manufacturing of these valves, as we could probably facilitate the turning by some special scheme.'[45]

Royce's interest in the way metals performed and how this might be improved unquestionably went well above that of most other designers/engineers of the day and led to Rolls-Royce subsequently establishing a department for metallurgical research.

Royce also had a virtual fixation about saving weight. Unnecessary weight was obviously a negative with an aero engine because it reduced its power-to-weight ratio, but finding the perfect balance between the weight and the strength required for its components remained a constant aspiration. In early 1915 he set out the importance of reducing weight:

> With reference to the weight of the 200hp aero engine, I am very pleased you have done this and I am pleased it has come out so satisfactory. We can

> no doubt reduce the weight in many parts ... Any cutting down such as this ought to be done before we commence testing and as you say there will probably be some strengthening up to do which will be more quickly found in experience with the lighter parts than by starting with heavy parts which have afterwards to be lightened for other reasons.[46]

Royce was particularly keen to reduce weight on the epicyclic drive gear to lessen the strain on the bearings: 'I propose we make it lighter than we think advisable and test in this condition with a view to increasing any parts which appear too delicate.'[47] Three days later he was reiterating his objectives here: 'My impression is that we still have to remove about 33% of the weight, even if we have to re-design in some way.'

The epicyclic gear was, of course, far from his only concern: 'Probably the shafts and the propeller hub are also on the heavy side. Kindly let me know what you are able to do.'[48]

With Royce it went beyond saving weight; the savings had to be well targeted and worthwhile: 'I did not realise that the parts were so small ... there must be places where we could save twenty times as much weight as on the small parts referred to here. Will you hunt all the time for metal which can be reduced where there are no heavy stresses.'[49]

He attempted to make his staff as keen on weight reduction as he was. In February 1915, he wrote: 'I was very disappointed at the weight of the epicyclic gear not being reduced more than we have been able to do at present'[50] and a week later he hoped that, 'You will be able to get in hand the urgent parts such as the chip forgings to the lightened design immediately.'[51]

The full extent of Royce's conviction about lightening is seen in his degree of concern about the relatively small piston pin involved in the installation of aluminium pistons: 'I am very pleased to hear that the Z aluminium pistons have done so well. They are indeed the lightest pistons and one can only complain that perhaps the piston pin is unnecessarily heavy. I should like to see it got down to 0.3lb.'[52]

Royce's convictions about continual testing, the investigation of the materials used and weight reduction all contributed to his unceasing drive towards engineering perfection in both function and form.

An instance of his remarkable concern with form occurred in December 1914 with his reference to the exit for water from the cylinder at the centre of the engine. He wrote:

> I had not written about this, as I was trying to find some better method of dealing with the difficulty. I think your way is very ingenious, but it seems to make such an inconvenient lump on the water jacket. I think we might be contented if the nut and the screw thread were ⅛ inch smaller in diameter, and I think it would be quite all right if it were the same size as the inside of the pipe. It would not make such a bulky-looking piece if it were ⅛ inch less in diameter and ⅛ inch nearer the centre of the cylinder.[53]

The 'bulky-looking piece' clearly offended his sense of configuration. He went on to say it 'should be made as close as possible round the pocket, as we do not want to carry a weight of water which is of no use to us, but it must be of a practical shape'.[54]

In May 1915, he wrote about a milling jig for machining a joint that faced the bottom half of the Eagle's crankcase. After making a number of comments, he ended by saying: 'This jig seems to have been well thought out, but might be improved a little in design to cut down the overall dimensions as much as possible.'[55]

Royce's aim for perfect functioning even extended to his construction of factory buildings for aircraft production. When considering the planning of a new aero-engine testing area he decided that:

> with the exception of 232 feet of partitional wall the whole of the work should be part of the very next extension of the Repair Shop. [As he remarked] I do not like spending money on corrugated iron buildings which are not of a permanent nature in English climates and would probably only increase the noise of the Test.[56]

Finally, whatever Royce's natural humility towards his unceasing search for perfection, he firmly believed that his and his team's painstaking work towards the construction of the Eagle engine should not be undervalued for Rolls-Royce's sake, and in May 1915, with its dimensions pretty well settled, he arranged for an elegant and dignified place to display the name of its parent company, which he decided should be on each side of the crank chamber.[57]

In the event Royce's expectations for his engines would be fulfilled, amd by 1918 five-eighths of the British aero engines used during the war were Rolls-Royces. Most were Eagles, with 4,651 produced, of which 3,123 had been installed in aircraft by the end of the war. The first Eagles were fitted during 1916 in a Handley Page O/100 heavy bomber serving with an RNAS squadron at Hendon, although it would not see active service until late in the year. The first aircraft type equipped with an Eagle engine to experience active service was the Royal Aircraft Factory's F.E.2d fighter. In June 1916, during the Allied Somme offensive, it helped oppose German fighters that Douglas Haig, the British Commander-in-Chief, had believed were faster, handier and capable of attaining a greater height than most British planes. Haig acknowledged that the F.E.2ds, equipped with Rolls-Royce engines, some 385 of which were built during the war, satisfactorily matched their German opponents. The Eagles were also installed in Airco's DH.4 light bombers that entered active service in France during March 1917, where they proved somewhat faster than the defending German fighters, and in the Felixstowe F.2a anti-submarine flying boats, over 100 of which entered service in December 1917.

The Eagle steadily increased in power until its Series VIII produced 360hp compared with the maximum 258hp of the Series I. Most of the Series VIII were produced in 1918, where their intended role from June of that year was to power day and night bombing attacks on the German Rhineland in retaliation for the German bombing of London the year before. They were vital to the so-called Independent Air Force commanded by Hugh Trenchard, with the Eagles powering Handley Page O/400 bombers – that followed on from the O/100s – for which an order for 700 was placed from August 1917. By 11 November, over 554 such aircraft had been built, although by August 1918 only some 200 were available to the Royal Air Force (RAF).[58]

The Independent Air Force's bombing operations could never have been mounted without the long-range capability and power of the Eagle engines, although the actual effects of these raids were to prove marginal at best. This was because the numbers used were always too low. On the night of 14/15 September 1918 a total of forty planes was reached for the first time, but their bombloads were still too light and lacked electronic aiming devices so there was little chance of their bombs hitting their targets, especially at night.

It has to be said that Henry Royce's magnificent Eagles, and arguably others of his family of wartime aero engines, could have been used to far better effect.

Royce was responsible for three other engines: the Falcon, Hawk and Condor. The Falcon was a faithful eight-ninths version of the Eagle designed

Pre-Series V12 Eagle engine dispatched in mid-August 1915 for installation in prototype Handley Page O/100 bomber. (Rolls-Royce Heritage Trust)

by Royce's Robert Harvey-Bailey. In April 1916 it developed 205hp, but this was extended steadily until, in July 1918, it produced 285hp when running at a standard 2,000rpm. Its most famous partnership was with Bristol designer Frank Barnwell's F2 two-seater fighter/reconnaissance aircraft, which he built round the engine. The plane became known as the Bristol Fighter or

Royce's first aero engine, the 200hp Eagle. (Rolls-Royce Heritage Trust)

Derby-designed Falcon III, always associated with the Bristol fighter. (Rolls-Royce Heritage Trust)

'Brisfit' and, after entering active service in April 1917, continuous upgrades to its engine power helped make it one of the most successful aircraft of the First World War with the ability, for instance, to dive faster than any other. It acquired a reputation on the Western Front for being able to fly for up to three times longer than its rivals without an overhaul and to continue to fly home even when severely damaged.

The Hawk was a half-size six-cylinder Eagle, without a propeller reduction gear, which was designed to produce 75hp but by 1918 was yielding 105hp. It was most distinguished for powering the Royal Navy's non-rigid airships, or blimps, designed to escort convoys in home waters and whose 250lb of anti-submarine bombs had an excellent record of discouraging U-boat attacks.

Both Falcons and Hawks were manufactured under licence by the Bristol-based firm of Brazil Straker & Co., whose 32-year-old engineering Director, Roy Fedden, enjoyed Claude Johnson's full confidence in maintaining Rolls-Royce's standards of workmanship.

The last in the family was the Condor, the largest of Henry Royce's first generation of aero engines, which, with a cylinder bore and stroke 1in larger than the Eagle, produced some 610hp. The Condor was intended for the new four-engined V/1500 Handley Page bomber designed to bomb Berlin on a round trip of some 1,100 miles. The Armistice came before such operations could begin but the Condor would be installed in the Hawker Horsley Bomber of the 1920s, and it powered Sir Alan Cobham's Short Singapore flying boat during its round-Africa flight of 1927–28. The Condor III would benefit from the post-war work of designer Arthur Rowledge, who reduced its overall weight by an astonishing 300lb.

During the war there was widespread admiration for the capability of Rolls-Royce aero engines, allied with some frustration about the time taken for them to come into service in the numbers required, a situation exacerbated by the Rolls-Royce factory being saddled with the task of not only producing new engines but also repairing those damaged in use. The reason for their popularity and outstanding performance was Henry Royce's rare ability to create units that, like his motor cars, gave 'unfailingly reliable and efficient service for long periods'.[59]

Their special qualities were highlighted in dramatic fashion at the end of the First World War in a book written for Rolls-Royce by author Boyd Cable. He emphasised, for instance, that:

> The need for speed, power of manoeuvre and other fighting qualities required another kind of reliability in the engines, in fact, in almost every fight in the air, the pilot under stress of circumstances has to handle his machine in a fashion that might well make the hair stand on end on the heads of the engine designers and builders. One instant the engine may be straining to the limit of its power to lift the machine nose up straight into the air; the next it may be racing wildly far beyond its laid-down number of revs per minute in an almost perpendicular dive. It may be throttled right down or shut off, and then with a jerk thrown into top speed; it has to keep running at any tilt and any rate of speed on its back, on its side, on its nose or tail, upside down or right side up ... All these things the Rolls-Royce 'Falcon' and 'Eagle' engines have done time and time again.[60]

A more detached but equally convincing tribute to the Eagle engine came in 1923 from eminent piston-engine designer Harry Ricardo, who wrote:

> This engine which was developed by Rolls-Royce during the war proved to be undoubtedly the most satisfactory and reliable engine in the hands of the Allies, and was of great value, not only on account of its magnificent performance but perhaps even more because of its encouraging effect on the morale of the Allied pilots. Official records computed in France during the war show that the average number of hours flown by these engines between overhauls was 103.2 or very nearly double that of any other aero-engine used in British service. This engine, also, is of interest because it is at once probably the most complicated and quite the most reliable engine yet built for aircraft.[61]

As for Royce himself, the most reserved of men, we have little evidence about his private life during the war years. Whatever his health problems, that he worked with notable energy during his accustomed long hours is incontrovertible and his authoritative voice comes to us clearly through his copious letters and minutes. For more personal information, however, we are restricted to vicarious comments from some of his acquaintances.

We know, for instance, that although Royce loved driving his Silver Ghost at speed, he believed he needed something more economical during the war and sent his designer Albert Elliott to London, where he bought a small second-hand Bugatti, whose designer Royce much admired. Elliott found it ran very badly and it actually caught fire as he drove it along the Embarkment Gardens. In spite of this, Royce had him bring it back to St Margaret's Bay and once he had tuned the engine he ran the little car – which never lacked fizz – during the course of the war.[62]

As the war progressed, St Margaret's Bay came to provide less of the detachment and steady rhythm of life that he sought. Among the unwelcome diversions were the regular security scares from the large number of military camps close by, with Albert Elliott actually put under temporary arrest during one of them, allied with the terrifying cross-Channel shelling from German warships and a growing scarcity of food and household materials. As a consequence, late in 1917 Royce and Nurse Aubin acquired a list of alternative residences along the South Coast into Sussex and Hampshire. Armed with these they went house hunting in Royce's Silver Ghost, for which they had hoarded petrol. At the end of a long and tiring day their very last appointment took them to Elm Tree Farm in West Wittering, which they both liked very much and decided to move in as soon as possible. They would stay there for the rest of Royce's life. West Wittering had much to suit him; it was a small rural village without gas or electricity about 8 miles from Chichester at the western end of the Selsey peninsula looking across to Hayling Island. We have some indications about the nature of Royce's life there through the reminiscences of two designers, Donald Eyre and Donald Bastow.

Donald Eyre's reminiscences, beginning in the early 1920s, referred to the spartan conditions. Eyre was young and lively, and during the winter he initially found the stark life very hard. After working hours he and a fellow designer would cycle to their lodgings along dark unlit lanes, have a short chat during their evening meal, then study or read before an oil lamp. His companion then took his glass of milk to his bedroom, leaving Eyre to sit close to a small wireless crystal set twiddling the cat's whisker to receive some light music in his earphones as free from distortion as possible.[63]

Whatever restrictions he endured, Eyre was an acute observer of Royce's methods and mental powers. While he had been selected because of his ability, he freely acknowledged that from the time Royce came into their drawing office for his daily visit he was the commanding and dominating figure. Eyre likened critical discussion of a design with Royce to a game of chess against a friendly but expert opponent whose playful wit and manner might lull one into forgetting his uncanny and constant alertness.[64] Eyre's

Master and plans at West Wittering. (Rolls-Royce Heritage Trust)

obvious hero worship was apparent from his remark that, 'As a very enthusiastic student in the presence of a master of engineering design, I learned more from each comment than years of my own experience would have taught me.'[65]

Donald Bastow's discerning description of the designers' working conditions in 1932, a year before Royce's death, showed they had hardly changed since Eyre's arrival a decade before. They still worked in a studio

The studio, West Wittering. (P.H. Vickers)

situated in the garden of a cottage called 'Camacha', which was owned by a Miss Ramsey. The studio had been converted from a barn and still had an earth closet and oil lamps. All was strictly utilitarian; in addition to four drawing boards and the tables to take the drawings, there were filing cabinets for blueprints of scale drawings. Their drawing boards were 30in by 40in, with moving straight edges across them. They were covered with cartridge paper as a white backing for the transparent paper on which they worked.

> Each had an adjustable set square for a fixed set of squares with 30, 60 and 45 degrees provided by themselves, a 12 inch nickel silver Chesterton ruler, pencils of assorted hardness and an India rubber. They all had an incandescent mantle oil lamp for working after dark. This was hung on the top left-hand side of their drawing board with its cylindrical wick needing frequent attentions. Royce's designers stood on a thick coconut fibre mat so that if they dropped a pencil, they probably wouldn't break the point and would not need to waste some pencil and their time re-sharpening it.[66]

Like Eyre, Bastow found their recreational opportunities strictly limited. There was sea bathing and tennis in the summer and, in the winter, badminton in the village hall. They could, of course, drive to Chichester for more sophisticated activities. Bastow endeavoured to find out more about his master and he talked extensively with Royce's niece Vi about Nurse Aubin, whom she roundly hated. He learned about Aubin's extreme possessiveness and jealousy of Vi, which he darkly concluded was very often indicative of a close physical relationship. He was told that Nurse Aubin (who was of a similar age to Vi) enjoyed acting as Royce's hostess, with Vi firmly believing Royce was mesmerised by her, although he did retain contact with Vi and his wife Minnie.

Whatever the increasingly serious question marks over Royce's health, both observers, with Bastow's more critical discernment contrasting with Eyre's hero worship, had little doubt about his rare capacity for work and his continuing importance to Rolls-Royce.

Neither was wrong, for whatever Royce's accomplishments with aero engines during the First World War, fresh demands upon his exceptional design skills during the 1920s and early 1930s would lead to further achievements that would eventually prove of even greater significance for his country.

PART 3:
POST-WAR CHALLENGES

8

The 1920s: Automobiles versus Aero Engines

In spite of the extended nature and extent of the First World War, its end in November 1918 came as something of a surprise to both the Directors of Rolls-Royce and the British military establishment. The massive plans made in 1917 for the expansion of British air power and the bombing of the German heartland – in response to the raids on London – were still in their early stages and none of the 1,500 Rolls-Royce Eagle engines due to be constructed in America had been completed by the time of the Armistice. With the sudden end of the war, the Rolls-Royce Directors faced the crucial question of how best the company's interests could be served in future. Whereas in Britain motor-car production had been largely suspended during the war, dependence on the petrol engine had grown and the prospects for the British domestic car market, including its top end, seemed bright.

These hopes did not appear misplaced, for while at the end of the war there were 160,222 vehicles on the road in the United Kingdom, by 1921 it had grown to an astonishing 478,538 registrations.[1] With such expectations there seemed good reasons for Rolls-Royce to be a significant player once more. Some indication that during the war, along with his primary concerns with aero engines, Royce had already been thinking about keeping the Silver Ghost up to date was seen when, on 7 July 1917, he told the Derby executives that all post-war chassis must have electric lighting and self-starters – developments that in fairness had been long required. These, plus the standardisation of aluminium pistons, which helped to increase power output by some 6 per cent over the standard pre-war engines, marked the company's determination to recapture its dominant role in high-quality automobiles. This was further demonstrated immediately after the Armistice with the factory's retooling for car production and the sending of the post-war Silver Ghost for testing in early 1919.[2]

A clear indication of the firm's optimism about its future motor-car production was seen in the increase of the Silver Ghost's chassis programme beyond the maximum of 500 per annum set before the war. There seemed good grounds for thinking the Silver Ghost was well capable of re-entering the luxury market when, following the first post-war Motor Show, *The Motor* credited it with a maximum speed of 78mph and spoke in glowing terms of its improved acceleration. Even so, there were indications that other firms were challenging the car that had for so long held a pre-eminent position. In England, although Napier was not the force of old and Daimler's double sleeve-valve engine was prone to emitting a cloud of nauseous blue smoke, Lanchester, with its new overhead-camshaft 'Forty' car, had become a more powerful competitor. In Europe the new Hispano-Suiza motor car that had appeared in 1919 arguably had a more efficient engine than the Ghost's side-valve, while in America there were other newcomers to the luxury car market.

Such developments, together with the anticipated social changes brought about by the war, had already helped to persuade Johnson that the single car policy needed to be amended and plans were in place for the Silver Ghost to be joined quite soon by a smaller car (code-named the Goshawk), that Royce had, in fact, worked on during the later stages of the war (for which in 1921 the company's Directors would authorise £25,000 towards jigs and tools for its manufacture).

In the case of aero engines, contrary to the optimism about the renascent automobile industry, the expected contraction of the Royal Air Force and limited expectations for civil aviation helped to convince Rolls-Royce that demand for such engines seemed bound to fall sharply. Royce's highly regarded Eagle, Falcon and Hawk engines had already been produced in relatively large numbers and future orders were expected to be in short supply. Although they were joined in August 1918 by the Condor, a scaled-up Eagle that used a spherical cylinder head and four valves instead of two, which produced 650hp at 1,900rpm and had originally been considered for the giant Handley Page V/1500 bomber, this was only likely to be purchased in relatively small numbers.[3] In fact, Johnson was soon to write to

Royce specifically asking him to economise on aircraft development work because he believed the company's survival depended on it producing its cars economically.

Whatever the contrasting expectations for automobile and aero engines, it was only to be expected that the Silver Ghost would soon be replaced and aero engines designed solely for wartime purposes would also need a major redesign.

As before, responsibility for maintaining the firm's reputation for engineering excellence and preserving its lead in a fast-changing world devolved to Royce, who, design genius or not, was now 55 years of age and in precarious health. Notwithstanding, with Claude Johnson as Managing Director, the devolved system – whereby Royce was separated from Derby – which had functioned so effectively both before and during the last war, was bound to continue.

Whatever the company's future prospects, during 1919 its aero engines were about to enjoy new fame from attempts by RAF airmen – supported by individual aircraft companies – to achieve long-standing aerial challenges dating back to before the war.

The pre-eminent one was for a non-stop flight across the Atlantic for which Claude Johnson's friend, Lord Northcliffe, had offered a massive prize of £10,000 before the war. Although at the war's end eleven aircraft manufacturers showed interest in attempting it, in fact only four British companies (Sopwith, Martinsyde, Handley Page and Vickers) would actually send teams to Newfoundland and attempt an unbroken journey of some 1,700 miles from there to Ireland. While using very different types of aircraft, the firms all relied on Rolls-Royce engines. The Sopwith Company designed a special two-seater biplane – appropriately called the 'Atlantic' – to be powered by a single Eagle engine; the entry by the Martinsyde Company involved another two-seater biplane called the 'Raymor', using a Falcon engine; Handley Page decided to make the attempt with a giant V/1500 bomber powered by four Eagle engines, while the final entrant from Vickers chose a Vimy bomber powered by two Eagles. Rolls-Royce played their part by sending Eric Platford, Head of Production Testing, to Newfoundland to supervise the final running of all the participating engines, while the company's Bob Lyons was appointed as mechanic for the Vimy team. All the engines were specially prepared by Rolls-Royce, with their water jackets rewelded to prevent leakage. The Vimy's engines were fitted with a crank damper to avoid over-vibration at full throttle, although for most of its projected journey they were intended to be flown throttled back.[4]

Sopwith's Atlantic set off on 18 May 1919 but was forced to ditch in mid-Atlantic due to a malfunction with its engine-cooling system before its two-man crew were rescued by the Dutch Steamer SS *Mary*. Martinsyde's entry also took off on 18 May, but it crashed on take-off, injuring both crew members, and a further take-off attempt resulted in another crash and the abandonment of their endeavour.

The Handley Page V/1500's attempt was delayed by a succession of frustrating if relatively minor faults, which led it to being leapfrogged by the twin-engined Vickers Vimy, the last aeroplane to arrive in Newfoundland, piloted by Captain John Alcock with Lieutenant Arthur Whitten Brown as his navigator, in which they embarked on their transatlantic bid on 14 June 1919.

Their flight in a fuel-laden aeroplane with an open cockpit was eventful from the start, with its wireless rapidly going out of service and the weather

Alcock and Brown taking off from Newfoundland in their Vimy, 14 June 1919. (Rolls-Royce Heritage Trust)

proving much worse than expected, compelling them to fly through 'lowering unscalable clouds, fog, rain, sleet and snow at higher altitudes' with the navigator having to rely on dead reckoning to find his way. After eleven hours they flew through the centre of a storm, where the plane went out of control and spiralled down from 4,000ft to some 60ft, looping the loop in the process before Alcock could attempt to regain height.

Even so, at 8:40 a.m. on 15 June 1919 they reached Ireland and made landfall in a bog at Derrygimla near Clifden, in Connemara, following a journey where, despite the exhaust manifold on their starboard engine splitting off quite early and deafening them with its noise, the engines continued to work perfectly over the whole journey.

The extent of their achievement can be measured by the fact that, despite a number of further attempts by other European countries, it would be almost eight years before the Atlantic was again crossed non-stop, this time by the remarkable lone American aviator Charles Lindbergh in his *Spirit of St. Louis.*

The other outstanding flying challenge was the Britain to Australia Air Race. On 19 March 1919, Australian Prime Minister Billy Hughes offered a prize of £10,000, similar to Lord Northcliffe's for the transatlantic crossing, to Australian nationals in British-constructed aircraft that could fly the marathon journey of almost 11,250 miles from Britain to Australia in under thirty consecutive days along specified routes under the most searching climatic conditions. The winning crew were pilot Captain Ross Macpherson Smith and his brother and navigator Lieutenant Keith Macpherson Smith, supported by Sergeants Jim Bennett and Wally Shiers, who acted as their mechanics. They travelled in another Vimy bomber powered by two Eagle engines; their journey involved fifty-five landings following flights varying from 20 to 730 miles for a total distance of 11,130 miles over a period of just under twenty-eight days, with a total flying time of 135 hours fifty-five minutes.

After taking off from a snow-covered Hounslow on 12 November 1919, Ross Macpherson Smith declared: 'The only cheerful objects of the whole outfit were our two engines – they roared away and sang a deep-throated song filled with contentment and gladness.'[5] With the aid of their two highly skilled mechanics, these continued to perform faultlessly over the whole arduous journey. In 1920 yet another Vickers Vimy, powered by two Eagle engines, set off on the first flight to South Africa although, after failing to take off at Bulawayo, the last stage was completed by a D.H.9.

Such successes gave particular prestige to both Rolls-Royce and Vickers, and an indication of Claude Johnson's delight with the non-stop Atlantic crossing was his instruction that the firm's Derby factory should be closed for a day's holiday.

Following the initial uncertainty over the company's wartime role, the move towards designing and producing aero engines had undoubtedly proved of immense benefit. In 1913 its net worth had stood at £421,679 but by 1919 this had grown to £1,175,413 (including an increase in its share capital of £87,176).[6] Another advantage for Rolls-Royce following the war was that it was accorded the privilege of being one of the Government's selected firms for aero-engine orders for, while the plant at Derby had also expanded, much of it was still only suitable for aero-engine work.

Understandably, when the Rolls-Royce Board met on 20 June 1919 – less than a week after Alcock and Brown's success, it was in a confident and celebratory mood. Prime subjects on the agenda were a resolution to congratulate Henry Royce on the success of his Eagle engines for the first non-stop transatlantic flight and to approve what appeared to be an exciting and important new venture with the flotation of an American Rolls-Royce motor company. This it was felt would help to increase its motor sales on a continent where the Americans imposed a 30 per cent duty on imported cars, and exploit the organisation set up towards the end of the war to make Rolls-Royce aero engines there.

The American market had interested Charles Rolls back in 1906, although at that time he had not been over-impressed by their engineering skills. However, following Claude Johnson's visit in 1917 to organise the Eagle engine's construction programme, 'the wealth of the country, the size of the upper income groups, the efficiency of American production methods and the relative freedom from restrictions of all kinds which American manufacturers enjoyed'[7] persuaded him to expand the organisation that he had established during the war. He also believed that undertaking production of Rolls-Royce chassis in America would act as a safeguard against any likely problems with his Derby labour force that might prejudice the future of the British company. Despite the amazing predominance of the popular Model T Fords, there appeared to be an opportunity for high-quality cars that other American firms were not properly exploiting.

Following protracted negotiations during 1919 conducted with the American financier J. E. Aldred, a prospectus was issued for the new company with an authorised capital of $15 million. This was oversubscribed and it was agreed that the products of the British and American companies would be 'identical and indistinguishable'[8] and that the English Board would act in an advisory capacity and supply 'prominent technical officials'. Initial production was agreed for 380 Silver Ghost chassis a year, well over half the annual production at Derby. A plant was purchased at Springfield, Massachusetts, which had long been a centre for the manufacture of service rifles. It had a skilled labour force and it was thought its isolation from an automobile manufacturing district such as Detroit would accentuate the difference between a Rolls-Royce and an ordinary car. The project, however, soon encountered a number of problems, including the need to counter the inclination of certain American buyers to think an American Rolls-Royce could not be as good as an English one. Another concerned the selling price of the chassis, which was settled at a price of $11,750 when the Springfield managers had suggested a lower $9,300. Buoyed by his confidence in Rolls-Royce's reputation, Johnson was unconcerned by the higher price, although in fact, he totally underestimated the US customer's cost consciousness.

By August 1920, other serious problems arose over the quality of some accessories, which were standardised in America and generally readily available locally. The Springfield management wanted to fit Bijur starters and Bosch magnetos, rather than Lucas dynamos, which they said gave more trouble than any other parts of the car. Royce inevitably became involved because all modifications to the car needed authority from England. He fully recognised that Bijur and Bosch electrics were better than Lucas ones and Ernest Hives, who was working under him as chief of the Derby experimental department, was sent to Springfield to meet its engineers and report back upon the different conditions in America. Hives concluded that the guarantees given by American manufacturers were better than those from the English suppliers and on cost grounds alone the evidence was overwhelmingly against importing accessories from England.

Hives also discovered that the Derby chassis experienced unforeseen problems on the uneven American roads and its right-hand drive, lack of a petrol tank gauge and the fact its filler caps were on the wrong side promoted considerable dissatisfaction, all problems Rolls-Royce should have anticipated. He recommended a number of important improvements and pointed out that 'the policy of making the Rolls-Royce car in America identical with the Derby car was far less important than the results of the car in the customer's hands which we want to be identical'. Hives also found that the chassis did not perform as in England because of the lower-quality American petrol and the wide range of atmospheric temperatures. The car was difficult to start and there were far more dissatisfied customers than in England. In response, Royce thanked Hives for pointing out the entire dissimilarity of procedure in the two countries. However, although he came to approve the use of the American Bosch magnetos and by April 1921 the policy of complete identity of product was abandoned because of its sheer impracticality, without going to America himself it was difficult for him to appreciate fully the rapid advances occurring there, particularly the benefits of mass production and the economies of scale. By the end of 1921 Johnson had visited Springfield again to help sort things out, although production had still only reached three chassis per week.

For Royce and the other Directors who lacked Johnson's and Hives' first-hand knowledge of the US car industry, the situation at Springfield usually seemed to pose some threat to the Derby firm. During 1920, the Board reluctantly agreed to guarantee a maximum of £125,000 to help Springfield through a crisis caused by a shortage of working capital, although in February 1921 a debenture issue of $2 million was finally agreed upon. Johnson was heavily involved in the prolonged negotiations, which had him returning to England in a state of near nervous exhaustion.

The debenture issue by no means ended problems at Springfield. The next major concern was over sales that in July 1922, amounted to just twenty-four of its chassis and twenty bodies a month, well below the planned output.[9] In November 1922, Johnson was forced to go over to Springfield again, where he learned that American customers proved very different from English ones. The latter would wait months for a hand-crafted car that was specifically made for them, whereas the Americans wanted their cars immediately.

During the same, year serious questions arose over the production of Royce's new 'Twenty' car that had already been introduced in England and which by prior agreement the American company was bound to manufacture.

It was eventually decided that its tooling-up costs would be prohibitive and in any case it would be unsuited to the American market, where several American cars offered a similar performance at a lower price.

During September 1923, the main issue in dispute with Springfield concerned four-wheel brakes. These were now virtually standard in the United States but Derby would not permit the modification to be introduced at

Springfield before it had been applied in England. Royce was reluctant to introduce them when his two-wheel system worked so well, but following pressure from Johnson, he agreed to authorise its adoption. Johnson cabled the news to Springfield but not before its first 600 left-hand drive Silver Ghosts still featureda two-wheel braking system contrary to the four on most US cars.

Policy differences also existed between Springfield and Derby with the trade-in system of second-hand cars. In America, a trade-in was crucial if a dealer was not to lose an order, whereas in England the reputation of the Rolls-Royce cars was so established that the company could virtually make its own terms of sale.

During 1924, the American company's trading figures showed little improvement with a first half-year loss of $79,000 – admittedly followed by a profit of $97,000 – although the full allowance for depreciation was not accounted for in either case.

In fairness, the undistinguished record of the American company so far was not only due to fierce local competition but also because it was much affected by its heavy debt and interest payments, along with the unimaginative control exercised by the parent Board members at Rolls-Royce, which in Royce's case meant his already heavy workload with designing was increased still further.

In fact, the British company was also experiencing problems with automobile sales. Although it had a considerable backlog of pre-war orders, this soon proved of mixed advantage because many customers had signed contracts at pre-war prices, which bore no relation to post-war costs, and lengthy negotiations with them were required. Although the company had been confident enough to raise the number of its chassis beyond the previous maximum, it soon found that when it made a necessary hike to its pre-war prices its customers (like those in America) were far more cost conscious than before the war. A 40/50hp chassis had originally been £506, but in December 1919 it had risen more than threefold, being set at £1,850. In April 1920, this was raised to £2,000 and in June to £2,250,[10] causing the cancellation of twenty-six from a total order book of 110 chassis. By November cancellations had risen to a massive 48 per cent of the total. During May 1921, in an attempt to clear stocks, the chassis price was reduced to £1,850 and arrangements were made for customers to purchase by instalments, while pressure was put on suppliers to reduce their prices.

Fortunately for Rolls-Royce, its competitors' prices were also high, with the Napier 40/50 costing some £1,750, but in fairness both Johnson and Royce had anticipated the likely new situation by recognising the need for a smaller car to attract a wider clientele. Royce's aim had been to design a car that cost 75 per cent of the Silver Ghost 'because owing to our reputation we ought to be able to sell a high quality small article at a figure above what it costs'.[11] In other words, it would be cheaper because it was smaller rather than having fewer costly components. After the war Johnson's friend Lord Northcliffe had urged him to improve Rolls-Royce's sales publicity (which he thought was awful), during which time Johnson revealed that although Royce had already designed a 20hp car it had, in fact, been considered too costly to manufacture and he was designing another of simpler and less costly design.[12]

When the first 'Twenty' Rolls-Royce was finally launched in 1922, the design broke new technological ground in having a six-cylinder twin-overhead-cam engine, with the head integral with the cylinder block and a transverse valve arrangement. Its ignition had an automatic advance and retard mechanism, with its gear change centrally mounted but with only three forward speeds.

While it proved a docile, comfortable and most reliable vehicle capable of a top speed of 62mph (confirmed in a road test conducted by *The Motor*), it undoubtedly lacked an exciting performance and, with an engine capacity of a little over 3 litres, it was a good deal smaller than most of its contemporaries. Its nearest English rival was the 'little' Lanchester of 21hp that came out in 1923 with its output performance superior to the Rolls-Royce 'Twenty' and with four-wheel braking giving better stopping power, 'although Royce's car scored for lightness and delicacy of control and for silence'.[13] Royce aimed his car at the professional middle classes, including women drivers, but the company's sales department proved less than enthusiastic, with Claude Johnson's brother, Basil, in charge of sales in the Conduit Street office, preferring to sell second-hand Silver Ghosts to new 'Twenties'. In fact, the firm did not even exhibit it at the 1923 Sixteenth International Motor Exposition, held at Olympia. Even so, in its first year it accounted for a £550,000 turnover against the £660,000 for the Silver Ghost and in all, 2,885 would be manufactured.

Apart from the car's mixed reception, Henry Royce became frustrated by the Sales Department failing to control the size and weight of the bodies being fitted to its relatively light chassis. He believed that 35cwt should be

The enclosed body of Royce's 20hp chassis made a nonsense of the weight limit of 35cwt. (Rolls-Royce Heritage Trust)

the loaded weight of the car, including passengers and luggage. He would forcibly repeat his concern here: 'We must once and forever cease to fit the large ponderous bodies (like the landaulette produced by Joseph Cockshoot of Manchester).'[14]

Following a Board Meeting where the 'Twenty' was compared adversely with the Silver Ghost for its lack of power, in July 1922 Claude Johnson issued a tetchy memo observing that: 'The serpent of speed and power has entered into this company and is likely to poison its existence ... Anyone encouraging in any way, the making or selling of high compression cars will be regarded as an unfaithful servant of the company and his services will be dispensed with.'[15]

Whatever Johnson's dark threats and implied criticism of W.O. Bentley's cars, he could not prevent the jibes in some quarters over the so-called Cinderella or 'Gutless Wonder', and by 1929 Royce would, in fact, replace the 'Twenty' with a more powerful 20/25.

In spite of this, customers who wanted quietness and refinement appreciated the 'Twenty's' Rolls-Royce characteristics and it gained a considerable, if not massive, following, although in fairness its near 3,000 sales over seven years compared quite well with the famous Silver Ghost's 6,173 over eighteen years. One of its strongest champions proved to be Royce's future biographer, the author Max Pemberton, as he showed in a letter to the company:

Dear Sirs,

It is with very real pleasure that I write to you about the remarkable performance of the 'Twenty' which I have now driven since the year 1923.

This car has accomplished 100,000 miles, it has done so without any road stop whatsoever and the engine is as quiet as the day it left your factory.

Your 'Twenty' has always been regarded – and deservedly – as the ideal town car for women; but I would like to say that I have driven this particular car for thousands of miles in all conditions of wind, weather and track and found it no less efficient on the open high road than in London…

It is surely one of the world's two great cars. The other is the Phantom.

Yours Sincerely,

Max Pemberton.[16]

In spite of Max Pemberton's enthusiasm and Claude Johnson's anger at the car's detractors, it has to be acknowledged that Royce's 'Twenty' Rolls was neither fish nor fowl. It inevitably lacked the beauty and panache of the much more powerful Silver Ghost and could never be expected to capture the upper end of the popular market because of its high price and marked docility. For the hostile Basil Johnson it was an ugly duckling produced for commercial necessity rather than on grounds of technical evolution. With its shorter and lighter chassis and comparatively small engine it would, of course, always play second fiddle to the Silver Ghost.

Whatever the concerns over the 'Twenty' car, the iconic Silver Ghost, whose emergence stretched back to 1906 and none of whose parts were interchangeable with those of the 'Twenty', was finally beginning to show its age.

Royce's own activities were also the subject of some criticism. While a strong admirer of the Silver Ghost and its designer, the astute Walter Robotham was surprised at the bewildering range of commitments undertaken by Royce and his team during the early 1920s and their continued involvement in the detailed design of almost all his cars' components, including electrical equipment, conductors, clutches, brakes, steering, shock absorbers engines and gearboxes.[17] Robotham noted that Royce was slow to buy components from accessory manufacturers – certainly those not contracted to Rolls-Royce – which in America were the products of vast and effective research facilities. Young draughtsman Donald Eyre also marvelled at the time Royce spent on designing even a simple component, in this case 'a hinged cap for a car engine and filter ... having to alter the shape, the hinge and fastening many times before Royce was satisfied'.[18]

While undoubtedly open to criticism for seeking perfection with some automobile components that could equally well have been bought in, and failing to make some of his cars' parts interchangeable, Royce undoubtedly still retained his shrewd understanding of the company's inherent interests.

He was, for instance, fully aware of the changing market for automobiles, especially upper-class ones. As early as 1919 he had struck a note of caution about the firm's luxury cars, writing to Ernest Claremont that one has the impression that there will be a somewhat limited use for such cars, probably more limited than before the war.[19]

In consequence, he retained his allegiance with aero-engine design to a greater extent than other Rolls-Royce Directors, including Claude Johnson. By 1921 Johnson had reduced the firm's aero department to carrying out repairs on the Eagle and Falcon engines and he neglected the development of the Condor, despite Napier and Bristol energetically marketing their Lion and Jupiter aero engines.[20] Rolls-Royce were therefore exceedingly lucky that during 1921, Lt Col. L.F.R. Fell, who was an admirer of Royce's work, became Assistant Director of Technical Development (Engines) at the Air Ministry. In that capacity he suggested that Rolls-Royce redesign the Condor and undertook to buy twenty of them. Royce allotted the work to two noteworthy designers, his highly regarded Albert Elliott and the outstanding Arthur Rowledge, who had just been recruited from Napier for whom he had designed the Lion engine. Royce gave them a relatively free hand with further development of the Eagle and Condor engines[21] and although Royce's request to the Board for the development of an experimental aero engine was rejected, by 1924, following his designers' comprehensive examination of the Condor and Eagle engines, he came to the decision that they were, in fact, obsolete with little scope for future development.[22]

As a result, he decided to design the 'F' engine – later to be called the Kestrel – which heralded a new family of advanced Rolls-Royce aero engines that eventually came to take economic precedence over the firm's luxury cars that were considered of premier importance during the firm's early post-war years. These would, of course, continue to be developed.

Condor engine after its redesign. (Rolls-Royce Heritage Trust)

The Kestrel was the first Rolls-Royce engine to be supercharged as standard. (Rolls-Royce Heritage Trust)

9

Royce's Aero Engine and the Schneider Trophy Contest of 1929

Although in 1926 Royce's construction of the 'F' engine, which subsequently became the Kestrel, marked the return of Rolls-Royce to mainstream aero-engine design, it was in fact, not until the early 1930s that the firm's output started to climb sharply and came to occupy a dominant national position.

The figures for aero-engine production by Rolls-Royce as a proportion of the total UK output for the years 1928–33[1] were as follows:

Year	Total Output (UK)	RR Output
1928	539	67
1929	721	35
1930	726	122
1931	637	315
1932	738	315
1933	730	545

The process was spearheaded by the Kestrel, whose chief attributes were succinctly summarised by Royce's designer Arthur Rubbra, 'for its use of aluminium cylinder blocks with steel liners instead of separate steel cylinders with welded-on jackets, a construction which considerably improved the beam stiffness of the crankcase and the ability to use higher rpm and powers without crankcase trouble'.[2]

At the time Royce was also concerned with another experimental unit, the Eagle XVI, a sixteen-cylinder engine arranged in banks of four that gave fundamentally the same power as the Kestrel. Although the Eagle XVI was initially favoured by Royce, it proved much larger than the 'F' engine and when installed in contemporary fighters, it hampered the pilot's view. This weighed against it, particularly in view of the streamlined nature of the Kestrel where wet liners could be introduced through the bores at the bottom of the cylinder block skirt, thereby helping to avoid the maintenance problems experienced by the American Curtiss D12 engines. Aviation author Harold Nockolds was convinced the Kestrel was a genuine landmark from an engineering point of view but, although the early marques developed some 480hp, Royce had already recognised the pressing need for a more powerful engine while still keeping to the same design.

This was achieved by his 'H' engine (later called the Buzzard) that produced 70 per cent greater cubic capacity, for which most of the detailed design work had been carried out by R.W.H. Bailey.

The Buzzard, known originally as the 'H' engine, is famous as the basis from which two versions of the 'R' Engine were developed. (Rolls-Royce Heritage Trust)

The extent of Royce's renewed interest in aero engines – and the Buzzard in particular – was seen in a rare telegram of thanks that he sent to Derby for their swiftness in developing it. This went as follows:

WORMALD, BAILEY, ROYCAR DERBY, EXTREMELY PLEASED
WITH EXCELLENT WORK DONE INTRODUCING LARGER
AERO
ENGINE SO QUICKLY THANKS TO YOUR EFFORTS AND
THOSE
ASSISTING - ROYCE.

With the engine's main components proving satisfactory, Royce urged them to produce still further power through the use of supercharging. This was made possible because in 1921, on Arthur Rowledge's recommendation, Royce recruited James Ellor, an expert from the Royal Aircraft Establishment who had reputedly advanced further than anyone else in what was then an embryonic science[3] and would make outstanding contributions to both the Kestrel and Buzzard engines. With the power of an engine depending on the mass of air it consumed in a given time, supercharging enabled additional air to be sent through it, which at this point was up to a maximum of 12¼lb/in^2. On the downside, this inevitably placed higher stresses on its working parts. Ellor also invented a forward-facing air intake that was unique at the time in that it converted kinetic energy into pressure energy, which allowed a reduction in both the engine's frontal area and its length.

The Buzzard was intended for use with large flying boats and its larger engine block enabled the cylinders' centres to be spread a little, which required the installation of additional cylinder holding-down studs. These proved effective not only on the Buzzard but with the very high boost pressures required for Royce's subsequent 'R', or racing, engine for the Schneider Trophy contests of 1929 and 1931.

The Kestrel series was destined to go on for fifteen years, with its horsepower increasing from 480 to 765 and the engine coming to power many of the Hawker company's iconic fighting aircraft, including the Hart, Demon, Fury, Audax and Osprey. Equipped with its Kestrel, the company's Fury fighter reached speeds of up to 250mph – an outstanding performance for the time. In such ways the Kestrel played a crucial role in helping

Rolls-Royce re-establish its position as the RAF's premier supplier of aero engines, although in the meantime Royce and his company were involved in an international competition that would propel their aero engines into world leadership to an even greater extent than the Silver Ghost did for their car engines prior to the First World War.

The story began in late 1928 with a discussion between Commander James Bird, Director of Supermarine Aviation, and his brilliant aircraft designer, Reginald Mitchell, about providing a suitable engine for the seaplane that the firm intended entering for the 1929 Schneider Trophy Contest (La Coupe d'Aviation Maritime), due to be held at Calshot on Southampton Water during 6 and 7 September, where opposition was expected from France, the United States and Italy. Mitchell was both Supermarine's outstanding aircraft constructor and a long-time contender for the international speed contests instigated in 1912 by French balloonist and airman Jacques Schneider. At the time Schneider had been shocked by the neglect of the seaplane, which he saw as the best means of spanning the oceans and bringing the four corners of the world closer. He believed it deserved a special national contest that combined a vision of aviation with a passion for speed for which he would present a trophy portraying water nymphs emerging from a wave to kiss a winged zephyr flying overhead.

His vision bore fruit when in the 1920s and 1930s the first transocean commercial air routes were opened up by flying boats, although they would quite soon give way to land-based aircraft. During the Schneider contests, seaplanes flew over a distance of at least 150 nautical miles, largely over water, following a triangular or quadrilateral course. (The 1929 race, for instance, covered seven laps of 50km each.) The contests were staged as time trials with aircraft setting off at pre-agreed intervals, usually fifteen minutes apart. Schneider's intention had been to hold them annually but, because of their high cost and the extent of the organisation required, they took place only eleven times between 1913 and 1929. By 1929, Schneider's own standing had long faded and he had died the year before in relative obscurity and in much reduced circumstances, although the contests themselves had taken on an ever-growing significance. The national teams that participated were represented by their aero clubs and limited to three entries each, with the winning country responsible for organising the succeeding contest. By the rules, any club that won the contest three times in five years would be judged to have taken the trophy outright.

The Schneider Trophy. (Author's Collection)

In spite of being restricted to seaplanes, the races proved popular due to the increased national prestige that accrued to the successful countries, namely France, Great Britain, the United States and Italy. The races also came to exert a massive influence on aviation with respect to the development of engine power, increasing engine reliability and 'clean' aircraft design.

Reginald Mitchell of Supermarine Aviation proved an outstanding seaplane constructor. He won his first Schneider Trophy for Britain in 1922 at the age of 27 with a flying boat powered by a 450hp Napier Lion engine. He repeated it in 1927 with the ultra-streamlined Supermarine S5 seaplane that was propelled by a far more powerful 900hp Napier Lion engine and flown by serving airman Flight Lieutenant Webster from the RAF's newly formed High Speed Flight, where the Air Council accepted full responsibility for both the race's finance and organisation.

In fact, it was a race that many thought Italy were unlucky not to have won and for the forthcoming race in 1929, Italy was expected to provide the strongest opposition to Britain. It was believed that this time the winning aircraft would have to be powered by an engine in the yet unattained 1,500–1,800hp category. There were two possible providers: the Napier company with its successful Napier Lion engine, which was by now reaching the limit of its development, although greater speed still seemed possible through relatively small improvements either in horsepower or by reducing its plane's aerodynamic resistance and weight; and Rolls-Royce with a new engine developed by Henry Royce that relied on supercharging but which reputedly had a tendency to crack its cylinder heads after very short service.

George Bulman, the Air Ministry's Director of Engine Development at the time, wrote in his memoirs how he met Mitchell three times over a short period when Mitchell sought his advice about whether or not to risk using the Rolls-Royce 'R' engine. Bulman remarked: 'We finally agreed to back it instead of the Napier Lion largely and for my part wholly on the faith I had in the Derby team.'[4]

Remarkably, powerful opposition existed within the Rolls-Royce company against becoming involved in such a hazardous, if not daunting, project. This was made plain by Rod Banks, latterly of Ethyl Corporation, in his book *I Kept No Diary*. He wrote that, 'Basil Johnson [Managing Director at the time] wanted none of it and felt their place remained in the automobile field, despite the success of the firm's aero engines, Hawk, Falcon and Eagle in the First World War.'[5]

However, three senior figures at Derby who were in favour, Ernest Hives, Arthur Rowledge and Cyril Lovesey, went down to see Royce at West Wittering in October 1928 to gauge his reactions. As they fully expected, they found him enthusiastic and up for the challenge. Banks explained:

> It was a bright autumn morning and Royce suggested a stroll along the beach; as they walked he pointed out places of interest. However Royce, who walked with a stick was a semi-invalid as Montague Napier had been, and he soon tired. 'Let's find a sheltered spot,' he said, 'and have a talk.' Seated on the sand dunes against a groyne, Royce sketched the rough outline of a racing engine in the sand with his stick. Each man was asked his opinion in turn, the sand was raked over and adjustments made. The key to the engine was simplicity, 'I invent nothing,' Royce declared ingenuously, 'inventors go broke'.

Like the Kestrel and the Buzzard, the new engine would have just twelve cylinders, against the eighteen of the Italian Isotta-Fraschini and the twenty-four of the American Packard aero engines. Its bore and stroke were a relatively modest 6×6 inches and its compression ratio 6:1, but the secret of its much-increased power would lie in supercharging.[6]

It was one thing for Royce and his designers being eager to take on responsibility for such an undertaking but despite his massive reputation and stature, he still needed the support of the present Managing Director and his Board.

In the event the British War Office would play a significant part in the outcome. The circumstances were again described by George Bulman, who, as its newly appointed Director of Engine Development, was closely concerned with the coming Schneider Trophy Contest and its likely technical advances in aero engines that would benefit the RAF in future years.

Following Bulman's discussions with Mitchell and their decision to support Rolls-Royce, his War Office Chief, Air Marshal Sir John Higgins, decided that the Managing Director of Rolls-Royce should visit the War Office to settle the deal in principle. Bulman wrote how at the meeting, to their utter amazement Basil Johnson begged to be excused the commission:

> Racing and all its aspects were things, he said, strictly to be avoided by his firm. Its reputation for sheer quality and perfection must not be compromised by sordid competition of this sort …
>
> As I listened to this miserable plea to be let off, knowing that the firm's engineers were straining at the leash to go ahead … I blurted out uncontrollably my fury in a single word unprintable in a polite context and essentially masculine.

> Higgins turned and looked at me for a long second, and then in a steely voice of real Air Marshal calibre said to our guest 'Mr. Johnson I order your firm to take on this job. We have complete faith in your technical team. The necessary arrangements will be made between our respective staffs. Good afternoon.'[7]

Upon this Bulman telephoned the good news to Rowledge and the specialist development of the Buzzard – now designated the 'R' engine in honour of Royce – went ahead. Practically every bit of the engine was altered during the detailed design phase, including bringing in a special supercharger that was needed to provide sufficient entry area into both sides of the impeller for the mass flows required.[8]

Bulman said that one of his most cherished memories at this time was a visit he made to West Wittering with Rowledge and the other designers on a spring day in 1929 to show Royce actual parts of the first real 'R' engine. These were laid out on his lawn where:

> This tall and bearded man with a magnificent head in profile examined each part in detail with Elliott explaining the why and wherefore. Frequently Royce would express his admiration, followed almost immediately by saying that he perhaps, bearing this and that in mind would have altered this face, or that angle, just a 'leetle' bit. Each such point was discussed at length, usually accepted, and a modification agreed, subject always to the factor of time.[9]

Thus, Royce played a very real part in the evolution of the 'R' engine with his exquisite art as a natural engineer.

Whatever the problems of a devolved system whereby the company's Chief Engineer and his core team of designers were divorced from the design and production facilities at Derby, Royce and his team were well used to tight deadlines and working night and day, where his confidence in their ultimate success inspired everyone working for him. Yet while they possessed the knowledge and appetite to raise their game to new heights, the final months leading up to the race provided ample opportunities for excitement.

By May 1929, within three months of starting work, they had advanced from the Buzzard that produced 925hp to the 'R' engine that ran for fifteen minutes at 2,750rpm and delivered an amazing 1,545hp.[10] Their aim was now to achieve runs of up to an hour at full throttle to prove its reliability.

Through the summer of 1929 the noise from the engine test beds at the Derby factory was stupendous and could be heard all over the town. In addition to the sound of the new engine, there was that of three auxiliary engines, one driving a blower, another blowing through giant pipes to cool the sump and a third in the yard with a propeller to blow away the toxic fumes. The test runs usually started at 08:00 and Rowledge, in his home outside Derby, could hear the roar of the engines over his breakfast. He timed his arrival at the factory for an hour after the test started. 'Thirteen times the engine – not always the same one – broke down before the hour was up but on 27 July, less than six weeks before the race it was still running as he drove through the gates.'[11] This was at 1,614hp at 3,000rpm. Time was becoming so critical that after another few days, when a run of 100 minutes had actually been made at 1,850hp, the engine was rapidly driven to Supermarine.

In the meanwhile, Rod Banks, the fuel expert from the Anglo-American Oil Company, was solving the problems that had led to overheating and the sooting up of plugs. Although he had no time for prolonged experimentation – in the manner of a medieval alchemist – he mixed a cocktail of 78 per cent benzol and 22 per cent aviation spirit, plus 3cc/gallon of tetra-ethyl lead for the suppression of detonation and attendant pre-ignition troubles.[12] Fortunately this worked as well as he could have hoped.

As for the engines themselves, after just five hours running time at Calshot, each engine had to be taken back to Derby for stripping, repair and testing. To achieve this and to always keep two working engines at Calshot, Rolls-Royce built a special Phantom-powered lorry with a cradle to hold an 'R' engine. In spite of its heavy load, it apparently travelled at speeds of 75mph or more between the two locations and despite police patrols it was never caught, although after every second trip the lorry's brakes needed relining.

Of unquestionable importance to the whole process were, of course, the pilots. From 1926 these had been provided by the RAF through its High Speed Flight and, although since then the Flight had been kept in being operationally, a team was reformed with the 1929 contest in mind. In February 1929 Squadron Leader Henry Orlebar was put in command. He had been carefully chosen for, at 33 years of age, he was already a Gallipoli veteran, a test pilot and a staff college graduate. Slim to the edge of gauntness, he was highly energetic, an excellent organiser, tactful and self-effacing. His team of four was made up by: Flight Lieutenant D'Arcy A. Greig, who had headed the Hendon Display aerobatic team the previous year; Flight Lieutenant George Stainforth, a former Sandhurst cadet and crack shot who was quiet and imperturbable; Flying Officer Dick Waghorn, winner of the sword of honour at Cranwell, extremely conscientious but even more reserved; and Flying Officer R.L.R. 'Batchy' Atcherley, winner of the Sword of Honour at Cranwell and best pilot of his year. They made up an utterly professional and balanced team with the seriousness of Stainforth and Waghorn offset by the high spirits of Atcherley and Greig.[13]

While they awaited their Supermarine S6 aeroplanes, the Flight flew S5s from the previous race and spent much of their time finding out the most efficient way of cornering the course, where two scientists from the Royal Aircraft Establishment (RAE) helped them evolve the perfect turn.

The team's first experience of the aircraft that were scheduled to fly in the race came on 5 August with aircraft S6 N247 delivered just one month before the race date of 6 and 7 September. Although Squadron Leader Orlebar did not intend to take part in the race, he carried out S6 N247's first tests, only to find he couldn't get the machine to rise out of water as

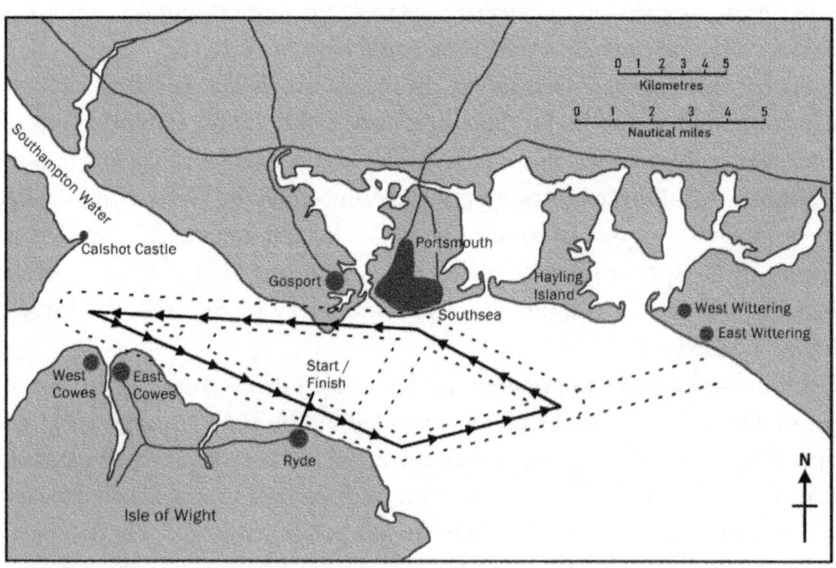

1929 Schneider Trophy Contest course. (P.H. Vickers)

Early Rolls-Royce 'R' Engine used for the Schneider Trophy. (Rolls-Royce)

the plane swung violently to port due to torque from its propeller. Mitchell rapidly solved the problem by the simple expedient of transferring most of the fuel to the starboard float and Orlebar then went on to rehearse the best take-off techniques. Waghorn did not have his first flight in the S6 until 19 August, with Atcherley following on the 20th and both flying it on the 21st, after which the plane had to be returned to Supermarine for the fitting of additional radiators.

With the relatively untried 'R' engines, it was decided that Britain's third entry should be a Gloster VI aeroplane using a Napier Lion engine that was boosted to 1,320hp. Although considerably less powerful than the 'R' engine, its aircraft was also smaller and lighter. However, after encountering repeated snags, the plane intended for D'Arcy Greig (who was more experienced with the Gloster than Stainforth) was withdrawn on the night before the race. Instead, it was decided that Greig would fly an S5 aircraft powered by an earlier 875hp Napier Lion engine.

On 25 August aircraft S6 N248 was air tested at Calshot for the first time, after which the weather clamped down for four days, making flying impossible.

A persistent problem with both S6s was leakage from the wing radiators after every flight. This was somewhat surprisingly cured with a patent sealing compound purchased earlier by Greig to seal the leaking radiator of his small Austin 7 car. Although by the eve of the race the British pilots had enjoyed precious little flying time, due to Waghorn's impressive handling of S6 N247 so far, he was made its first choice, and S6 N248 was therefore to be flown by the brilliant Atcherley, who was in great demand at air shows all over the world.[14]

The team was completed by Greig flying the S5 N219 with its proven Napier Lion as a reassurance against unforeseeable troubles arising with the 'R' engines.

In fact, the problems experienced by the other competing nations proved far more serious and served to demonstrate the hazardous nature of such international racing. On 6 August, the French ace Florentin Bonnet crashed and was killed and within forty-eight hours the French team had withdrawn, citing lack of time for adequate pilot training. As for the Americans, after their pilot A.L. Williams experienced repeated take-off problems with a new mid-wing monoplane powered by an improved version of the Packard X engine (X-2775), the US Navy Department withdrew its support and refused permission for him to compete.

This left the Italian team as Britain's sole opponents. The Italians had created an equivalent of the RAF's High Speed Flight in their Reparto Alta Velocita (RAV) and sponsored a design competition for new racers and engines. They were expected to be very good but their chances suffered a major blow when, while practising on Lake Garda on 22 August, their second-in-command, Captain Giuseppe Motta, dived steeply into the water and was killed. This brought a strong likelihood of the Italians withdrawing from the contest and, although their team of six aircraft arrived at Calshot on Thursday, 29 August, by the time of the race's navigation trials on 6 September, only one of their two new Macchi M.67 aircraft had flown and then for only fifteen minutes.

Amazingly, the British had not done that much better with their flying practice. S6 N248 and S5 N219 were still undergoing repairs until 4 September before their intended pilots, Atcherley and Greig, were able to get a final run in them. Waghorn, in 6N247, completed his run, although it ended with him hitting a barge with his wing-tip – fortunately he only suffered slight damage.

While all went well for the Italians with the navigation and seaworthiness tests, further problems would arise for the British. Although they completed their navigation tests successfully, on their return Atcherley's S6 N248 was seen to have a leak in one of its floats.

The morning tests lasted six hours overall and to touch the machine before this elapsed meant disqualification. Although Mitchell had worked through the night on the final preparations, he was raised from his sleep to look at the plane. To the team's relief, he estimated that the plane should continue to float for the three hours required. He was proved right for although at the end of the period the plane had a definite list, it did not capsize and it was able to be brought ashore where the float was emptied and repaired.

There remained the final inspection, servicing, tuning up and refuelling, which it was estimated would be completed by 22:00. Again all went well for the Italians, but when one of the Rolls-Royce mechanics was changing a spark plug on Waghorn's aircraft he discovered a heavily scored cylinder. The cylinders were in blocks of six and the damage meant changing the whole block. After frantic enquiries it was found that although changing parts of an engine was permissible, the engine number had to remain the same and the work would have to be carried out with the engine still installed in the machine.

Although the other S6 due to be flown by Flying Officer 'Batchy' Atcherley was considered the most likely to win, the redoubtable Ernest Hives decided not to take the risk of having just one S6. He and Cyril Lovesey, who was in charge of the engine party, drove to the hotel where a group of Rolls-Royce fitters were staying before watching the race the following day. There they found a group, including two teetotallers, whom they took back to Calshot to work through the night to change the engine block. The detailed work had to be carried out in the cramped nacelle of the aircraft and it was only because one of the fitters, Jack Marsden, was left-handed that a vital gudgeon pin could be knocked out and an impossible job completed on time.[15]

At 06:00 Lovesey warmed up the engine and gave it a twenty-minute run at full throttle, during which time it worked perfectly, even developing a few more revolutions than before. Squadron Leader Orlebar arrived the next morning to learn of the night's activities, but when Waghorn arrived later the news was kept from him.

Hives' and Lovesey's persistence had an unexpected but vital reward during the race. Of the two S6s, Waghorn in his newly repaired plane went off first with orders not to allow his engine temperature to exceed 95°C.

Flying Officer H.R.D. Waghorn climbing into his cockpit for the winning performance in the 1929 Schneider Trophy. (Royal Aeronautical Society/ National Aerospace Library)

He still averaged 328.63mph over the seven-lap course, with Italy's Tomasso Dal Molin following fifteen minutes later and flying a magnificent race in the old Macchi M.52R, averaging 284.20mph. D'Arcy Greig came next in the Napier Lion-powered S5, averaging a very creditable speed of 282.11mph but still 2mph behind Molin. The first Italian Macchi M.67 then set off but failed to complete the race due to mechanical troubles and exhaust fumes entering the cockpit. It was now Atcherley's turn. He was given permission to risk an engine temperature of 98°C and was confidently expected to break all the previous race times. In the event, with an average speed of 325.54mph, he was behind Waghorn, but more importantly he was adjudged to have passed within the Seaview turn and was disqualified.

The second Machhi M.67, piloted by the highly regarded Lt Giovanni Monti then also failed to finish, leaving victory to Waghorn in a plane that, but for Hives and Lovesey's determination and the skills of Rolls-Royce fitters, would never have entered the race. If it hadn't, victory – however unlikely – would have gone to the Italians.

With Waghorn's success the alarms that came about before the race and the disqualification of the most favoured British entry were largely forgotten.

Whichever of the S6s won, it represented a triumph for Royce's supercharged twelve-cylinder 'R' engine and Mitchell's highly streamlined but sturdy airframe, supported as they had been by Government funding, access to the National Physical Laboratory's wind tunnel and the expertise of the RAE. A few days after the contest, on 12 September 1929, S6 N247 set a new world absolute speed record of 357.7mph whilst piloted by Squadron Leader Orlebar.

For Rolls-Royce and Vickers Supermarine, together with the instruments and accessory producers, the victory meant larger marketing opportunities and for both chief designers, whether the young 34-year-old Mitchell or the 66-year-old Royce, the race helped galvanise them and their teams into seeking new materials and techniques to increase performance, while their association with the young airmen of the RAF's High Speed Flight brought a deep appreciation about the risks being taken. Royce visited the pilots while they were training at Calshot and during the frequent design conferences held there. He was later accustomed to tell his staff at West Wittering about all the technical and practical points that had been discussed.

Reginald Mitchell and Henry Royce at Calshot in 1929. (Rolls-Royce Heritage Trust)

Both designers witnessed the thrills of the race, Mitchell first-hand, while Royce watched it through powerful binoculars while lying on top of a haystack opposite his home at nearby West Wittering. Following Flight Lieutenant Waghorn's victory his first remark was: 'Thank God the boys are safe', thereby revealing his great anxiety for them.[16] The race preparations were helped by the fact that Royce and Mitchell clearly felt at ease in each other's company, with their obvious rapport caught in a joint photograph taken at Calshot.

Royce was particularly concerned that nothing should spoil the beautiful aerodynamic lines of Mitchell's aircraft, while Mitchell's regard for Royce's work was evident in a subsequent article he wrote for *The Aeroplane*, published on 25 December 1929, where he paid high tribute to both Royce's engines and the spur of international competition to the design of British aircraft:

> During the last ten years there has been an almost constant increase in speed in our racing types. To maintain this steady increase very definite progress has been essential year by year. It has been necessary to increase the aerodynamic efficiency and the power-to-weight

1929 at Calshot

7 laps of 50 Kilometres each (350 kms)

Race No.	Pilot	Representing	Aircraft	Engine	Speed / Remarks
2	Fg. Off. H. R. Waghorn	Great Britain	Supermarine S.6	1900 hp Rolls-Royce 'R'	328.63 mph
4	Wt. Off. T. Dal Molin	Italy	Macchi M.52R	1000 hp A.S.3	284.20 mph
5	Flt. Lt. D. D'Arcy A. Greig	Great Britain	Supermarine S.5	875 hp Napier Lion	282.11 mph
7	Lt. Remo Cadringher	Italy	Macchi M.67	1800 hp Isotta-Fraschini	Retired on second lap
10	Lt. Giovanni Monti	Italy	Macchi M.67	1800 hp Isotta-Fraschini	Retired on second lap
8	Fg. Off. R. L. R. Atcherley	Great Britain	Supermarine S.6	1900 hp Rolls-Royce 'R'	325.54 mph, but disqualified for cutting a pylon

1931 at Calshot

7 laps of 50 Kilometres each (350 kms)

Race No.	Pilot	Representing	Aircraft	Engine	Speed / Remarks
1	Flt. Lt. J. N. Boothman	Great Britain	Supermarine S.6B	2350 hp Rolls-Royce 'R'	340.08 mph

No challenger. Flt. Lt. Boothman flew around the course alone to win the trophy outright.

Summary of race performances for the Schneider Trophy. (P.H. Vickers)

> ratios of our machines; to reduce the consumption at the frontal areas of our engines; to devise new methods of construction and to develop the use of new materials.
>
> It is quite safe to say that the engine used in this year's winning S6 machine … would have taken at least three times as long to produce under normal processes of development had it not been for the spur of international competition. There is little doubt that this intensive engine development will have a very pronounced effect on our aircraft during the next few years.[17]

For Royce, apart from the triumph of his 'R' engine, there was the belated offer of a baronetcy in the 1930 Birthday Honours that Johnson, for one, believed should have been offered to him at the end of the First World War. Apart from any personal awards, following the success of Rolls-Royce engines in Mitchell's airframes, there was every expectation of them continuing their partnership in the forthcoming Schneider contest of 1931, which if they won would give Britain outright ownership of the trophy and added prestige for their companies.

It was a hope echoed by Ramsay MacDonald, Prime Minister of Britain's new Labour Government, who said: 'We are going to do our level best to win again.'[18] In the event it was a hope that was not by any means shared by other members of his Cabinet.

PART 4: MASTER DESIGNER

10

Automobiles – Preserving the Marque

In 1924, when Royce authorised the further development of aircraft engines, Rolls-Royce's two current automobiles were expected to provide the bulk of the company's profits. Both, however, required major revisions. Royce's masterpiece, the Silver Ghost, now some seventeen years old, was due for replacement and the smaller 'Twenty' car that had come out two years before, with the hope that it would be cheaper and easier for the owner driver to handle and maintain,[1] would need an enhanced engine before long. It was a time when the company faced challenges of a magnitude last seen by its predecessor during the opening years of the twentieth century. Across the Atlantic, formidable American cars, notably Cadillacs, Packards and Lincolns, posed major opposition for Rolls-Royce's subsidiary company at Springfield, Massachusetts. While in Britain, although the automobile industry was comparatively fragmented, Rolls-Royce faced home-based competitors such as Daimler, Sunbeam and Lanchester. From 1921, W.O. Bentley had begun to produce fast, high-quality sports cars that could double as racing machines, whose output by 1924 had grown to over a third of Rolls-Royce's.

The problems experienced at Springfield had raised questions about production costs at Derby and Royce's reluctance to install new systems that had already been incorporated elsewhere. Post-war British owners of the Silver Ghost, for instance, demanded improved front suspension and braking systems on all four wheels, features that were standard on most American

'Twenty' on the road at Glencoe in Scotland. (Rolls-Royce Heritage Trust)

cars but which were not fitted to the Ghost until 1924 when Royce was about to bring out its long-anticipated successor.

The first glowing references in the press to this car, which would be called the 'New Phantom', appeared in *The Motor* of 15 May 1925. This explained that:

> In the course of developing the design of the new chassis Rolls-Royce Ltd. have made and tested a six-cylinder overhead camshaft engine, a 12-cylinder engine of the V type and an engine having eight cylinders in line; but for various reasons, none of those was considered to be so good as the engine now standardised, which is of the six-cylinder type with overhead-valves operated by push-rods. Simplicity, silence and the necessity for the engine to be capable of years of service without attention were determining factors of this choice.[2]

Development of the Phantom engine undoubtedly involved much protracted work for Royce and his team, with the firm's sales catalogue claiming that it took seven years of research to perfect, also revealing that, although the selected engine was only just larger at 7,668cc than the Silver Ghost's 7,036cc, it produced three and a half times more power at the same speed and was said to be the best it was possible to obtain.

Claude Johnson had high hopes for the car and he had earlier ruled that absolute secrecy would be kept about its construction, with Ernest Hives, who was responsible for producing it, even leaving pieces of armoured plate around the factory to maintain the pretence that it was an EAC (Eastern Armoured Car). As Johnson anticipated, it succeeded in restoring Rolls-Royce's place at the head of the quality car market and, whatever cloak-and-dagger precautions were taken on its appearance, the car's performance certainly impressed the Americans. Maurice Olley, who worked for Rolls-Royce in the United States during both world wars, tells of a singular incident relating to it. In 1928 General Motors opened a 4-mile speed loop at Milford, Michigan, where no cars of American manufacture by General Motors or otherwise could cover more than two laps at full throttle without running out their big ends. But the Phantom I, with a massive Barker seven-passenger landaulette body, covered the loop at 80mph, lap in and lap out, without the slightest sign of trouble. The wisdom of Claude Johnson in keeping it under wraps as long as possible was seen by the subsequent decision of General Motors, after its laps at Milford, to dismantle and examine the car with the result that within two years every American car had durable big ends.[3] The relative shortness of its four-year life compared with the Silver Ghost's was a clear indication of the much fiercer opposition and the growing speed of technical advances elsewhere.

Following the successful launch of the Phantom, Johnson approached Royce about raising the standard of his 'Twenty' car by giving it a four-speed gearbox and a four-wheel braking system. With his other major design commitments Royce proved most reluctant, believing that a three-speed gearbox and an effective two-wheel brake system were perfectly adequate for the smaller car. Johnson persisted for by this time practically all other British and American cars, however modest, had four-speed gearboxes. Johnson telephoned Royce at West Wittering and Royce's designer Ivan Evernden reported that the line between them 'became white-hot'. Finally, the conversation ceased and Royce came from the line shaking with anger, but he said rather ruefully, 'I suppose I must do what he wants – he always knows best.'[4] Since 1911, when Johnson had taken Royce to Egypt to convalesce

Sir James Percy and Henry Royce and Phantom I at Le Canadel, 1928. (Rolls-Royce)

Another Phantom I with sporting drophead coupe bodywork. (Magic Car Pics)

from serious illness, they had enjoyed a close and warm personal relationship – which included their respective families – and because of which Johnson could fearlessly make demands of Royce where marketing the firm's products was concerned. In January 1926, Royce's new gearbox and braking system for the 'Twenty' were road tested by *Autocar*, whereupon it referred to it as 'the Ultra-refined Six, a car which may be said to disarm criticism'. With the new Phantom and a revived 'Twenty', Rolls-Royce appeared to be maintaining their dominant position in the high-quality car market.

Yet unbeknown to both Johnson and Royce, their close and fruitful partnership was shortly to end. On 22 December 1925, as Royce set off for Le Canadel, he met Johnson on what would be the last occasion for, on 12 April 1926, Johnson would die suddenly from pneumonia. Although he was succeeded by his brother Basil, there was never any prospect of a similar affinity between them. Apart from early clashes over sales of Royce's 'Twenty', in 1927 Basil suppressed a report by L.F.R. Fell in favour of Rolls-Royce's aero engines[5] and in the following year he refused to support the development of Royce's 'R' aero engine for the 1929 Schneider Trophy Contest. The upshot was that Royce helped force Basil Johnson's resignation. As the company's founder capable of producing streams of novel technological ideas and with his canny beliefs about the company's best interests, Royce understandably continued to exert a crucial influence. He would, however, never again be as close to the company's leading figure nor be challenged in the same fashion.

Basil Johnson was succeeded by his protégé Arthur Sidgreaves, who would serve as General Manager until after Royce's death. Sidgreaves was a shrewd and effective administrator who actively supported Royce's singular innovations with aero engines without enjoying the close personal relationship of Johnson. By now, as the last of the old guard, Royce had inevitably become a somewhat remote figure working from his home base surrounded by his favoured design team. Any critical comments about his growing conservatism and continuing reluctance to delegate were, however, less likely to come from Sidgreaves than powerful emergent figures like Hives and Robotham – whatever their immense regard for his talents.

Regardless of the changes among Rolls-Royce's senior management, the years 1924–30 – including those of the British National Strike and the start of the Great Depression – were in the main unfavourable for luxury motor cars, and like other Directors Royce was compelled to watch the serious problems developing with their American company. Although in

1925, during the mini boom that preceded the great slump, Springfield's business prospects improved and the company felt strong enough to take on the additional expenditure by purchasing the local Brewster & Co. Car Body Company, Claude Johnson returned from his last visit to the United States in sombre mood about Springfield's economic environment. He told his fellow Directors: 'The difficulties are enormous. One can buy three or four fine American cars for the price of a Rolls-Royce car. The American citizen cannot believe that the Rolls-Royce car can possibly be superior to his own cars to this extent and turns his back on the Rolls-Royce.'

In spite of such fears, deceptively favourable trading conditions meant thateven when Springfield lost nine weeks production when switching to the New Phantom and incurred exceptional tooling costs of $450,000, it could still declare a profit of $368,281. The best year for Springfield was, in fact, 1928 when nearly 400 Phantom Is were produced, although during the next year, when Derby started supplying the new Phantom II, this dropped to fewer than 200.

Such instances of favourable trading together with the energetic leadership of H.J. Fuller tended to increase the American managers' dissatisfaction with the firm's dependence on Derby. In 1926 they aired three possible solutions. One was for Derby to sell its common stock and thus end its influence on Springfield. The English Directors, including Royce, were against this on the grounds that it would allow Springfield's unrestricted use of the name of Rolls-Royce in the United States. A second was for Springfield to transfer its financial responsibility to Derby, to which the English Directors were also opposed, being unwilling to take on such extended financial responsibilities. The third was for the American company to acquire a majority holding in Rolls-Royce's parent company in England, which Claude Johnson had been utterly against and which the English Directors continued to oppose after his death. Any such considerations were shelved when in 1929, the Wall Street crash crippled the American market for high-priced luxury cars. As a result, the American Board decided to cut back production and rely on a much-reduced staff, including 50 per cent of the previous sales organisation. They also requested a visit by a senior figure from Derby to discuss the future. At Springfield things were made worse when Fuller decided to produce further obsolete Phantom I chassis to use up his remaining stock of materials.

In Britain, Henry Royce was notably unsympathetic with the American company's misfortunes. In a letter to Arthur Sidgreaves of 3 September 1929 he said:

> They have created a disastrous situation from which I fear there is no cure … We did our utmost to stop them from this stupid enterprise which is exactly the opposite of my recommendations. I said, avoid obsolete stock at any cost; rather starve your market and slow up your work.[6]

Royce was obviously out of patience with the American organisation and tended to believe it was pointless to spend much further time and resources on it.

Other members of the Rolls-Royce Board were far more prepared to help Springfield and in February 1930, agreement was reached for it to import 200 left-hand-drive Phantom II chassis from England at a price of £1,330 a chassis, while Managing Director Arthur Sidgreaves journeyed to America. There he made an extensive tour of its automobile industry and was most favourably impressed by American quality cars like the sixteen-cylinder Cadillac and the current Studebaker. He concluded that Rolls-Royce would have to introduce synchromesh gear changing on its cars and found the springing of the latest Studebaker better than that of the Phantom II. During his meeting with Fuller he reiterated that Springfield should import the Phantom II chassis from Derby, which, despite the current 33 per cent import duty he believed could still be sold at a profit – if only a small one. In fact, the expenses that bore down the heaviest were not the chassis prices but the additional ones involved in trying to sell its cars in a highly competitive US market.

Unlike his Managing Director, Henry Royce had little opportunity and much less patience to consider overlong the failing American venture. The year 1929 was proving a frantically busy year for his small design team, with aero engines required for the Schneider Trophy and launching the Phantom II motor car, for which Robotham had been pressing in view of the rapid improvements elsewhere. Here he had Royce's strong support, expressed in a letter to him:

> I have long considered our present chassis out of date. The back axle, gearbox, frame springs, have not been seriously altered since 1912. Now we all know it is easier to go on the old way but I so fear disaster by being out of date and having a lot of stock left and by secrets leaking out … that [the Phantom II] must be in production soon after midsummer 1929.[7]

The Phantom II with a body by Park Ward on a 1930 chassis. (Magic Car Pics)

Fortunately, with its redesigned chassis and luxurious interior the car did not disappoint, although the chief excitement was in its 7.6-litre straight-six-cylinder engine. This was fully in the Rolls-Royce tradition, remarkably docile but easily capable of speeds of over 80mph.

For customers liable to be attracted by competing Bentleys, the Phantom II was followed within a few months by the Phantom II Continental sports variant with a low-raked steering column and special springs on the rear axle. This was capable of 75mph in third gear and 92.3mph in top with acceleration from 0 to 60mph in 19.4 seconds, despite its splendid but heavy Park Ward Saloon coachwork. However, during its seven-year life just 1,680 Phantom IIs would be manufactured (including 278 Continental models) compared with the 2,269 Phantom Is manufactured at Derby and 1,243 at Springfield.

Yet another of Royce's automotive responsibilities during 1929 was the updating of his 'Twenty' motor car into the more powerful 20/25, which involved enlarging its six-cylinder engine from 3,127cc to 3,669cc, thereby giving it a maximum speed of 67mph that would subsequently be increased to an impressive 76mph. Although its sales did not fully live up to Royce's best hopes, in Rolls-Royce terms it proved a popular car with 3,827 models produced, half of which were after Royce's death.

In sum, during 1929 Royce's design team succeeded both in producing a high-class motor car with an exciting sports version and updating the firm's smaller model. The three models gave Rolls-Royce a wider choice of products, although they were entering a uniquely competitive environment where, apart from rival quality cars, the more popular ones were enjoying massive technical improvements with frequent model changes accompanied by a steady fall in their average prices.

Draughtsmen Donald Eyre painted a vivid picture of Royce and his designers working to the limits of their ability during 1929, where Eyre's own register of work in progress revealed a wide range of tasks, including drawings for Royce's 'H' and 'R' aero engines together with a medley of automotive assignments, including engine mountings, suspensions and cylinder-head bores. Throughout this, their normal sheltered pattern of working was being shattered by the roar of aero engines practising close by for the coming Schneider Trophy Contest. Their diverse tasks contrasted with the lone ones often undertaken by the American design teams. That they kept ahead of developments elsewhere – even by narrow margins – said much for the designers and their leader, who was one of the very few men who could make notable contributions with both car and aero-engine projects at every point. In such circumstances it was all the more important that Royce should maintain a handsome margin of superiority with his aircraft projects, where there were far fewer competitors and price constraints.

By 1930 Royce, who had traditionally put quality above everything else, was coming to appreciate the increasing importance of cost with motor cars, particularly in America, to where he sent Edward Hives to explore the situation at Springfield. Although Hives reported back that he could still see a future for the American company as a sales outlet, he also described his visits to several US factories, where he found extreme cost consciousness allied to most impressive production facilities. In response, Royce freely acknowledged that to make cars at Derby and to sell them in the United States at a profit was very difficult if not impossible – 'like a single firm against a nation'.[8] He also came to the conclusion that to compete in the US (with the Phantom II chassis) they had to make Rolls-Royce's operations more efficient. 'Either we have to increase our productions or to decrease our

Henry Royce and Arthur Rowledge at West Wittering. (Rolls-Royce Heritage Trust)

establishment charges because no matter how good our work is technically, we cannot expect to get the present prices.'[9]

In fact, neither Ernest Hives' hopes for a continuing role for Springfield nor Royce's concept for Derby embarking on a degree of mass production with quality safeguards (an objective fully shared by Hives and Robotham rather than long-time Works Manager Arthur Wormald), would be realised.

In 1931 Springfield stopped production, although not before the Derby factory had sent them 127 left-hand-drive Phantom II chassis for testing and fitting with Brewster bodies. Things actually staggered on until August 1935, when the factory was finally sold and responsibility for Rolls-Royce car sales returned to Britain. Any meaningful scrutiny of Rolls-Royce production methods at Derby would be overshadowed by the company's takeover of Bentley Motors, arguably its most dangerous home rival in recent years.

The acquisition served to bring together the British automobile industry's two most distinguished designers, with Walter Owen Bentley's background undoubtedly having some parallels with Royce's. Although he suffered none of Royce's early privations, being born into a prosperous London family and attending Bristol's Clifton College, he had left school at 16 to start work, like Royce, as an apprentice engineer with the Great Northern Railway. In Bentley's case it was at the railway's headquarters' workshops at Doncaster and, unlike Royce, he joined the Great Northern on a premium five-year apprenticeship (1905–10), which cost his father £75. At Doncaster he was taught to design complex railway machinery, and he also acquired practical experience in the technical procedures of casting, manufacturing and building it. W.O. showed an early love of speed when in 1909 and 1910 he competed in the Isle of Man Tourist Trophy races for motorcycles, although he failed to finish in either event. After studying theoretical engineering at King's College, London, he found employment with the National Motor Cab Company, overseeing the maintenance of its 250 vehicles. In 1912 he joined his brother Horace in a company, Bentley and Bentley, that sold French Doriot, Flandrin et Parant (DFP) cars. W.O. had aluminium alloy pistons fitted in them and a DFP with such pistons and a modified camshaft achieved several records at Brooklands during 1913 and 1914.

At the beginning of the war W.O. was commissioned into the Royal Naval Air Service, where he worked under Royce's own contact, Commander Wilfred Briggs. W.O. visited manufacturers to emphasise the advantages of his aluminium pistons, and his visit to Ernest Hives at Rolls-Royce, for instance, led to Royce incorporating them in his Eagle aero engine. The Royal Navy put W.O. in charge of a team of designers and he demonstrated his advanced engineering skills by modifying the design and manufacture of Clerget engines for the Sopwith Camel and Sopwith Snipe aircraft. These became known as the BR1 (Bentley Rotary I) and the BR2 engines, and were constructed by Humber Ltd and other manufacturers. In 1919 he was awarded an MBE and £8,000 cash by the Royal Commission of Awards to Inventors for this work. On 18 January 1919 he would use the proceeds to found Bentley Motors Ltd together with Frank Burgess, Harry Varley and Colonel Clive Gallop. As a team they succeeded in building a potent 3,000cc straight-four engine on a sturdy car chassis.

The first Bentley 3-litre car was constructed in the firm's cramped premises at New Street Mews, London. It began its road tests in January 1920 and was delivered in September 1921 to widespread acclaim for its attention to detail, high quality and durability. W.O.'s declared aim was 'to build a good car, a fast car, the best in class'. He decided that the best way to spread the word about his cars was through competition successes. Bentley entered a team of race-prepared 3-litre cars in the 1922 Isle of Man Tourist Trophy (TT) Race, where he drove one of them. In the event they were the only team to finish and their receipt of the team award launched Bentley's reputation. A Bentley 3-litre won at Le Mans (Grand Prix d'Endurance de 24 Heures) in 1924, with others of his models winning in 1927, 1928, 1929 and 1930. In 1930 wealthy supporter Woolf Barnato, in Bentleys, won all three races he entered. An envious Ettore Bugatti was said to have remarked that W.O. made 'the fastest lorries in the world' in an oblique reference to his amazingly strong chassis, where Royce had earlier set the standard with his own robust chassis for the Silver Ghost. In this respect both men appeared to have been influenced by their earlier training in railway engine shops.

By 1924, with Bentley's increasing output, Royce began to take notice, writing from West Wittering that 'the makers are evidently out to capture some of our trade', although he concluded that 'we do not think we can learn much by buying a car because we can see in which way it can be better than we are – that is – for high-speed performance because it has four valves per cylinder'.[10] The idea of another car capturing the rich enthusiast market concerned him more than he was prepared to acknowledge, and in 1926 he wrote from Le Canadel that he would like 'to design a high-speed sports car, not expecting much in the way of sales, but for the good quality of ordinary sales'. His wish was still evident the next year for one of the visitors to Le Canadel reported to Derby that Royce was very keen on seeing a very smart sports car on our stand at Olympia. The Rolls-Royce Board, however, remained firmly opposed to entering such a precarious market. They were proved right for in 1921 Bentley Motors got into such financial trouble that it led to rich enthusiast Woolf Barnato having to purchase the business' assets, and in 1929 he become Chairman, with W.O. continuing his design work as Barnato's employee. This arrangement certainly worked for a time, with W.O.'s six-cylinder Speed Six (introduced in 1928) proving the most successful Bentley in competition. In spite of this the sums still did not add up, with indirect costs averaging 34.7 per cent of the direct costs of production.[11]

Although the company sold 100 of its 8-litre model designed for the ultra-rich, which was in direct competition with Royce's Phantom II, the Great Depression took a heavy toll and with Barnato's financial support diminishing the company was forced to go into voluntary liquidation.

The most likely purchasers appeared to be D. Napier and Sons because they not only wanted to re-enter the motor business but to secure the services of a first-class designer. Rolls-Royce's Managing Director, Arthur Sidgreaves, was understandably most anxious that this did not happen and the Rolls-Royce, under the cover title of the British Equitable Trust, succeeded in buying all of Bentley's assets, including its founder, the name Bentley and its trademark, for a bargain £125,175.

In his biography Bentley recorded that it was more than a week before he learned that the Trust was, in fact, acting for Rolls-Royce Ltd. The circumstances were as follows:

> His wife returned from a cocktail party where she overheard a man saying something which she understood to mean that his company had recently taken over the old Bentley firm. Later in the party she managed to find out the man's name from her hostess. 'It was Arthur Sidgreaves' my wife told me. 'Who is he?' 'He's the Managing Director of Rolls-Royce, I told her.'[12]

According to a court ruling, W.O. was required to join Rolls-Royce under contract from 1 May 1932 to the end of April 1935. He anticipated that he would be given an independent design and drawing office with its own

Bentley taking first and second at Le Mans, 1930. (Bentley Motors)

team, but this was something Royce would not allow. There was a reputedly difficult initial interview between them that began with Royce saying, 'I believe you're a commercial man, Mr Bentley?' and W.O. replying, 'Well, not really – primarily, I suppose I'm more a technical specialist.' Royce persisted, 'You're not an engineer then, are you?' This annoyed W.O., who responded with, 'I think you were a boy in the GN running sheds at Peterborough a bit before I was a premium apprentice at Doncaster.'[13] The upshot was that W.O. was kept occupied in a rather nebulous sort of job on not ungenerous terms liaising between customers and Rolls-Royce's Derby works, test driving cars at Brooklands and giving them test runs across the Continent and the Alps. While he was free to comment on the design for the latest Rolls/Bentley sports saloon of 1934, there was no question of him becoming involved in its design. This was regrettable for, although it was very late in Royce's life, if only the two distinguished engineers had made a better start and had been prepared to work together, they might still have achieved significant and different results. In fact, W.O. came to feel a warm admiration for Rolls-Royce's Design and Experimental Departments, in particular for Ernest Hives, but in 1935 he left Rolls-Royce to become Technical Director at Lagonda and his technical expertise was lost to the company.[14]

On purchasing Bentley, Rolls-Royce faced the problem of how best to relaunch the marque. In the event this proved far from easy. By now the 3-litre model was dated, they were not happy with the 4½-litre model and the 4-litre one, which had been produced quickly in an attempt to stave off bankruptcy, had a Ricardo engine. This left the 8-litre, which competed with Rolls-Royce's Phantom II Continental. The solution appeared to be a brand new car but, although Bentley had been working on a smaller car to undersell Rolls-Royce's 20/25, work had stopped at an early stage. While Rolls-Royce's Experimental Department was involved with Royce's Peregrine, a scaled-down version of the 20/25, its role was still uncertain. The chance of benefitting from the takeover seemed to be slipping by when Hives proposed putting the 3,669cc engine for the 20/25 into the smaller Peregrine, so creating a new car with the liveliness beloved of Bentley owners and the smoothness acceptable to Rolls-Royce ones. Royce accepted the solution, although his death occurred before the first Rolls-Bentley was produced and proved one of the successes of the 1930s. Nonetheless, as Rolls-Royce's W.A. Robotham correctly remarked, 'It should be emphasised that all the Peregrine and 20/25 components that went into the first Rolls-Bentley were designed by Royce. All we did was to rearrange their disposition in the Derby Experimental Department.'[15] Even W.O., whose only involvement had been in the car's testing – at which he was brilliant – and had no reason to be over-complimentary, wrote to Derby: 'Taking all things into consideration, I would rather own this Bentley car than any car produced under that name.'[16]

In such ways Royce and his team of designers succeeded in keeping Rolls-Royce as the classic contenders in the luxury automobile market during the 1920s and early 1930s. The Phantom III would be produced in 1936 after Royce's death, although he had earlier agreed on its dimensions, while the Wraith, which did not appear until 1937, was a development of Royce's 25/30 with a new 4.25-litre engine and independent suspension.

From the time of his first motor car, and particularly with his Silver Ghost, Royce was rightly renowned for his universally high engineering standards and technological refinements. However, during the last five years of his life, when confronted by a rapidly advancing US car industry with its massive companies and extensive design teams, he found himself open to specific criticisms for not incorporating systems and components that had been designed and produced to similarly exacting standards more cheaply elsewhere. Rolls-Royce fuel gauges, for instance, cost £5.20[17] each when the US equivalent was $3.40, while electrical components showed a far larger differential still. In addition, the time taken by Royce during 1930 on designing a perfect system of compression ignition when so much large-scale experimental work had already been carried out by American firms brought such criticism that it led to one of his strong rejoinders. In a memorandum of September 1930 he wrote:

> Believe me we are doing our best to get our work equal to our competitors and you will realise that it is not easy to produce designs sufficiently good to be worth making; one firm fully engaged against many. Very few indeed care to strive for hours, days, weeks, months on the drawing board to produce something worthy of the name of a design.[18]

One can positively hear the cry of a master designer who under massive pressure was still not prepared to compromise his standards nor surrender the initiative to others. The nature of the dilemma was evident in one of his final decisions when he authorised work to go ahead on an advanced Phantom III motor car that he decided should be powered by a complicated new V12 engine. There was no denying that the 7.3-litre, all-aluminium engine was both intricate and expensive, which in the Phantom III's case would be installed in the most costly car the company ever produced. Yet for a firm that claimed it made the finest car in the world, a car of this calibre had to be produced. To some extent it was influenced by American luxury cars. Both Packard and Cadillac had V12 and V16 engines on show at the 1930 London Motor Show at Olympia, while in the same year Daimler had also produced a car with a V12 engine.[19] Royce traditionally believed that engineering excellence was paramount and it was actually not until 1936 that a determined attack on price was launched by Rolls-Royce's Walter Robotham.

The Phantom III was certainly a large and heavy car, weighing 4,050lb (1,837kg). Even so, it was capable of accelerating from 0 to 50mph in 12.6 seconds and from 0 to 70mph in 24.2 seconds and was much superior at fast cornering than its predecessor, with a synchromesh gearbox on its second, third and top speeds.

Although Ernest Hives for one believed that in certain respects it was actually inferior to some current American models, after road testing it the British magazine *The Autocar* concluded that 'Somewhere is an ultimate in the highest expression of road travel, comfort and performance, and the Phantom III is beyond question the nearest approach to it yet.'[20]

The very powerful Phantom III. (Magic Car Pics)

Phantom III's magnificent V12 engine. (Magic Car Pics)

Even so, with no major components common to the company's other cars and an anticipated production of some 200 a year, there was no chance of it being profitable. Its actual sales totalled 715.

In fairness, as early as 1919 Henry Royce had publicly expressed his fears about luxury cars having a more limited role than before. With his 'educated instincts' about the company's future it was somewhat ironic that he was forced to spend the last fourteen years of his life struggling to disprove his 1919 prediction, although, given Rolls-Royce's traditions and past accomplishments with motor cars, he had no choice. There was, however, a limit to how far he could row against the tide when in an increasingly egalitarian age, in spite of serious economic convulsions, the motor car was becoming a utilitarian vehicle for both wealthy and ordinary families. This together with unprecedented opposition from across the Atlantic meant that British luxury cars – including Rolls-Royces – were destined to command a smaller market.

Even so, at the time of his authorisation of a large and sophisticated motor car whose advanced engine was likely to require further development, Royce also sanctioned the development of a private venture, twelve-cylinder aero-engine programme based on the Kestrel[21] that in time would prove of immense national importance, lead to a positive transformation of the company's economic prospects and permanently change its main thrust from cars to aero-engine technology.

11

Winning the Schneider Trophy Contest of 1931

Following Royce's achievements with his 'R' engine in the Schneider Trophy Contest of 1929 it seemed beyond belief that at first, the chances of British participation in the next one, scheduled to be held again at Calshot, seemed non-existent.

One of its highest profile opponents was the Chief of the Air Staff, Sir Hugh Trenchard, who on 10 September 1929, three days after Britain won the 1929 race, and just before relinquishing his post after the best part of a decade, wrote to the Secretary of State for Air declaring that, 'I am frankly against this contest. I can see nothing of value in it.'[1]

Although Trenchard had supported RAF involvement for the 1927 and 1929 races, deep down the man, who had never been in favour of ace pilots in the First World War, had always been ambivalent about his pilots entering the Schneider contests because he felt it distinguished them from their colleagues, which he considered bad for discipline. While the greatest champion of an independent air service, he had been an undistinguished pilot and was not inclined to believe that such contests gave an important boost to RAF recruitment when in a time of high unemployment he could always attract good recruits.

He was also not prepared to acknowledge the especial momentum that such contests brought for design teams like Royce's and the telescoping of development cycles that George Bulman, Head of the Air Ministry's engine team, estimated would compress[2] into six months more than five years of normal engine development. Trenchard was sure that progress could equally he achieved through normal scientific and research programmes.

Whatever Trenchard's opinions, at a time of deepening economic troubles there were inevitable questions about weighing the high cost and perils of such races against their possible benefits, especially for the host country. On 30 September 1930, the Air Ministry issued a statement that an RAF team would not be entered for the 1931 Race and that any British participation would have to be made by private venture under the auspices of the Royal Aero Club.

The American Government had already decided not to give its official support, although their aviation objectives were already moving strongly towards the development of civil aeroplanes, but France and Italy still pledged their backing for the coming race, where both were intending to enter new aeroplanes.

However, if Italy and France did plan to compete with more advanced aircraft, Britain appeared to have no choice but to match them with improved machines of its own. How this could be achieved was less clear for, on 8 December 1930, the Royal Aero Club put the costs of the projected race at £100,000, far beyond its own resources or perceived ability to raise funds. Although by the end of the month Italy's and France's entries were confirmed, on 15 January 1931 the Air Ministry reiterated the Government's determination not to give any assistance, either direct or indirect, whether by the loan of pilots, aircraft or other material, by the organisation of the race, the policing of the course or in any other way.[3]

Although the Royal Aero Club met later that month to consider what further action might be taken, any change of mind on the part of the Government seemed remote, especially as Philip Snowden, its Chancellor of the Exchequer, was a strong pacifist who went so far as to announce that he wanted to end the race's pernicious rivalry between nations.[4] On the other hand, Sir Samuel Hoare, as a long-standing Conservative Minister of Aviation, wrote to *The Times* arguing that while heretofore:

> The British aircraft industry was almost at its last gasp. Now the export of our aircraft to foreign countries, already to be valued in many millions, is steadily rising. The change I mainly assign to the reputation we have won for ourselves in foreign markets, and that we should not have won to the same degree without the resounding victories in the Schneider Cup races.[5]

Even as relentless pressure from both the public and the press seemed to be bringing Prime Minister Ramsay MacDonald back to his former supporting stance, the financial situation was unexpectedly resolved by the colourful figure of Lady Fanny Lucy Houston, philanthropist, political activist and suffragette. Born in 1857, Lucy was the ninth child of wool warehouseman and draper Thomas Radmall. With her striking looks and strong personality she became a chorus girl known as 'Poppy' and proceeded to marry into wealth and society. Her three husbands were older than her and she outlived them all. Her third husband, Sir Robert Houston, was a reputedly hard, ruthless and unpleasant bachelor, shipping magnate and Member of Parliament. Yet after marrying Lucy he came to dote on her and at his death he left her £6 million and his yacht, *Liberty*. Fiercely right wing, she publicly scolded the Labour Government for not supporting the race. In her telegram to the Prime Minister she wrote: 'To prevent the socialist Government being spoilsports, Lady Houston will be responsible for all extra expenses necessary beyond what Sir Philip Sassoon [Chairman of the Royal Aero Club] says can be found, so that Great Britain can take part in the race for the Schneider Trophy.'[6]

With Lucy's unqualified support and with Trenchard's successor, Sir John Salmond, deciding that. 'On balance I'm bound to come to the view that Britain ought to take part in the race,' the country's participation was finally guaranteed, with the RAF again providing the pilots and the other services being responsible for making the supporting arrangements.

Lady Lucy Houston, who paid for the contest. (Rolls-Royce)

Remarkably, Royce's own support seemed conditional before he fully accepted the undertaking. In July 1930 he wrote to his Managing Director, Arthur Sidgreaves, saying:

> It was agreed with you that we all wished there would be no race in 1931 and that we had derived considerable benefit from the last year and my impression was that we should get some benefit from future development work, but nothing like the same amount ... We feel however that if pressure is brought to bear on us by the Government or elsewhere we feel it our duty to do our best to uphold British prestige.[7]

Whatever his reservations about not getting the same value as two years before and, even more important, his high concerns with the risks being run by the young RAF pilots, Lady Houston's gift put special obligations on him. Whatever his health issues and continuing heavy commitments, he could hardly deny the race's prestigious nature nor an undoubted number of benefits for Rolls-Royce. It was now down to Supermarine and Rolls-Royce to provide the aircraft and engines needed for a race scheduled for 12 September 1931, just seven months away.

Sir Henry Royce. (Rolls-Royce)

By 31 January, whatever Royce's earlier reservations, it was on his authority that Arthur Sidgreaves promised a staggering 400hp increase of power for the 'R' engine intended for the race. With time too short to construct a new aircraft, Mitchell had to adapt his S6 aeroplane (to be called the S6B) to carry Royce's more powerful engine. Part of the increased power was required for take-off because this time the regulations required a fully loaded take-off and re-alighting on the sea prior to the take-off

Henry Royce and Nurse Aubin. (Rolls-Royce Heritage Trust)

for the race itself. These extra manoeuvres required reductions in fuel and oil consumption that, following initial setbacks, would be achieved through another of Rod Banks' special fuel cocktails, which on this occasion contained 10 per cent alcohol.

The limited time led to a frantic engine redesign programme, with Royce achieving the astounding 2,350hp required 'by making its crankshaft and centrifugal blower run faster by increasing the air intake while at the same time strengthening the connecting rods and other reciprocating parts to withstand the extra loads'.[8] 'The load on the centre main bearing went up to nine tons and the blower took 360hp to drive it – the full output of the Eagle [engine] of the WWI.'[9] To improve the engine's extraction, sodium-cooled valves were incorporated, with a hollow stem filled with liquid sodium that helped to dissipate heat by conducting it away rapidly down the stem of the valve guides. These had been invented in America and Rolls-Royce took out a licence for their use from the Bristol Aeroplane Company.

A massive problem for Mitchell was the need to dissipate the extra heat generated by the more powerful engines. He did so by increasing the efficiency of the air coolers by about 40 per cent and improving the dissipation of water heat by covering the top surface of the floats with radiators.[10] The floats were also lengthened in order to hold more fuel and provide better take-off capability. With the greater speed Mitchell faced fresh problems from control flutter, which he cured by fitting mass-balancing weights to the rudder and the ailerons.

In Royce's case one difficulty after another was experienced in testing the engine, which resulted in further work on the drawing board, in the metallurgist's laboratory and in the experimental workshops. It was one thing producing much increased power, quite another extending the life of such an engine to the estimated five hours needed for practising and taking part in the race itself. The method used to achieve it was excessively demanding, i.e. running it in the testing house for a full sixty minutes at maximum power. This had already worked in 1929, but this time the stresses on the engine were much higher and by the end of April it had only lasted a maximum of twenty minutes before some failure occurred. To save time in rebuilding wrecked engines the decision was taken to replace each part when its expected duration had been reached.

This experimental work led to hundreds of refinements in design and an entirely new type of connecting rod being developed.[11] Another result of the increase in engine speeds over the 1929 engine was that the oil consumption jumped from 7 to an astounding 50 gallons an hour. Oil was being flung out of the crankcase breathers and after one test run of twenty-five minutes, oil consumption actually rose to 112 gallons an hour. Weeks of intensive work were spent on the design of the scraper rings, breathers, the scavenging system and crankcase capacity until oil consumption was reduced to an acceptable 14 gallons an hour.

By mid-July the engine's life had been extended to half an hour, whereupon it was decided that some practice engines should be delivered to Calshot. The noise of the engine being run full out resounded across the city of Derby as it had two years before, but this time it went on day and night to the near despair of the town's citizens and, with the simulated airflow raised to 400mph, it reached unbelievable levels.

Despite regular objections, General Works Manager Arthur Wormald somehow managed to win the protestors over until on 12 August – to Ernest Hives' delight – the rebuilt engine roared out its defiance for the hour required, while producing the full 2,350hp at 3,200rpm.

Thanks to intensive metallurgical research by Rolls-Royce (which Royce had always regarded as being of the greatest importance), lighter materials were able to be used: the engine finally weighed just 1,630lb, giving it 21 per cent more power for a weight increase of only 6.5 per cent. With the engines

1931 Supermarine S6B, outright winner of the Schneider Trophy. (Rolls-Royce Heritage Trust)

in sound heart, the next issue was who among the RAF personnel would fly in the race.

Squadron Leader Harry Orlebar was again appointed team leader and Flight Lieutenant Stainforth, who had lost out in 1929, was retained. They were joined by five others: Flight Lieutenants J.N. Boothman, F.W. Long, E.J.L. Hope, Flying Officer L.S. Snaith and Lt G.L. 'Gerry' Brinton of the Fleet Air Arm. With too few racing aircraft for them all it was decided to release Brinton and Snaith. However, it was not long before the hazards of the job, which were always in the minds of both Royce and Mitchell, became apparent. Prior to receiving the new S6Bs, practice started with the earlier S6s and it was during this time that the first mishap occurred when the wash of a large liner capsized S6 N248, during the course of which Eustace Hope sustained a cracked eardrum and had to be posted out. To his delight, Lt Jerry Brinton was recalled as his replacement.

On 21 July, the pilots received delivery of one of the new S6Bs. The experienced Orlebar decided to put it through its paces, but despite a

Sir Henry Royce in conversation with Squadron Leader Orlebar. (Rolls-Royce Heritage Trust)

number of attempts as in 1929 he failed to lift it off the sea. The fault was traced to the propeller and following its replacement by one of exactly 9ft 6½in, take-off was successful. On 11 August, another S6B was delivered and it was flown the next day. There followed five days of strong winds when flying was impossible, but on 18 August, under Orlebar's guidance, Gerry

Brinton attempted his first take-off in S6AN247. His initial run was smooth and well-executed, but to Orlebar's concern the tail went up a little and he watched in alarm as the machine sank back in the water. It then jumped off at a steeper angle, fell again, hitting more heavily this time, then bounced up to 30ft before nosing forward and plunging in. The floats were torn off and the machine turned over, killing the pilot outright.[12]

The possibility of such a tragedy had always been in Royce's mind, a fact corroborated by young designer Donald Eyre, who was at West Wittering at this time. He believed that, although 'Royce thought the contests were certainly worthwhile and of the utmost importance to the nation and the engineers because so much was learned from them, the risks of the loss of valuable lives worried him.'[13]

Despite the accidents to the S6As (which would soon be repaired), both S6Bs remained sound, although their time in the air so far was hardly impressive, with one flying for less than an hour and the other less than ninety minutes. Even so, during the rest of August bad weather limited further flying opportunities before rumours started circulating about their Italian and French opponents still being a long way behind with their preparatory work. Both also suffered fatalities: the French with their pilot Lt Georges Bougault and the Italians with Lt Monti, who had raced at Calshot in 1929. Sure enough, on 3 September a joint Franco/Italian message was received by the Royal Aero Club to the effect that unless a postponement of at least six months was granted they would be unable to compete. The Royal Aero Club pointed out that the rules of the contest did not allow any postponement except from day to day and on 5 September, the Air Ministry received confirmation that neither nation would compete. In spite of this it was decided that after so much effort and expense a race that would secure the Schneider Trophy outright for Britain should go ahead.

Although it was bound to be something of an anticlimax, with an unprecedented number of 200,000 people expected, it was decided to try to give them a worthy spectacle by having one of the two S6Bs enter the race. It was hoped this would complete the course successfully in a faster time than before, with the other making an attempt on the current air-speed record.

For the RAF High Speed Flight the decision meant that following months spent training – with all the risks, involved – only two pilots would be required. Orlebar decided that the two lucky pilots should be selected on the grounds of their seniority with the flight: George Stainforth, who had been left out in 1929, was picked first and John Boothman, who was the senior among the remaining pilots, took the second berth. Stainforth had the choice of which challenge to take up. He decided on making an attempt on a new air-speed record with Boothman, who joined the RAF in 1921, being nominated to complete the course and, opposed or not, register what would be an historic victory.

In the meanwhile, there were still issues to be solved with the possible aerodynamic effects of an immensely powerful engine on a relatively tiny machine while struggling to take off from the water, and, when airborne, flying at around 400mph low over the sea.[14]

The two S6Bs were modified to bring their centre of gravity forward and when they flew on 6 September, a great improvement was seen in their take-off capability. The other persistent problem was the effect of Banks' potent fuel cocktail on the compound that sealed the plane's fuel tanks and fuel pipes that, when it loosened, polluted the fuel and clogged the filters, even causing the engines to cut out in flight. Fortunately, Mitchell found that the joints themselves were unaffected and he ordered his pilots to keep flying 'until all that stuff comes off'.

Bad weather conditions on 12 September caused the contest to be postponed for a day but on the 13th it was perfect and crowds gathered along the Solent. Flight Lieutenant Boothman in aircraft number S6B1595, which up to this point had flown for less than twenty-seven minutes, prepared to attack the course record. The Air Ministry made it clear that if he completed the course successfully, there would be no further flights and Boothman had strict orders to keep the engine's coolant temperature at 95°C.[15] In the event he made an excellent take-off, landing, taxi test and second take-off and, although he took the turns by a wide margin, successfully completed the course at 340.08mph. This was some 12mph faster than Waghorn in 1929, who by now had been killed testing a Hawker Horsley at Farnborough, and Boothman laconically reported that during the race 'the engine ran like a clock'.[16]

His success meant that the Schneider Trophy, which had first been won in 1913 by Maurice Prévost at a speed of 45.75mph, now became the permanent property of the Royal Aero Club.[17]

For those at Supermarine and Rolls-Royce nerves, had been tauter than for a normal race, for being beaten by a superior opponent, however regrettable, was acceptable, whereas a solo failure was bound to raise many questions about the constructors.

This time an ailing Royce followed the race from his bed by using a stop-watch and following the notes of Boothman's engine, which enabled him to chart its progress with uncanny accuracy.

There remained the attempt to set a new air-speed record to confirm Britain's air superiority. This became even more significant following an Italian attempt over Lake Garda on 10 September 1929, two days before, in which their pilot Stanislao Bellini had been tragically killed. All such apprehensions proved groundless for in S6B1596 George Stainforth made 'his four high-speed runs of three kilometres each off Lee on Solent, two with the wind and two against [that] broke all previous records with an average speed of 379.05 miles per hour to send the vast crowd home happy.'[18]

One final attempt remained with Rolls-Royce's sprint engine, with which they hoped to raise the speed record over the magic 400mph. It had not been ready for 13 September and any chance of setting a new record seemed to have been lost when the Air Ministry gave orders to clear Calshot and stand down the RAF High Speed Flight. It took a personal intercession by Royce on behalf of the Flight to have the process halted and for George Stainforth in his silver and blue aeroplane, S6B1595, aided by another fuel cocktail from Rod Banks to flash across the Solent, to become the first man, on 29 September 1931, to exceed 400mph on a measured run for a new world of record at 407.5mph.[19] Afterwards the engine was stripped down at Derby. No defects were found and, apart from possible fatigue in the metals, it could have been reassembled to repeat the performance. The 28mph increase over Stainforth's earlier speed attempt was attributed to a number of factors: 'an increase in engine power [39%], reduction in drag [10%], increase in propeller efficiency 14% and improvement in piloting of 37%.'[20]

It was only to be expected that Royce's aero engines, which had won the Schneider Trophy, should play an important part in maintaining Rolls-Royce's towering reputation in engine construction during his final years. Shortly after the race other representatives from Rolls-Royce emphasised the manifest virtues of the 'R' engine.

In 1931, Senior Designer Arthur Rowledge proudly spoke to the BBC about its future prospects:

> [I]n preparing the engines for the 1929 Contest we were in many ways at the beginning of the development of this particular engine. In 1931 we had more knowledge and data to enable us to tackle the job but at

> the same time we had a smaller field for development. The 1931 engine, besides giving more power, was a more efficient engine than its predecessor ... with almost every piece of material in the engine working at its limit of stress or heat capacity even for the short life required of such an engine ... However, the limit of development has not yet been reached as regards engine construction ...[21]

Also in 1931, Rolls-Royce's Managing Director, Arthur Sidgreaves, acknowledged the contributions made by both engines and airframes in the last two successful Schneider Trophy races towards his country's and his company's high reputation in aircraft construction: 'For the last few years Britain's supremacy in the manufacture of aircraft is generally recognised and is due to the experience and knowledge gained in contests such as that for the Schneider Trophy.'[22]

Distinguished Rolls-Royce Engineer Alec Harvey-Bailey, speaking in retrospect, then emphasised the vital commercial advantages accruing to the company from the Schneider Trophy races:

> Although Rolls-Royce had developed an enviable reputation in the aero engine field by 1918 and had subsequently powered the great pioneering flights, including the start of civil aviation, the 1920's saw the company slip into third place behind Bristol and Napier. At the end of the decade it was the performance of the 'R' type racing engine which overshadowed the competition, both British and foreign, in the Schneider Trophy contests and put Rolls-Royce into serious contention for major RAF contracts.[23]

For Henry Royce, who had but three years to live, the 'R' engine tested his convictions about what he believed was the classic aircraft engine with its twelve-cylinder conformation and liquid cooling system capable of being given massive power boosts by means of supercharging. For its construction he brought together a design team of unrivalled ability with the likes of Rowledge, Elliott, Lovesey and Hives, although he was still always prepared to adopt superior systems from outside, such as sodium-cooled valves to enhance its performance. As a believer in constant experimentation, he fully supported the team's practice of having the engine subjected to the most massive strains in testing. In this regard, Alec Harvey-Bailey described the awe-inspiring sight of the test engine at full throttle with ram air playing on the intake, simulating flight conditions:

> The 'R' engine was run with stub exhausts with blue flame gushing from them at high power. In an adjacent bed a Kestrel was driving a Roots blower to produce ram air and in [an adjoining] hangar a Buzzard was driving a propeller to blow scavenging air through the racing engine bed.[24]

The upshot, followed by further testing in 1931, was the strongest and soundest aero engine in the world that was in due course capable of being transformed by Royce's conceptual skills and Hives' construction abilities into a new, advanced form.

There are also good grounds for believing that Royce's involvement in the Schneider Trophy races had an emotional impact on him that went beyond some of his other projects. While West Wittering was 200 miles away from Rolls-Royce's Derby Factory, it was so close to the site of the race at Calshot that he only needed to make the shortest of journeys to become involved with the race's arrangements and meet with other participants, like the pilots and his fellow designer, Reginald Mitchell. In fact, the course of the 1931 Schneider Trophy Contest had to be slightly altered to include a turning point pylon actually on the beach at West Wittering.

As a result, the publicity-shy designer was able to relax his near monkish existence with his designers to put himself about a bit. There was, for instance, a photograph taken of him with Nurse Aubin talking to Flight Lieutenant Stainforth and Squadron Leader Orlebar at Calshot, and another with all of the High Speed Flight. The effect of such visits was such that in 1929, on his return to West Wittering, he had felt bound to share with his fellow designers the technical points discussed there. This he repeated in 1931. Most importantly, he was able to obtain unique feedback from the lionhearted young men using his engines. Much additional information was also obtained from the frequent multi-disciplinary conferences that he chaired, which were attended by the test pilots, Rolls-Royce officials from Derby and, on some occasions, by Reginald Mitchell.

The ageing Royce was an enthusiast at heart and he was sure to have been affected by the earnestness of the professional pilots, together with the audacity of his fellow designer, Reginald Mitchell, whose imaginative boldness matched his own engineering vision to take full advantage of the relative smallness of the potent 'R' engine to create beautifully streamlined yet amazingly sturdy aircraft.

Watching the planes practising at great speed some few feet over the water was also bound to remind him about the vulnerability of the pilots whose lives depended on his engines and whose performances he followed with unashamed apprehension. He was plainly delighted when the races were not only successful but concluded safely. In 1929 he was so pleased to win the Schneider Trophy that he invited his six personal designers to take tea with him on the lawn of his house at West Wittering. With the intense and prolonged nature of their normal work schedules, this was such a special event that young designer Donald Eyre asked permission to take a photograph, which Royce readily agreed to and then had his nurse take a second with Eyre in the picture. Being Royce, it was fully appropriate that Eyre should observe that 'the meal was merely scones, bread and butter and honey, the latter being so hard that I could only scratch the surface and pass the jar to my neighbour'.[25]

Schneider Trophy tea party at Elmstead, 1929. Clockwise from back: Ethel Aubin, H.I.F. Evernden, Henry Royce, A.G. Elliott, B.I. Day, W.G. Hardy, R.L. Marmont, C.L. Jenner. (Rolls-Royce Heritage Trust)

The short deadlines and constant changes associated with the Trophy work were also likely to have taken a physical toll, far beyond most men, but for Royce the essence of life lay in his work. An instance of this occurred while Donald Eyre was at West Wittering during 1929. When Royce came to examine his designers' work, he was usually accompanied by his black labrador, Rajah. Afterwards the two would go paddling along the seashore. Whatever his obvious enjoyment with the dog, when Royce returned for another critical session he would frequently tell them about the ideas that had come into his mind while on the beach. However enjoyable the immediate experiences, the challenges of current engineering problems were rarely out of his thoughts.

Yet however much he deliberately sought to maximise every second of his life, by late 1931, his health was deteriorating fast. Meeting visitors had to alternate with increasing time in bed before, on 22 April 1933, he finally succumbed at 70 to the terminal illness that had dogged him during so many of his later years. For his funeral it was typical of this most private man that he would specify no mourners nor flowers and at his cremation he allowed just two people to mourn him: one of his solicitors, Mr G.H.R. Tildesley, and Mr Albert Claremont, the brother of his old partner at Manchester.

Whatever the physical challenges during the final phase of his life, Royce retained the capacity to visualise a far broader application of his high-output 'R' engine and the acuity to authorise in October 1932 'the development by Rolls-Royce of a new aero-engine bigger than the Kestrel but smaller than the Buzzard and incorporating as much "R" technology as possible'.[26] This would be the company's PV12 (Private Venture 12 cylinder) engine of some 1,000 horsepower, which when developed into the form of the robust and ever-dependable Merlin (described overleaf) would play a major strategic role during the coming war by powering the fighting planes that won the most important air battle of all time.

The Standard Merlin Engine

It is a twelve-cylinder, liquid-cooled, supercharged engine. The twelve cylinders are arranged in two banks of six mounted on the crankcase in 'V' formation, the angle of the 'V' being 60 degrees. Four valves per cylinder, two inlet and two exhaust, are operated by overhead camshaft through the medium of rockers. One camshaft, carried in seven forged aluminium bearings is used for each cylinder block. The exhaust valve stems are hollow and filled with sodium to assist cooling. A balanced, hollow crankshaft, carried in seven main bearings of special lead-bronze transmits the drive to the airscrew. Connecting rods are of 'H' section steel forgings. The aluminium pistons are provided with three pressure and two scraper rings. The pistons work in high-quality steel liners inserted in the cast-aluminium cylinder blocks. A centrifugal-type, two-stage supercharger driven by a special two-speed gear mechanism delivers the mixture at above atmospheric pressures. Each cylinder is fitted with two spark plugs served by two separate twelve-cylinder magnetos so that the complete ignition system is duplicated. One carburettor of twin-choke up-draught is used. High-pressure, dry-sump lubrication delivers oil at pressure to crankshaft and camshaft bearings and all the bearings and gears throughout the mechanism. The coolant is a mixture of 70 per cent water and 30 per cent ethylene glycol circulated by a centrifugal-type pump. The complete engine stands 3ft 5in high, 2ft 5in wide and 7ft 3in long – it takes up no more than the space of a single bed. It gives a maximum power unit when the low supercharger gear is used of 1,260hp at 12,250ft altitude, maximum output with the high gear ratio is 1,175hp at 21,000ft. The engine weighs 1,450lb, something over half a ton. It produces more horse-power per pound weight than any other similar engine in the world. It has been produced in greater quantities than any other single operational type built in the history of British aviation.

(Taken from *The Power Behind Their Wings*, pp. 43–44.)

The Merlin engine. (Rolls-Royce)

Addendum

Sir Henry Royce, OBE left an estate of £112,598, less than the majority of people expected, but over £8 million at today's valuation. The terms of the will were as follows:

He bequeathed:
To Ethel Aubin, 'my nurse for over 20 years, and who has done so much to prolong my life', his property, Elmstead, and lands and his furniture, etc.

The residue of the property as to:
One tenth as his executors may think fit to research, or for the distribution of knowledge, for the purpose of improving the health of, and preventing disease to the human race. £100 to Margaret Carroll, if still in his service. An annuity of £75 to Martha Norman, similarly. An annuity of £50 to his wife's companion, Betty Freeman, and then:
Two-fifths upon trust for his wife for life, with remainder as to half to follow the above one tenth. And half to the children of his late sister, Mrs Willison, two-fifths upon trust for the said Ethel Aubin for life, and then for her children; or should she not leave issue as to half for the children of his said sister, and half to follow the above one-tenth.
One tenth to the children of his late sister Mrs Willison, and one-tenth to Albert William Claremont, Solicitor of Vernon House, Bloomsbury Square.

(Taken from *The Life of Sir Henry Royce*, p. 249.)

12

Royce: The Man and His Achievements

Anyone in a professional capacity would be unlikely to forget a meeting with Henry Royce, for he was a rather scary figure who even after mellowing in middle age never lost his aura of authority and capacity to take charge, a man who over long years would routinely make heavy demands on those in his design team and never allow them to forget that their role was special. Broad-shouldered and 6ft 2in tall, his wide blue eyes never lost their piercing and interrogative gaze. Although his rather squeaky voice was a surprising feature, in his younger years at least he was quite liable to raise it to a high level and lace his observations with devastating invective, where his memory would come into full play. Conversely, he warmly praised sound work and he was a cogent observer and good listener when attempting to obtain the fullest information. Throughout his life those in the workplace who abused metals or performed shoddily swiftly attracted his fury, although his outrages often tended to be short-lived and to give way to ironic humour.

His early struggles left him with a longing for knowledge that he saw as the doorway to success and he was notably intolerant of what he saw as false learning, like the Latin tags bandied around by his somewhat pompous Company Secretary, John De Looze, who was often the butt of his sharp humour.

In reality, despite his lack of formal education Royce possessed an instinctive and impressive grasp for design. As his Senior Designer Albert Elliott observed:

Sir Henry Royce on the drive entrance to Elmstead House. (Rolls-Royce Heritage Trust)

> Henry Royce never claimed to be a good draughtsman but he had a wonderful eye for line and proportion and instinctively knew the right shape for every piece. Nor was he a trained mathematician but he had his own way of doing calculations, by using simplified methods, showing that he had a highly developed sense of the fundamental principles of mathematics.[1]

Royce's early poverty also led him to be extremely careful with money where, for instance, he used his designing pencils to their last stub and abhorred his designers' waste of electricity. Even so, the acquisition of money would never come anywhere near his quest for mechanical perfection. Royce (and Johnson) willingly took large salary cuts during the First World War and whatever the financial climate Royce invariably purchased the very best machine tools for the Derby factory and quality, if unshowy, furniture for his own home.

Another likely result of his lack of early home life was his liking to be shown respect and addressed as Sir or Mr Royce. Only his original partner, Ernest Claremont, dared to address him as 'Fred', and although like other

Elmstead House, West Wittering. (P.H. Vickers)

Stone plaque at Elmstead House, erected by the Rolls-Royce Enthusiasts' Club. (P.H. Vickers)

Rolls-Royce executives he came to be habitually referred to by his initial 'R', it was made clear that there was only one 'R'.

Royce undoubtedly possessed rare powers of concentration and so intent was he on the success of his business that in the early years his only appreciable hobby was gardening, and then usually after a long day's work. Typically, his garden was productive for he became an expert on pruning and his roses and fruit crops were renowned. Towards the later stages of his life he felt more able to indulge in outside interests, which invariably involved research

Sign on Royce Way, near Elmstead House. (P.H. Vickers)

and new skills. At West Wittering he became a successful small farmer due to his thoroughgoing inquiries into soil and crop patterns and, through the help of his draughtsman Donald Eyre, he became a proficient water-colourist.

On the vexed question of whether Royce was just a copyist rather than an inventive genius, motoring authority C.W. Morton, for instance, had no doubts. He maintained that:

> [When] faced with a new problem Henry Royce would carefully examine the attempts made by others and if in his opinion a satisfactory solution existed he would use it. If he could find a sound approach, even if the outcome had been unsuccessful, he would use the approach, refine and develop it until it worked, but if he could not find a successful solution or a sound approach he could and did explore many possible new ways and his well of ideas never ran dry.[2]

Throughout his life Royce possessed a level of enthusiasm and drive, which when allied to his natural ability and unassailable self-confidence must to some observers have appeared well-nigh unstoppable. While fully recognising this, one of his designers, Donald Bastow, believed that early on, at least, 'The one thing he had no time for, up to the age of twenty-one when he was again without a job, through no fault of his own, was fun.'[3] This was possibly correct during the years before his twenty-first birthday prior to him embarking on his independent role, but it also reveals as much about Bastow, who failed to fully appreciate Royce's obsession and delight in mechanical excellence, rather than conventional leisure pursuits. This tended to place him apart, but he was never solitary. While he did not overvalue the approval of others, he valued loyalty and could give affection. He enjoyed a genuinely warm relationship with his niece Violet (Vi) and there are many instances of his genuine regard for both young people and animals. He was particularly kind to Claude Johnson's two daughters,[4] famously giving a donkey to Tink, and when Royce went to stay in Claude Johnson's London flat it was decided that he should sleep in the room of Johnson's elder daughter, Betty. This was filled with her treasures, including many pictures of celebrities. When one of the staff suggested she should remove most of them along with vacating the room she refused, confidently declaring that, 'He was one of the nicest people you could possibly meet and he is interested in all sorts of things apart from motor cars, my room can stay as it is.' When Royce arrived, he duly went from picture to picture courteously asking her why she had it on view and listening to her explanations most attentively.[5] He had, of course, a close and warm relationship with her father, who in turn was one of the leading lights in having Royce's statue erected at Derby.

He was capable of taking on the role of father figure – if a stern one – in the workplace to the three young apprentices who helped him build his first car. Whatever passion was lacking in his marriage may have been connected to his wife's natural temperament, for his relationship with his nurse was of the closest. That they did not marry, as she appears to have wanted, might well have been due to their wide differences in age and his undoubted ill health. He certainly made generous financial provision for her for life and even authorised a bequest for her future children. This said, his early privations seemed to have left him with a natural caution and the need to establish and maintain control of both private and public situations.

Whatever his other activities, Royce's endless quest for mechanical excellence was fundamental. It applied to any task he undertook, whether making

Regd. Telegraphic Address. "Royce, West Wittering."
Station— Passenger & Goods. Chichester—7 Miles. L. B. & S. C. Railway.

"Elmstead," West Wittering, Nr. Chichester.

July 2/23

My dear C.J.

The great success of your work in connection with the statue to be erected to me at Derby should be some satisfaction to you.

Needless to say I cannot adequately express in words my gratitude to you in this matter or my admiration of the incomparable way in which it has all been carried out, no one I ever knew of could have done it so but you

The great success of the RR company and the pleasure it has given to my life could not have come about except for your wonderful influence & the enthusiasm that you have created, the pros & cons of the small pieces of metal could not have come to much without your great guiding genius

Again thanking you my dear C.J. for your very many kindnesses to me. Believe me one of the many admirers of your greatness of both heart & mind

Excuse this most inadequate of notes

Yours v. sincerely
F H Royce

Royce's affectionate letter to Johnson regarding his statue. (Originator unknown)

a small engine component, a hand tool or even repairing a farm gate. He acknowledged this dominant motivation to the local vicar at West Wittering, the Rev. Arthur Gill, whose noisy lawnmower he felt compelled to strip down and rebuild. By this time his achievements were no secret and one of the Rev. Gill's sons, the eminent sculptor Eric Gill, gained permission on behalf of his father to carve Royce's favoured inscription on his fireplace overmantle: '*Quidvis recte factum quamvis humile praeclarum*', which translated means 'Whatever is rightly done, however humble, is noble'.

Although Royce never underrated his own capacity, he possessed an essential humility and whether noble or not he understood that his labours could never guarantee commercial success, although his zeal and high aims undoubtedly led him to attract a number of talented men with organisational and marketing skills who would help to propel his affairs forward. While they proved of cardinal importance to his commercial undertakings, Royce possessed the priceless ability of being able to develop his ideas into impressive reality that, combined with a gifted sense of timing and capacity to sense what was going on, served him well.

Derwent Wood's life-sized bronze statue of Henry Royce and the inscription on the front, which was unveiled on 27 June 1923, outside the headquarters of Rolls-Royce in Derby. (P.H. Vickers)

Such capacity was fully apparent in his business career. With his initial commercial venture, Royce's minute capital of £20 could hardly have been enough without the aid of his partner's additional £50, while his comprehensive business skills reinforced Royce's engineering accomplishments. Even so, whatever their joint achievements, it was Royce's decision to enter the electricity industry (where he was as skilled as most) when it was enjoying major expansion that proved crucial to their success.

This knack of good timing was again apparent in the late 1890s, when despite Royce's inventions of wireless dynamos and his excellent electric-powered cranes, a trade depression caused large German and American companies to enter the British market and pose serious threats to the continuing prosperity of Royce Ltd. In response, against strong opposition from Claremont and his firm's other Directors, Royce decided to enter the fledgeling automobile business, where the outstanding qualities of his first three cars convinced the redoubtable Charles Rolls and Claude Johnson about the benefits of selling them.

His subsequent development of the superb 40/50 chassis enabled Rolls-Royce to enjoy a most auspicious period until the outbreak of the First World War. When Johnson was temporarily searching for the means of the company continuing, it was Royce's agreement to build the Eagle aero engine and its successors that not only guaranteed Rolls-Royce's survival but led to its much increased importance as an aero-engine constructor during the First World War.

In 1924, following the war, when the firm's aircraft engine production was being neglected by other Directors of Rolls-Royce and its automobiles faced a raft of problems in an increasingly competitive market, Royce embarked on the development of a new range of aircraft engines. Their novel features led to them being adopted for the final two Schneider Trophy races, where their victories brought Rolls-Royce to new levels of success.

Finally, in late 1932, less than five months before his death, he agreed with Ernest Hives that they should proceed with a twelve-cylinder private venture aero engine (PV12) with its vast potential, together with a new twelve-cylinder luxury car.

Henry Royce was thus instrumental in five crucial decisions: entering the electrical industry; producing automobiles; undertaking aero-engine construction; revitalising the company's aircraft programme; and supporting the PV12 programme leading to the Merlin engine. Such achievements are

The Rolls-Royce tile in the Made in Derby Walk of Fame, Exchange Street, Derby. (P.H. Vickers)

surely enough for him to be admitted to the elite band of pre-eminent British engineers, but to be responsible for designing such advanced car and aircraft engines for some twenty years while battling serious ill health and when detached from Rolls-Royce's Derby factory, represents an outstanding achievement, even for someone with his exceptional powers and relentless determination.

For the firm to have its founder and chief engineer removed from its headquarters and parent factory for so long and succeed as it did is without parallel in British industrial history, although Royce was undoubtedly helped by the very able team of designers who accompanied him. In the early days at Le Canadel they included such distinguished men as Elliott, Olley, Jenner, Day, Evernden and Hardy. Yet eminent as they were, they followed his distinctive and highly demanding work pattern where he visited them daily and discussed each feature of the scheme on which they were working before a final decision was reached.

During 1928, at West Wittering, designer Donald Eyre watched in wonder at Royce's finessing of design 'by continually changing, simplifying and improving every part of a mechanism or unit … Making definite improvements at each step was the general practice and drawings were often patched where the paper had worn through with rubbing.'[6] While seemingly a laborious process, under Royce's remorseless prompting the final results were as good as could possibly be achieved. Eyre soon realised that he possessed the capability of visualising alternative ways of a diagram from which the best could be carefully selected and the required standard of perfection could be realised. Highly privileged or not, working under Royce involved long hours, in surroundings where extraneous noise was heavily frowned upon. For a long period at West Wittering there was no phone in the studio at Camacha, with messages delivered by Royce's Secretary, Monty Marmount, on his bicycle. Jackets were worn until Royce removed his and suits were expected to be plain and quiet; moderate drinking habits and no smoking were the order of the day. Although in the late 1920s Royce was no longer capable of working the punishing hours he had spent designing the Eagle engine, his day did not end with those of the designers. It was his practice to return to the office after his evening meal and spend further hours studying their progress. The next day they found their boards covered with scribbled notes and criticisms and they had to make the modifications required before his next scheduled visit. The demands on them were undoubtably high, but such was his ability and their joint achievements that with very few exceptions they remained steadfastly loyal.

Such conditions eminently suited Royce's unwavering interest in work, and Eyre talked of his reluctance to part with his designers for evenings and weekends, habitually keeping them beyond their appointed leaving time discussing design problems. Following one Saturday afternoon when he saw Eyre and Jenner carrying tennis racquets, on the following Monday he outrageously berated the two young men saying: 'I've been working hard all the weekend, I have no time to go playing games.' To Royce such recreation was a waste because it was non-productive unlike, for instance, gardening.

Such behaviour led Ivan Evernden, who worked with Royce in the 1920s, to conclude that Henry Royce 'ruled the lives of the people around him, claimed their body and soul, even when they were asleep'.[7]

Royce's demands also featured in the reminiscences of Walter Robotham, who was later to become a key figure at Rolls-Royce. As a young car tester he visited both Le Canadel and West Wittering, and in 1923 at Le Canadel he was regaled by lurid accounts from Royce's personal staff who were visiting. As he wrote: 'Stories told of these periods of solitary confinement were many and varied. One designer maintained that whenever he had any spare time he was put to work collecting fir cones for the fires instead of bathing.'[8] Robotham's own experience was somewhat different, for at West Wittering his discussions with Royce on technical matters were followed by lunch accompanied by an excellent bottle of local wine. But even the independent and highly talented Robotham bowed before Royce's authoritarian work ethic when he felt unable to take his test car into Saint-Raphaël or Cannes after finishing work in case he attracted Royce's displeasure. It was made quite clear to him that urgent problems at Derby would not allow any deviation from the direct route home, leaving no opportunity to explore Monte Carlo or Nice.

When almost ten years later Robotham visited America as a senior Rolls-Royce executive, he would be overwhelmed by the disparity between Rolls-Royce's engineering resources for its motor cars and those in Detriot.[9] During further visits to the separate divisions of General Motors he saw the massive research facilities compared with those of Royce and his team. With such disparities it was hardly surprising that Robotham should remain a huge admirer of Royce, attributing the Silver Ghost to Royce's tremendous energy, vitality, ability and devotion to quality but justly concluding that following the war, although Royce could not work as hard as before, he still would not rationalise his design work by buying in superior components from accessory manufacturers. Robotham fully acknowledged the massive workload on the West Wittering team, where with the emergence of the 20hp chassis there were two motor cars needing detailed designs for two different sets of components.[10] In reality this was far from the whole story for by 1929, along with the car work there was the redesigning needed for the 'R' aero engine to participate in the Schneider Trophy Races of 1929 and 1931, while by 1932 Royce was also working on a small supercharged car of 2½ litres. With such responsibilities it has to be acknowledged that under Royce's demanding but fulfilling system his designers produced more than could ever have been anticipated. Outstanding men like Albert Elliott and Arthur Rowledge, the brilliant designer of the Napier Lion engine, stayed with Royce because they fully recognised his overall genius.

Along with the author, readers have shared Royce's thought patterns through the stream of observations and directives he sent to Derby when constructing the Eagle engine and in later memos revealing his growing concerns about the stern competition facing Rolls-Royce during the late 1920s, together with the relentless pressures on the costs of manufacture.

These show that, despite Royce's lifelong pursuit of excellence, his long-favoured mantra that 'The quality remains long after the price has been forgotten', which was fully appropriate during the glory days of the Silver Ghost, was no longer so pertinent at a later date due to the rapid advances of the American car industry where, with quality being taken ever more for granted, price would assume premier importance.

By 1930 Royce was writing to Hives that:

> We are not vain enough to think that we are the only good pebble on the beach … we are all agreed that it is possible to make great economies without loss of perfection which as before must be our very first requirement but we might sacrifice 1% of perfection for 10% in cost …[11]

He came to the latter conclusions because he recognised that, 'Materials in England are higher in price than in the U.S.A. This supports my statement that with us it falls more heavily upon our Company because the whole country is less efficient.' While he actually believed this justified the amount of time spent by him and his designers on accessories, arguing that,

'We have always found this forces us into making many things that similar people in the USA bought from specialists,'[12] it was Royce's continuing hope that Rolls-Royce could continue to stay ahead technologically by increasing the efficiency of the firm's technical staff at Derby. At the same time he acknowledged that the company would soon have to part with their products for considerably less money and he was, in fact, already showing his concern over the marketing of his new 20/25 car when he told Managing Director Arthur Sidgreaves that, 'You know how terribly anxious I am to get this model right as quickly as possible so that we can sell it at such a price as to be able to make enough number to be profitable.'[13]

Royce's conversion to fully competitive costing was neither quick nor complete. He had previously cited a whole number of special ideas in support of his drive for perfection, including the conviction that there would always be a market for superlative quality in automotive engineering; that Rolls-Royce would emasculate its goodwill by producing in quantity, because quantity and quality were incompatible; that selling a few hundred costly cars always paid; that an inferior component, however cheap, was never justified if something better could be produced, however costly; that Rolls-Royce would antagonise the industry by entering the quantity market.[14]

He was patently reluctant to reject them and the extent to which he was prepared to accept the latest economic situation was brought into some doubt by his agreement in 1932 to the production of the Phantom III, a large new car with a highly complex engine, unashamedly luxurious with a continued lack of common components. Yet once again Royce's engineering instincts and his faith in his designers' skills in the car's detailed development proved sound, when after significant teething troubles it turned out to be much superior to the current British Daimler, handier to drive than the superb 7.7-litre Grosse Mercedes and having a distinct advantage over the latest American Packards and Cadillacs for stability and road worthiness.

Whether it could ever make money was another thing and the reform of Derby's cost arrangements for motor cars became Robotham's responsibility, with price reforms still under way at the beginning of the Second World War. In any case, whatever the financial penalties of Royce's conservatism towards the economics of car design, they were massively offset by the returns from Rolls-Royce's advanced aero engines and, despite Royce's later struggles with fast-changing conditions for his bespoke products, his lifelong aim 'to take the best that exists and make it better. When it does not exist, design it …'[15] remained irrefutable.

It is therefore unsurprising that, close to ninety years after his death, when personal memories of Royce, the man, have long faded, that his standards and achievements should continue to resonate with so many people. For aeronautical historians he is the artist of all things mechanical, with the outstanding reliability of his Eagle engines that carried Alcock and Brown on the first transatlantic flight; and for antique car buffs there is the Silver Ghost, Royce's most beautiful motor car, which probably had its greatest moments as the trusted mount for Lawrence of Arabia during his renowned desert campaign. For a later generation his genius might be exemplified by the snarl of Merlin engines in 1940 engaged in dogfights over Southern England against a Fascist invader and for contemporary citizens at large who still acknowledge particularly fine products by attributing them to the standards of Rolls-Royces.

A notable instance of Royce's unyielding commitment was tellingly described by the author G.R.N. Minchin in an unashamedly partial account:

> Royce said to 'the boys' that such a fast car should have a means of varying the stiffness of the suspension with which they agreed. This was not an easy thing to achieve, however. No car manufacturer had so far made any such device that was at all satisfactory, but Royce's spirit gave him strength to respond to the challenge. The night before he died, he sat up in bed and on the back of an envelope sketched out his design. He told his nurse to be sure that it reached Derby safely, but he was gone before the boys received it. Suffice to say that until recently all Rolls-Royce and Bentley cars have had this device practically unaltered from the sketch made in bed. It is still by far the best thing of its kind in the world.[16]

Finally, although she could have had few doubts about his belief 'that your soul was not your own but it belonged to your work which was the purpose for which you lived,'[17] it was made starkly apparent to Ethel Aubin while she was with him during his last moments. She told Sir Max Pemberton that he whispered to her, 'If I have any regrets, it is because I think, I might have worked harder.'[18]

For the author, there will always be the enduring image of a 4-year-old boy charged to stand in a field and wave his arms to keep the birds off the corn under a sky free of aeroplanes with the nearby lane still frequented by ponderous horse-drawn carts. By the time of his death sixty-six years later, his engines had not only powered record-breaking aeroplanes but motor cars that were the very epitome of luxury, power and smooth running. The small boy who enjoyed mixed success in deflecting the birds from their intended food supply subsequently became the patrician figure who in the workplace captivated highly skilled designers and constructors alike with his singular and elegant conception of engine workings and of mechanical perfection.

Notes

Preface

1. Nockolds, Harold, *The Magic of a Name*, 1953, p. 19.

Chapter 1: Early Struggles

1. Kirby, M.W., 'George Stephenson, 1787–1848', *Oxford Dictionary of National Biography*, 3 January 2008, p. 2 of 12.
2. Reese, Peter, *Transforming the Skies: Pilots, Planes and Politics in British Aviation, 1919–1940*, 2018, pp. 182–6.
3. Pemberton, Sir Max, *The Life of Sir Henry Royce*, 1936, p. 32.
4. Bastow, Donald, *Henry Royce: Mechanic*, 1989, p. 9.
5. Pemberton, Sir Max, op. cit., p. 20.
6. Evans, Michael H., *In the Beginning: The Manchester Origins of Rolls-Royce*, 2004, p. 22.
7. Pemberton, Sir Max, op. cit., p. 29.
8. Evans, Michael H., op. cit., p. 23.
9. Bastow, Donald, op. cit., p. 10.
10. Pemberton, Sir Max, op. cit., p. 18.
11. Evans, Michael H., op. cit., p. 23.
12. op. cit., p. 24.
13. ibid.
14. Nockolds, Harold, op.cit., p. 25.

15. At this time Frederick Rouse was the District Locomotive Superintendent at Peterborough.
16. Pemberton, Sir Max, op. cit., p. 34.
17. op. cit., pp. 34–35.
18. Evans, Michael H., op. cit., p. 36.
19. op. cit., p. 50.
20. Evans, Michael H., op. cit., p. 49.
21. op. cit., pp. 50–1.
22. ibid.
23. King, Peter, *Knights of the Air*, 1989, pp. 69–70.
24. Evans, Michael, op. cit., p. 59.

Chapter 2: Royce and Claremont – Branching Out

1. Evans, Michael H., op. cit., p. 63.
2. Tritton, Paul, *The Godfather of Rolls-Royce: The Life and Times of Henry Edmunds, Science and Technology's Forgotten Pioneer*, 1993, p. 92.
3. Clarke, Tom C., *Ernest Claremont: A Manchester Life with Rolls-Royce and W.T. Glover and Co.*, 1995, p. 1.
4. Pugh, Peter, *The Magic of a Name: The Rolls-Royce Story, The First 40 Years*, 2000, p. 30.
5. Evans, Michael H., op. cit., p. 373.
6. op. cit., p. 64.
7. Pemberton, Sir Max, op. cit., p. 42.
8. Clarke, Tom C., op. cit., p. 10.
9. Bastow, Donald, op. cit., p. 40. Bastow believed that both were, in fact, arranged marriages.
10. Pugh, Peter, op. cit., pp. 298–9.
11. Evans, Michael H., op. cit., pp. 86–8.
12. At today's prices (2019) £6,000 represents £759,719 and £9,000 £1,139,579 (Consumer Price Index 'CPI' inflation calculation). Despite its progress, Royce and Co. Ltd was still a relatively small firm.
13. Bastow, Donald, op. cit., p. 41.
14. Clarke, Tom C., op. cit., p. 15.
15. Following the Second World War Errol returned to Derby, where for over a decade he would run Rolls-Royce's photographic section. He continued living there until his death in 1967.
16. Morton, C.W., *A History of Rolls–Royce Motor Cars: Volume 1: 1903–1907*, 1964, p. 9.

17. Evans, Michael H., op. cit., p. 104.
18. Morton, C.W., op. cit., p. 10.
19. op. cit., p. 11.
20. Clarke, Tom C., op. cit., p. 15.
21. On his death Claremont left generous provision for Misses Hamett and Clare Jane McKnight of £500 each, along with his personal items and six months continuation at his house. It is quite possible that Clare Jane McKnight had been living with Claremont as his de facto wife, although different appearances would be kept up, Clarke, Tom C., op. cit., p. 40.
22. Tritton, Paul, op. cit., p. 107.
23. Clarke, Tom C., op. cit., p. 16.
24. Evans, Michael H., op. cit., pp. 108–109.
25. Lloyd, Ian, *Rolls-Royce: The Growth of a Firm*, 1978, p. 5.
26. Evans, Michael H., op. cit., p. 126.
27. op. cit., p. 128.
28. Morton, C. W., op. cit., p. 25.
29. ibid.

Chapter 3: Royce and His Motor Car

1. Evans, Michael H., op. cit., pp. 128–129.
2. Morton, C.W., op. cit., p. 26.
3. Pemberton, Sir Max, op. cit., p. 172.
4. Lloyd, Ian, *The Growth of a Firm*, p. 7.
5. ibid.
6. Evans, Michael H., op. cit., p. 135.
7. Morton, C.W., op. cit., pp. 28–29.
8. op. cit., p. 80.
9. Evans, Michael H., op. cit., p. 142.
10. *The Power Behind Their Wings: An Account of the part played by Sir Henry Royce and the Rolls-Royce engineers in the development of the in-line liquid cooled Aero-Engine in Great Britain*, 1944, p. 11.
11. Buist, H. Massac, *Rolls-Royce Memories*, 1926, p. 4.
12. Tritton, Paul, , p. 11.
13. ibid.
14. Mr. H. Edmunds, Obituary, *The Times*, Tuesday, Nov. 22, 1927.
15. Tritton, Paul, op. cit., p. 102.
16. op. cit., p. 112.
17. op. cit., p. 132.

18. op. cit., p. 116.
19. Evans, Michael H., op. cit., p. 171.
20. op. cit., p. 172.
21. ibid.
22. ibid.
23. ibid.
24. op. cit., p. 173.
25. ibid.
26. 'Two Men Came Together', *Rolls-Royce News*, 19 May 1954, p. 8.
27. Evans, Michael H., op. cit., p. 186.
28. It was, in fact, Royce's second prototype car.
29. Oldham, Wilton J., *The Hyphen in Rolls-Royce: The Story of Claude Johnson*, 1967, p. 63.
30. Evans, Michael H., op. cit., p. 194.
31. op. cit., p. 193.

Chapter 4: Rolls and Royce

1. Oldham, Wilton J., op. cit., p. 49.
2. Lord Montagu of Beaulieu, *Rolls of Rolls-Royce*, 1966, p. 24.
3. op. cit., p.41.
4. Morton C.W., op. cit., p. 52.
5. *Oxford DNB*, 2004, Jeremy, David J., Charles Stewart Rolls, p. 2.
6. Evans, Michael H., op. cit., p. 208.
7. Meynell, Lawrence, *Rolls: Man of Speed*, 1953, p. 97.
8. op. cit., pp. 98–9.
9. Evans, Michael H., op. cit., p. 271.
10. Nockolds, Harold, op. cit., p. 62.
11. Morton, C.W., op. cit., pp. 225, 226.
12. Harvey-Bailey, Alec and Evans, Michael, *Rolls-Royce: The Pursuit of Excellence*, 1984, p. 7. Sykes was an illustrator for *The Car Illustrated*, founded by Montagu, and Eleanor Thornton had previously been Claude Johnson's Secretary at the Automobile Club, before she was employed by Montagu and may have also been Montagu's mistress.
13. Nockolds, Harold, op. cit., p. 62.
14. Buist, H. Massac, op. cit., p. 32.
15. Lord Montagu of Beaulieu, op. cit., p. 140.
16. op. cit., p. 144.
17. ibid.

18. op. cit., p. 168.
19. op. cit., p. 178.
20. 'A flight in the Wright Aeroplane', typescript of 9 October 1908 by C.S. Rolls, with amendments by the author (National Aerospace Library Collection).
21. Pugh, Peter, op. cit., p. 74.
22. Lloyd, Ian, *The Growth of a Firm*, p. 31.
23. ibid.
24. Lord Montagu of Beaulieu, op. cit., p. 199.
25. op. cit., p. 219.
26. He was an enthusiastic member of the Army Motor Reserve in which he held the rank of Captain.
27. Lord Montagu of Beaulieu, op. cit., p. 233.

Chapter 5: Johnson, Royce and the Silver Ghost

1. Oldham, Wilton J., op. cit., p. xix.
2. Brendon, Piers, *The Motoring Century: The Story of The Royal Automobile Club*, p. 39.
3. Pugh, Peter, op. cit., p. 29.
4. Oldham, Wilton J., op. cit., p. 39.
5. Nockolds, Harold, op. cit., pp. 41–2.
6. Oldham, Wilton J., op. cit., p. 66.
7. op. cit., p. 72.
8. The car is still the property of Rolls-Royce Ltd and it remains one of their most treasured possessions.
9. Morton, C.W., op. cit., p. 266.
10. Nockolds, Harold, op. cit., p. 69.
11. *The Power Behind Their Wings*, op. cit., p. 12.
12. Braun, Andreas (ed), *Rolls-Royce Motor Cars*, 2013, pp. 77–9.
13. Oldham, Wilton J., op. cit., p. 81.
14. Nockolds, Harold, op. cit., p. 73.
15. Wilton, J. Oldham, op. cit., p. 76.
16. Morton, C.W., op. cit., p. 399.
17. Buist, H. Massac, op. cit., pp. 25–27.
18. Lloyd, Ian, *The Growth of a Firm*, p. 31.
19. ibid.
20. op. cit., p. 34.
21. op. cit., p. 35.

Chapter 6: The Silver Ghost in Peace and War

1. Oldham, Wilton J., op. cit., p. 91.
2. Bastow, Donald, op. cit., p. 18.
3. Oldham, Wilton J., op. cit., p. 93.
4. Bastow, Donald, op. cit., p. 42.
5. Nockolds, Harold, op. cit., p. 84.
6. *Motor Sport*, January 1941, p. 265.
7. Nockolds, Harold, op. cit., p. 92.
8. Lloyd, Ian, *The Growth of a Firm*, p. 42.
9. op. cit., p. 45.
10. ibid.
11. op. cit., p. 52.
12. Tagg, A.E., *Power for the Pioneers, The Green and E.N.V. Aero Engines*, 1990, p. 19.
13. Lloyd, Ian, *The Growth of a Firm*, pp. 52–3.
14. op. cit., p. 53.
15. Samson, C.R., *Fights and Flights*, 1930, p. 7.
16. Nockolds, Harold, op. cit., p. 98.
17. op. cit., p. 99.
18. op. cit., p. 103, 104.
19. Fletcher, David, *The Rolls-Royce Armoured Car*, 2012, p. 5.
20. Hobbs, David, *The Royal Navy's Air Service in the Great War*, 2017, p. 158.
21. ibid.
22. Churchill, Winston, *The World Crisis*, vol. II, 1923, p. 71.
23. Nockolds, Harold, op. cit., p. 106.
24. Fletcher, David, op. cit., p. 16.
25. ibid.
26. Nockolds, Harold op. cit., pp. 110, 111.
27. op. cit., p. 111.
28. op. cit., p. 113.
29. Lawrence T.E., *Seven Pillars of Wisdom*, 1997, p. 589.

Chapter 7: Royce's Move to Aero Engines

1. Nockolds, Harold, op. cit., p. 115.
2. Preface to Royce, F.H., *The First Aero Engine Made By Rolls-Royce Ltd*, Rolls-Royce, 1916; hereafter called the 'Blue Book'.

3. Green's engine, in fact, proved of little consequence in the coming conflict.
4. Oldham, Wilton J., op. cit., p. 107.
5. Blue Book, Letter from Royce to GMD of 26 August 1914.
6. ibid.
7. Blue Book, Letter from Royce to GMD of 1 September 1914.
8. Blue Book, Second letter from Royce to GMD of 1 September 1914.
9. Blue Book, Letter from Royce to GMD of 8 September 1914.
10. Such gearing involved a metal circle rolled around the circumference of another fixed circle.
11. Blue Book, Letter from Royce to Works of 21 October 1914.
12. Blue Book, Letter from Royce to Works of 26 October 1914.
13. Blue Book, Letter from Royce to Works of 27 November 1914.
14. Blue Book, Second letter from Royce to Works of 27 November 1914.
15. Blue Book, Letter from Royce to Works of 9 December 1914.
16. Blue Book, Letter from Royce to Works of 12 December 1914.
17. Blue Book, Letter from Royce to Works of 23 December 1914.
18. Blue Book, Letter from Royce to Works of 16 January 1915.
19. Blue Book, Letter from Royce to Works of 6 February 1915.
20. Blue Book, Letter from Royce to Works of 23 February 1915.
21. Blue Book, Letter from Royce to Works of 1 March 1915.
22. Blue Book, Letter from Royce to Works of 10 April 1915.
23. Blue Book, Letter from Royce to Works of 9 April 1915.
24. Blue Book, Letter from Royce to Works of 19 April 1915.
25. Blue Book, Letter from Royce to Works of 15 May 1915.
26. Blue Book, Letter from Royce to Works of 16 October 1915.
27. Blue Book, Letter from Royce to Works of 25 November 1915.
28. Blue Book, Letter from Royce to the Admiralty of 5 March 1915.
29. Blue Book, Letter from Royce to Aero Engine (Admiralty) of 8 March 1915.
30. Blue Book, Letter from Royce to GMD of 5 July 1915.
31. Blue Book, Letter from Royce to the Admiralty of 4 May 1915.
32. Blue Book, Letter from Royce to the Admiralty of 4 October 1915.
33. Blue Book, Letter from Royce to the Admiralty of 25 October 1915.
34. Blue Book, Letter from Royce to the Admiralty of 4 November 1915.
35. Blue Book, Letter from Royce to Works of 25 May 1915.
36. Blue Book, Letter from Royce to Works of 25 May 1915.
37. Blue Book, Letter from Royce to Works of 27 May 1915.
38. Blue Book, Letter from Royce to Works of 28 May 1915.
39. ibid.

40. Blue Book, Letter from Royce to Admiralty of 9 June 1915.
41. Blue Book, Letter from Royce to Works of 15 September 1914.
42. Blue Book, Letter from Royce to Royal Aircraft Factory of 6 November 1914.
43. Blue Book, Letter from Royce to Works of 8 April 1915.
44. Blue Book, Letter from Royce to Works of 22 June 1915.
45. Blue Book, Letter from Royce to Works of 23 November 1915.
46. Blue Book, Letter from Royce to Works of 12 January 1915.
47. Blue Book, Letter from Royce to Works of 15 January 1915.
48. Blue Book, Letter from Royce to Works of 18 January 1915.
49. Blue Book, Letter from Royce to Works of 6 February 1915.
50. Blue Book, Letter from Royce to Works of 16 February 1915.
51. Blue Book, Letter from Royce to Works of 23 February 1915.
52. Blue Book, Letter from Royce to Works of 22 September 1915.
53. Blue Book, Letter from Royce to Works of 7 December 1914.
54. Blue Book, Letter from Royce to Works of 7 December 1914.
55. Blue Book, Letter from Royce to Works of 15 May 1915.
56. Blue Book, Letter from Royce to Works of 13 April 1915.
57. Blue Book, Letter from Royce to Works of 12 May 1915.
58. Taulbut, Derek S., *Eagle: Henry Royce's First Aero Engine*, 2011, p. 315.
59. op. cit., p. 240.
60. Cable, Boyd, *The Soul of the Aeroplane: The Rolls-Royce Engine*, 1915, pp. 18–21.
61. Taulbut, Derek S., op. cit., p. 240.
62. Oldham, Wilton J., op. cit., p. 108.
63. Eyre, Donald, *50 Years with Rolls-Royce: My Reminiscences*, 2005, p. 30.
64. op. cit., p. 33.
65. op. cit., p. 35.
66. Bastow, Donald, op. cit., p. 38.

Chapter 8: The 1920s: Automobiles versus Aero Engines

1. Pugh, Peter, op. cit., p. 107.
2. Lloyd, Ian, *The Years of Endeavour*, 1978, p. 1.
3. Lloyd, Ian, *The Growth of a Firm*, p. 135.
4. Taulbut, Derek S., op. cit., pp. 246–248.
5. Reese, Peter, op. cit., p. 69.
6. Lloyd, Ian, *The Growth of a Firm*, Appendices I & VI.

7. Lloyd, Ian, *The Years of Endeavour*, p. 23.
8. Pugh, Peter, op. cit., p. 111.
9. Lloyd, Ian, *The Years of Endeavour*, p. 48.
10. Pugh, Peter, op. cit., p. 96.
11. Lloyd, Ian, *The Years of Endeavour*, p. 86.
12. Harvey-Bailey, Alec, *Rolls-Royce: Twenty to Wraith*, 1986, p. 25.
13. Bird, Anthony and Hallows, Ian, *The Rolls-Royce Motor Car and Bentleys built by Rolls-Royce*, B.T. Batsford, 1975, p 125.
14. Pugh, Peter, op. cit., p. 102.
15. op. cit., p. 100.
16. op. cit., p. 102.
17. Robotham, W.A., *Silver Clouds and Silver Dawn*, 1970, p. 92.
18. Eyre, Donald, op. cit., p. 42.
19. Lloyd, Ian, *The Years of Endeavour*, p. 5.
20. Lloyd, Ian, *The Growth of a Firm*, pp. 135–6.
21. Lloyd, Ian, *The Years of Endeavour*, p. 18–19.
22. op. cit., p. 96.

Chapter 9: Royce's Aero Engine and the Schneider Trophy Contest of 1929

1. Lloyd, Ian, *The Years of Endeavour*, p. 247.
2. Rubbra, A.A, *Rolls-Royce Piston Aero Engines: A Designer Remembers*, 1990, p. 19.
3. Barker, Ralph, *The Schneider Trophy Races: The Extraordinary True Story of Aviation's Greatest Competition*, 1971, p. 190.
4. Bulman, George Purvis, *An Account of Partnership: Industry, Government and the Aero Engine: The Memoirs of George Purvis Bulman*, (ed. M.C. Neale). 2002, p. 150.
5. Banks, Rod, *I Kept No Diary*, 1983, p. 87.
6. ibid.
7. Bulman, George Purvis, op. cit., p. 150.
8. Rubbra, A.A., op. cit., p. 60.
9. Bulman, George Purvis, op. cit., p. 151.
10. Nockolds, Harold, op. cit., p. 143.
11. Barker, Ralph, op. cit., p. 193.
12. op. cit., p. 194.
13. op. cit., pp. 191–192.
14. op. cit., p. 209.

15. Robotham, W.A., op. cit., p. 272.
16. Eyre, Donald, op. cit., p. 39.
17. Barker, Ralph, op. cit., p. 252.
18. Pegram, Ralph, *Supermarine Rolls-Royce S6B, 1931 (S1595 and S1596) Owners' Workshop Manual*, p. 134.

Chapter 10: Automobiles – Preserving the Marque

1. Oldham, Wilton J., op. cit., p. 140.
2. op. cit., p. 140.
3. Nockolds, Harold, op. cit., p. 176.
4. Oldham, Wilton J., op. cit., p. 166.
5. Pugh, Peter, op. cit., p. 127.
6. Lloyd, Ian, *The Years of Endeavour*, p. 65.
7. Pugh, Peter, op. cit., p. 104.
8. Lloyd, Ian, *The Years of Endeavour*, p. 72.
9. op. cit., p. 73.
10. op. cit., p. 106.
11. op. cit., p. 107.
12. Bentley, W.O., *My Life and My Cars*, 1967, p. 164.
13. Dymock, Eric, *A Name That Launched a Style of Life*, 2009, p. 4.
14. Bentley, W.O., op. cit., p. 176.
15. Robotham, W.A., op. cit., p. 81.
16. Pugh, Peter, op. cit., p. 125.
17. Lloyd, Ian, *The Years of Endeavour*, Note 11 to Chapter 3, p. 238.
18. op. cit., Note 6 to Chapter 9, p. 244.
19. op. cit., p. 121.
20. Pugh, Peter, op. cit., p. 134.
21. Schlaifer, Robert and Heron, S.D., *Development of Aircraft Engines and Development of Aviation Fuels*, 1950, p. 216.

Chapter 11: Winning the Schneider Trophy Contest of 1931

1. Barker, Ralph, op. cit., p. 218.
2. Bulman, George Purvis, op. cit., p. 157.
3. op. cit., p. 222.
4. Reese, Peter, op. cit., p. 121.
5. *The Times*, Letter of 23 January, 1931.

6. Nockolds, Harold, op. cit., p. 146.
7. Lloyd, Ian, *The Years of Endeavour*, p. 102.
8. Nockolds, Harold, op. cit., p. 146.
9. Bulman, George Purvis, op. cit., p. 158.
10. Barker, Ralph, op. cit., p. 235.
11. *The Power Behind Their Wings*, op. cit., p. 33.
12. op. cit., p. 239.
13. Eyre, Donald, op. cit., p. 39.
14. Bulman, George Purvis, op. cit., p. 158.
15. Pegram, Ralph, op. cit., p. 143.
16. Nockolds, Harold, op. cit., p. 147.
17. It is presently on display at the Science Museum in London alongside Submarine S6BS1595.
18. Barker, Ralph, op. cit., p. 250.
19. Rod Banks' skills were again evident when on 23 October 1934 he helped the Italians regain the world record for piston-engine seaplanes with their diminutive pilot Francesco Agnello recording a new record of 440.68mph. This record still stands today.
20. Pegram, Ralph, op. cit., p. 145.
21. Pugh, Peter, op. cit., p. 166.
22. op. cit., p. 167.
23. op. cit., p. 168.
24. Harvey-Bailey, Alec, *Roll-Royce: Hives, The Quiet Tiger*, 1985, p. 15.
25. Eyre, Donald, op. cit., p. 41.
26. Pugh, Peter, op. cit., p. 174.

Chapter 12: Royce: The Man and His Achievements

1. Peter, Pugh, op. cit., p. 126.
2. Morton, C.W., op. cit., p. 7.
3. Bastow, Donald, op. cit., p. 40.
4. Wilton, J. Oldham, op. cit., pp. 134–5.
5. op. cit., p. 109.
6. Eyre, Donald, op. cit., p. 33.
7. Peter, Pugh, op. cit., p. 125.
8. Robotham, W. A., op. cit., p. 45.
9. op. cit., p. 73.
10. op. cit., p. 92.
11. Lloyd, Ian, *The Years of Endeavour*, pp. 72–3.

12. op. cit., p. 73.
13. op. cit., p. 74.
14. Lloyd, Ian, *Rolls-Royce: The Merlin at War*, 1978, pp. 159-160.
15. *Rolls-Royce Motor Cars Strive for Perfection*, Catalogue for Rolls-Royce Exhibition at the BMW Museum in Munich 2013, page 15.
16. This incident was related by Donald Eyre in his reminiscences on page 56.
17. Buist, H. Massac, op. cit., p. 10.
18. Pemberton, Sir Max, op. cit., p. 40.

Select Bibliography

Newspapers

The Times
The Daily Telegraph
The Daily Sketch
The News Chronicle

Aeronautical Journals and Magazines

Aeroplane, 1918–37
L'Aeronautique Paris, 1930–32
Aircraft Engineers, 1931
Automobile Engineer, 1920
Autocar, 1919
Engineering, 1920
Flight, 1917–37
Interavia, 1936
Rolls-Royce News, 19 May 1954

Lectures, Articles and Pamphlets

'A Century of British Aeronautics: The Royal Aeronautical Society, 1866–1966', The Royal Aeronautical Society, 1966.

Evernden, Ivan, 'The First Sir Henry Royce Memorial Lecture: Sir Henry Royce, Bart', *Royal Aeronautical Society Journal*, vol. LX, Jan–Dec 1956, pp. 769–84.

Hildersheim, Erik, 'A German Appreciation of the Rolls-Royce Aero Engine', *Aeroplane*, November 1919, pp. 1729–34, 1789–94, 1803–4.

Jeremy, David J., 'Charles Stewart Rolls', *Oxford Dictionary of National Biography*, Oxford University Press, 2004.

Keith, Sir Kenneth, Hooker, Sir Stanley and Higginbottom, Samuel L., 'The Achievement of Excellence: The Story of Rolls-Royce', Addresses to National Meeting of the Newcomen Society, 28 October 1976.

King, Horace Frederick, 'The Two Rs 1904–1954: A Commemorative History of Rolls-Royce Aero Engines', Rolls-Royce, 1954.

Kirby M.W., 'George Stephenson 1787–1848', *Oxford Dictionary of National Biography*, Oxford University Press, 2008.

McCarthy, Roy, 'Two Men Came Together: Commemorating the First Meeting of Henry Royce and the Hon C.S. Rolls', May 1904, Rolls-Royce Ltd, 1954.

Pearson, Sir Denning, 'The Development and Organisation of Rolls-Royce Ltd', 17 November 1964.

Pemberton, Sir Max, 'An Appreciation of Mr. Royce', Unveiling of a Statue to Mr F. Henry Royce: A Living Engineer, 27 June 1923.

Robins, Ralph H., 'To the Standards of Sir Henry Royce', 24th Annual Sight Lecture, Wings Club, 20 May 1987.

Ruffles, Philip, 'His Legacy to Power For Land, Sea And Air', 1st Hon C.S. Rolls Lecture, Institution of Mechanical Engineers, 8 May 2002.

Skinner, Sandy, 'The First Aero Engine Made By Rolls-Royce Ltd', *Torque Meter: Journal of the Aircraft Engine Historical Society*, vol. 7, no. 2, Spring 2008, pp. 37–42.

Books

Primary Source

The 'Blue Book': Royce, F.H., *The First Aero Engine Made By Rolls-Royce Ltd*, Rolls-Royce, 1916.

Rolls-Royce Publications

Bastow, Donald, *Henry Royce: Mechanic*, Rolls-Royce Heritage Trust, 1989.

Bruce, Gordon, *Charles Rolls: Pioneer Aviator*, Rolls-Royce Heritage Trust, 1990.

Cable, Boyd, *Rolls-Royce Aero Engines and the Great Victory*, Rolls-Royce, 1919.

Cable, Boyd, *The Soul of the Aeroplane: The Rolls-Royce Engine*, Rolls-Royce, 1919.

Clarke, Tom C., *Royce and the Vibration Damper,* Rolls-Royce Heritage Trust, 2001.

Driver, Hugh, *Lord Northcliffe and the Early Years of Rolls-Royce*, Rolls-Royce Heritage Trust, 1998.

Evans, Michael H., *In the Beginning: The Manchester Origins of Rolls-Royce*, Rolls-Royce Heritage Trust, 1984, rev. 2004.

Eyre, Donald, *50 Years with Rolls-Royce, My Reminiscences*, Rolls-Royce Heritage Trust, 1905.

Harvey-Bailey, Alec and Evans, Michael, *Rolls-Royce: The Pursuit of Excellence*, Rolls-Royce Heritage Trust, 1987.

Harvey-Bailey, Alec, *Hives the Quiet Tiger*, Rolls-Royce Heritage Trust, 1985.

Harvey-Bailey, Alec, *Rolls-Royce: The Formative Years, 1906–1939*, Rolls-Royce Heritage Trust, 1983.

Harvey-Bailey, Alec, *Rolls-Royce: The Sons of Martha*, Rolls-Royce Heritage Trust, 1987.

Harvey-Bailey, Alec, *Rolls-Royce: Twenty to Wraith*, Rolls-Royce Heritage Trust, 1986.

Hooker S., Reed H. and Yarker A., *The Performance of a Supercharged Engine*, Rolls-Royce Heritage Trust, 1997.

Instructions for the Installation, Running and Maintenance of Rolls-Royce 'Kestrel' and 'Buzzard' Aero Engines, Rolls-Royce Limited, 1932.

Lea, Ken, *Rolls-Royce: The First Cars from Crewe*, Rolls-Royce Heritage Trust, 1997.

Levin E., *The Rolls-Royce Armoured Car: Its Substance and Place in History*, Rolls-Royce Heritage Trust, 2016.

Montague, Lord Edward, *The Early Days of Rolls-Royce and the Montagu Family*, Rolls-Royce Heritage Trust, 1986.

Rolls-Royce 1904–2004: A Century of Innovations, Rolls-Royce Group plc, 2004.

Rolls-Royce Aero Engine Instruction Book, 'Eagle' Series I to VIII, 'Falcon' Series I, II and III, Rolls-Royce, December 1917.

Rubbra A.A., *Rolls-Royce Piston Aero Engines: A Designer Remembers*, Rolls-Royce Heritage Trust, 1990.

Taulbut, Derek S., *Eagle: Henry Royce's First Aero Engine,* Rolls-Royce Heritage Trust, 2011.

Selected Books

Abbiss, Reg, *The Bentley Story*, The History Press, 2014.

Banks, Air Commodore F.R. (Rod), *I Kept No Diary: An Autobiography*, Airlife, 1983.

Barker, Ralph, *The Schneider Trophy Races: The Extraordinary True Story of Aviation's Greatest Competition*, Chatto and Windus, 1971.

Bentley W.O., *My Life and My Cars*, Hutchinson, 1967.

Bird, Anthony and Hallows, Ian, *The Rolls-Royce Motor Car and Bentleys Built by Rolls-Royce*, B.T. Batsford, 1975.

Bowman, Martin W., *Famous Bomber Aircraft*, Stephens, 1989.

Braun, Andreas (ed.), *Rolls-Royce Motor Cars: Strive for Perfection*, Hirmer, 2014

Brendon, Piers, *The Motoring Century, The Story of the Royal Automobile Club*, Bloomsbury, 1997.

Buist, H. Massac, *Rolls-Royce Memories*, Cambridge University Press, 1980.

Bulman, George Purvis, *An Account of Partnership: Industry, Government and the Aero Engine: The Memoirs of George Purvis Bulman* (ed. M.C. Neale), Rolls-Royce Heritage Trust, 2002.

Clarke, Tom C., *Ernest Claremont: A Manchester Life with Rolls-Royce and W.T. Glover and Co.*, Hulme Press, 1995.

Clarke, Tom C., *The Rolls-Royce Wraith*, J.M. Fasal, 1986.

Coles, David and Sherrard, Peter, *The Four Geniuses of the Battle of Britain: Watson-Watt, Henry Royce, Sydney Camm and RJ. Mitchell*, Pen & Sword, 2012.

Cross and Cockade International, *Lawrence of Arabia and Middle East Air Power*, Cross and Cockade International, 2016.

Dalton, Lawrence, *Those Elegant Rolls-Royce*, Dalton Watson, 1970.

Fletcher, David, *The Rolls-Royce Armoured Car*, Osprey, 2012.

Gunston, Bill, *Rolls-Royce Aero Engines*, Patrick Stephens, 1989.

Harker, R.W., *Rolls-Royce from the Wings: Military Aviation, 1925–71*, Oxford Illustrated Press, 1976.

Harker, R.W., *The Engines Were Rolls-Royce: An Informal History of that Famous Company*, Macmillan, 1979.

Heron S.D., *History of the Aircraft Piston Engine*, Ethyl Corporation, 1961.

Hobbs, David, *The Royal Navy's Air Service in the Great War,* Seaforth Publishing, 2017.

Johnson, Claude, *The Early History of Motoring*, E.J. Burrow and Co. Ltd, 1927.

Keegan, John, *The First World War*, Hutchinson, 1998.

King, Peter, *Knights of the Air: The Life and Times of the Extraordinary Pioneers Who Built British Aeroplanes*, Constable, 1989.

Leasor, James, *Wheels to Fortune: The Life and Times of William Morris, Viscount Nuffield*, James Leasor, 2011.

Lloyd, Ian, *Rolls-Royce: The Years of Endeavour*, Macmillan, 1978.

Lloyd, Ian, *Rolls-Royce: The Growth of a Firm*, Macmillan, 1978.

Lloyd, Ian, *Rolls-Royce: The Merlin at War*, Macmillan, 1978.

Meynell, Laurence, *Rolls: Man of Speed*, Bodley Head, 1953.

Minchin, G.R.N., *Under My Bonnet*, G.T. Foulis and Co. Ltd, 1930.

Mitchell, Gordon, *R.J. Mitchell: School Days to Spitfire*, Tempus, 2002.

Montagu, Lord Edward, *Rolls of Rolls-Royce: A Biography of C.S. Rolls*, Cassell, 1966.

Morgan, Bryan, *The Rolls and Royce Story*, Collins, 1971.

Morriss H.F., *Two Brave Brothers*, Richard J. James, 1939.

Morton C.W., A *History of Rolls-Royce Motor Cars: Volume 1: 1903–1907*, G.T. Foulis, 1964.

Nockolds, Harold, *The Magic of a Name*, G.T. Foulis, 1950.

Oldham, Wilton J., *The Hyphen in Rolls-Royce: A Biography of Claude Johnson*, G.T. Foulis & Co., 1967.

Pegram, Ralph, *Supermarine Rolls-Royce S6b: 1931 (S1595, S1596) Owners' Workshop Manual*, Haynes Publishing, 2018.

Pemberton, Sir Max, *The Life of Sir Henry Royce*, Selwyn and Blount, 1936.

Pugh, Peter, *The Magic of a Name, The Rolls-Royce Story, Part Three: A Family of Engines*, Icon Books, 2002.

Pugh, Peter, *The Magic of a Name: The Rolls-Royce Story: The First 40 Years*, Icon Books, 2000.

Reese, Peter, *Transforming the Skies: Pilots, Planes and Politics in British Aviation 1919–1940*, The History Press, 2018.

Robotham, W.A., *Silver Ghosts and Silver Dawn*, Constable, 1970.

Roland, John, *The Rolls-Royce Men: The Story of Charles Rolls and Henry Royce*, Lutterworth Press, 1969.

Samson, C.R., *Fights and Flights*, Ernest Benn, 1930.

Schlaifer, Robert and Heron, S.D., *The Development of Aircraft Engines [and] the Development of Aviation Fuels Two Studies of Relations Between Government and Business*, Harvard University, 1950.

Sewell, Brian, *The Man Who Built the Best Car in the World*, Quartet Books, 2015.

Tagg, A.E., *Power for the Pioneers: the Green and ENV Aero Engines*, Crossprint, 1990.

Taylor, James, *Rolls-Royce*, Bloomsbury, 2017.

The Power Behind Their Wings: An Account of the part played by Sir Henry Royce and the Rolls-Royce engineers in the development of the in-line liquid cooled Aero-Engine in Great Britain, HMSO, 1944

Tritton, Paul, *The Godfather of Rolls-Royce: The Life and Times of Henry Edmunds M.I.C.E., M.I.E.E., Science and Technology's Forgotten Pioneer*, Academy Books, 1993.

Ullyett, Kenneth, *The Book of the Silver Ghost*, Parrish, 1963.

Wilson, Gordon A.A. and Hinton Jnr, Steve, *The Merlin: The Engine that Won the Second World War*, Amberley, 2020.

Index

The History Press
The destination for history
www.thehistorypress.co.uk